Training the Racehorse

Training the Racehorse
Tim Fitzgeorge-Parker

J. A. Allen
London

British Library Cataloguing in Publication Data.
A catalogue record for this book is available
from the British Library.

ISBN 0.85131.586.0

Published in Great Britain in 1993 by
J. A. Allen & Company Limited,
1 Lower Grosvenor Place,
London, SW1W 0EL.

First published by Pelham Books in 1973

Printed in Hong Kong by Dah Hua Printing Press Co. Ltd.
Typeset in Hong Kong by Setrite Typesetters Ltd.

Designed by Nancy Lawrence

Contents

List of Photographs

Foreword to First Edition by Sir Noel Murless

Tim Fitzgeorge-Parker needs no introduction to the racing public. In his time he has been an amateur rider, a trainer and press correspondent. Also, he has had the great advantage of learning his profession under such a master as the late Mr Atty Persse, with whom both Sir Cecil Boyd-Rochfort and Major Geoffrey Brooke started their careers.

Training racehorses, however, is an individualistic business. Obviously the basics are the same, as any horse, to race, must be fit.

The diversion lies, I think, in the way the horse is brought to the peak of fitness, and the tricky part is in maintaining that degree of fitness over a period of time.

I feel sure that this book will give a great amount of pleasure to all who are interested in racing.

Foreword by Martin Pipe

Training Racehorses is really about getting a horse fit and keeping him well and happy. This book goes through in a very thorough way, everything that one would need to know. When I first started to get interested in training my own horses and not having had the advantage of working for an established trainer and getting to know the routine of training I read *Training the Racehorse* and found it a wonderful guide to the daily routine and care of the horse. Tim Fitzgeorge-Parker's knowledge of horses has been gained over many years of experience as an amateur rider and successful trainer and I am sure everyone who reads this book will gain a greater understanding of training and the horse, as I did.

Martin Pipe

Acknowledgements

The plans of the courses are reproduced by kind permission of Raceform. The British Racecourse Locations map is reproduced by kind permission of The Racecourse Association Ltd.

The photographs are reproduced by kind permission of: Sports and General Press Agency, pages 12, 19, 22, 44, 45, 49, 57, 83, 116, 150, 189, 212, 227, 254; W.W. Rouch & Co., pages 5, 6, 7, 54, 155, 156; Lesley Sampson, pages 35, 111, 112; The Press Association, pages 3, 26, 152.

Many thanks to Martin Pipe for his generous foreword, to Martin Diggle for his editing and to Charlotte Fanshawe for her help with 'Reams of Bumf'.

And a special 'thank you' to my wife Eleanor and daughter Lucy for encouragement and for their hard work typing and editing, without which this new edition would not have completed the course.

CHAPTER ONE

'Lest We Forget'

'Blinkers? What d'you mean blinkers? I'm damned if I'll have those things on my horse. They look awful. Besides, you've always told me he was perfectly honest. They'll think he's a rogue if he runs in them and I'll certainly never be able to sell him on.'

Unfortunately this is a true, typical modern owner's reaction to the innocent suggestion that his horse should run in blinkers next time out. If he does, the trainer knows that he will win. The animal is very fit, but in his last two races he's been looking about him, not paying attention to the job in hand. So would you, if you were a big horse with no other form of impulsion than a little man riding with ultra-short stirrup leathers, scrubbing about on top like a chimp on an elephant. In the last race, however, the horse, who was as honest as the day is long − as the trainer had told the owner − had received a harsh, unnecessary beating, which could well have soured him off − unnecessary because all he needed was blinkers to keep his mind on the job.

Our grandfathers, born in the happy years before motor cars, had to rely on the horse for everything; to do their shopping, to travel around, to get the doctor for a sick child. Inevitably they had to know more about the animal than we can today in an age of universal mechanisation. So often their ideas are plain common sense and considerably kinder than methods employed today.

At the turn of the century, when the American jockey Tod Sloan's influence began to be felt and all riders started to ride with short stirrup leathers, 'like a monkey up a stick', as it was

1

then described, the trainers had to find some other means of impulsion. The power of the driving legs had been diminished and excessive use of the whip would only sour the horse off. So, whenever necessary, they fitted blinkers. They knew their value. After all, every cart and carriage horse had to be equipped with blinkers to stop him shying at things in the hedge, to keep his mind on the job, to make him a safe conveyance. They were as normal and necessary as side lights on a motor car.

It was no reflection on the horse's honesty. Some of the most genuine animals in Turf history have been useless without them; Felicitation, Alycidon, National Spirit, Durante (one of the best and bravest handicappers of my time) and his sister, Royal Hunt Cup winner Val d'Assa. The last two were among the many fine horses that Atty Persse trained in the last years of his long and glorious career while I was his assistant trainer. Nearly all our three- and four-year-old colts wore blinkers. The late Lord Sefton's flying Nasrullah filly Nassau was never without them, even at exercise, after she had whipped round at the start when heavily fancied first time out at Kempton. Nothing daunted, Atty fitted blinkers next time. He, Sefton and Jack Olding doubled their bet and she flew in. Nassau won six of her twelve starts that season, but from that moment she never even left her box without her black hat. Blinkers had another use with her. They stopped her looking behind her and thus selecting targets to kick. She could go backwards almost as fast as she could go forwards to deliver a well-aimed *coup de pied*. We had a court case when, freed from her blinkers so that the jockey could weigh in after the Queen Mary Stakes at Ascot, she kicked a woman and broke her jaw. But in a race she was as game a battler as you would ever find and, if her owner had not insisted on having her home and turning her out at Croxteth during the winter, she would, according to her trainer, have won the One Thousand Guineas instead of finishing fourth.

Unhappily, between the wars, a racing journalist described blinkers as 'the rogue's mask'. The phrase stuck and was used again and again. I hope that ignorant fellow turns uncomfortably in his grave every time a trainer is discouraged from fitting blinkers and a horse suffers an unnecessary hiding.

I once asked Atty how much blinkers improved Durante, winner of two Jubilees. 'At least two stone', he replied.

Take another example. A chronic rearer. Always a nuisance, frequently dangerous. Incidentally, a colt or a gelding will not

Durante, a good and genuine horse who ran in blinkers, winning the Rosebery Stakes.

normally come backwards unless he is pulled by his rider, whereas a thoroughbred filly will whip over onto her back with terrifying speed. 'Like some ladies I have known!', as Atty would say with those big blue Irish eyes twinkling.

So many people think they know the answer. It's usually rough, cruel and so seldom one hundred per cent effective that such horses are often condemned as unrideable. The whip between the ears, the bottle of oil smashed over the head to give the feel of blood, the savagely placed Chifney, and so on.

Our grandfathers had no need for such treatment. They would simply remove the horse's hind shoes and ride him out on sharp gravel. I always use this method. It's fuss-proof and most effective. The last thing he wants to do is to rear and place all his weight on his soft frogs. Above all, it's practical common sense.

It is absolutely vital that the ideas and practices of the old masters should be recorded for posterity before they are forgotten and it is too late. They must be remembered and, where necessary, adapted to modern conditions.

Certainly it is true that with horses we are always learning, but, unlike motor cars, television' or aircraft, it has all been learnt before. Any young trainer who thinks he knows better than his forebears is in for a rude awakening.

So in this book, with the help of the great trainers who have collaborated so wonderfully, I have tried to look at the art of training the racehorse through ancient and modern eyes.

There are, of course, a number of do's and don'ts; elementary principles which must be followed. But in general it would be quite wrong to lay down the law, because in many ways apparently strictly opposed methods can be equally successful. For example, the fresh-air fiend who favours little clothing and top doors open in every kind of weather can achieve the same success as the man who insists on keeping his charges warm at all times. The only essential is to be consistent.

So we can only guide, pointing out ways of training that have been successful over the years and still produce many winners despite the changed racing scene in and out of stables — antibiotics, air travel, starting stalls, etc.

Certainly, good horses make good trainers, just as they make good jockeys. And I am inclined to disagree with my old Guv'nor, Atty Persse, who wrote: 'Good trainers, like good wives, are born, not made. Without natural flair it is far better to keep away from racing stables and to run a garage, for no amount of teaching will transform a horseman into a trainer of horses.'

If for 'good' we substitute 'brilliant' the generalisation makes more sense. Trainers like Atty himself, George Lambton, Fred Darling, Noel Murless, Vincent O'Brien, Paddy Prendergast, Etienne Pollet and Tommy Smith were indeed naturals. The vast majority of the other good trainers — and we are lucky to have many in this country — owe their success to dedicated learning, an eye for and understanding of the horse, real hard graft and that little bit of luck which is so essential in the acquisition of the necessary good horses and in keeping them free from accident or disease.

The main obstacle to good training in these islands is undoubtedly the lack of realistic training fees, so that in all but a few cases trainers are subsidising their owners. No wonder

Atty Persse, top trainer and the author's mentor, at home at Stockbridge.

George Lambton.

Fred Darling.
Top trainers of the old school.

there are more horses in training than ever before. I shall deal with this question in some detail in a later chapter, so suffice it to say here that in 1939, when you could buy a packet of twenty good cigarettes for $11\frac{1}{2}$d (5p) and a brand new motor car for £100, you had to pay 5 guineas a week to keep a horse in training. Translate that into modern money and you will see what I mean. The Jockey Club, most of whom are, of course, racehorse owners, must take the blame for not announcing a minimum training fee and keeping the figure constantly under review. This is the one way to keep the sport in a healthy state by ensuring a proper living wage for members of an arduous profession, who should not have to rely on betting, dealing and tax evasion in order to live and raise their families.

'Before the war', said Atty, 'the 5 guineas a week training fee was your bread and butter, which provided you with a living even in a bad year. The ten per cent of winning stakes, betting and dealing were the jam. Now we have to try and live on jam.'

And he said one of the saddest things I have ever heard. 'If my son John had lived, I would have done my damnedest to dissuade him from becoming a trainer today.' This from one of the all-time greats, who had devoted a long life to riding and training the thoroughbred horse and who loved the profession which he adorned.

Perhaps one of the most extraordinary things about Atty was his memory. I find that this applies to myself and to nearly everyone who has ridden or been associated with horses all his life. Instead of forgetting whole periods like most old men, he always had at least one horse every year on whom to hang the memories.

CHAPTER
TWO

Buying

Even if it is only half true that anyone can train a good horse, it must be obvious that selection is the most important factor in training. It may not be quite so vital for the man whose annual intake consists mainly of home-bred yearlings from his owners' own studs, but he, too, has to select those he wishes to train and advise on the discards. The ordinary trainer, Flat or jumping, owes his livelihood to his ability to choose the right animals. This requires a lot of skill and knowledge, a fact which is still not properly recognised in this country.

In France a trainer receives ten per cent of all sales and purchases by law in the same way as he receives ten per cent of all place money down to fourth position. In England his counterpart still often gets ten per cent of winning stakes only. As far as sales and purchases are concerned he must fend for himself. And, as in most cases he is subsidising his owners on their training fees, it appears (not for the first time) that there is no British justice for trainers.

Of course the lack of a fixed percentage system leads to many abuses. A horse bought privately can be passed on to the owner at a considerably higher figure than the original purchase price. A horse bought at public auction may well have his price inflated if the vendor lets it be known that he will give a handsome percentage to the buyers of his offerings.

Forgetting the more sordid details, however, it is essential for a successful trainer to have an eye for a horse. Moreover, he must possess the psychology to enable him to fit horse to owner.

When yearling time comes round again even before the end of summer, most trainers have already earmarked the older horses they plan to dispose of and are busy persuading owners to replace them with new talent.

As the breeders who can afford to race their horses themselves grow fewer, so the number of Classic winners sold at public auction increases. Keeneland, Saratoga, Dublin, Newmarket, Deauville, Doncaster; all present opportunities. All provide hope for the future. And hope is what racing is all about.

Of course, owners come from all over the country. But there are certain areas which always seem to contain more than their fair share. Ascot and Sunningdale and the country near Birmingham (around Stratford-upon-Avon, for example) are already full of owners, but are still the most promising coverts for trainers to draw.

One of the most difficult tasks confronting the trainer is to persuade his patrons that they must up the ante every year if they want to buy any worthwhile horse. It is always said, with reason, that training owners is much more difficult than training horses. More and more owners have no knowledge of animals and regard them as machines.

As a result, patience, that essential quality when dealing with horses, is becoming rarer all the time. I have known so many owners who, suffused with a holy glow at sales time, have declared, 'I'm not interested in two-year-old racing. I want a yearling who will make into a good stayer as a three- and four-year-old.' Nevertheless, halfway through the animal's two-year-old season they start complaining: 'When is my horse going to run?' Which soon develops into: 'When is he going to win?'

The ideal is to buy such a man or woman a quick type as well, who will show form as a two-year-old, to keep them happy while waiting for the other one to mature.

For most people any auction sale has a fascination, and it always surprises me that more horse-lovers do not come to what must be, for them, the most intriguing and exciting auction sales of all.

There is no charge for car park or admission. The only essential expense is for a catalogue, which contains full details of every lot to be sold and a comprehensive register giving, in concise notebook form, a summary of the racecourse and stud performances of every stallion represented by yearlings at the sale.

Armed with catalogue and pencil, the horse-lover can enjoy an unparalleled feast of expert instruction: just why did Paul Cole buy that particular animal, and why did he and the other experts ignore that magnificent-looking individual? But wait, perhaps they were not so right: although he fetched such a small price, was he not knocked down to Richard Hannon, who is fast becoming one of the best judges of a yearling in the land.

Then there are the contrasting thrills — on the one hand those magnificent battles way up in the six and even seven figures, and on the other, the bargains. Perhaps you were at Ballsbridge one memorable sunny afternoon. Did you wonder why the late Sir Victor Sassoon bothered to buy a Hard Sauce yearling for only 270 guineas? Or did you take a fancy to the colt, follow his fortunes, notice that his new owner had christened him Hard Ridden and had entered his cheap purchase in the Classics? If you did, you had fun and made money, culminating in a good win on the Derby.

What are the factors which influence the experts buying their two-year-olds for the following season?

First, the catalogue. If you want to buy a good winner and are not prejudiced by the need for a certain bloodline, your catalogue is not nearly as important as it is when buying foals. There are a few good judges of a foal, but in the main the little animal is so unformed that the saying 'Fools and foals go together' has strong foundation. While the yearling will probably change considerably before he is fully grown, he has reached the stage where his own physical attributes are a fairly reliable guide.

A famous old trainer, Ted Gwilt, who specialised in very cheap yearlings, had one golden rule. The dam must be either a winner or dam of a winner. He had considerable success. Naturally, the greater the number and the higher the class of the winners on the dam's side of the pedigree, the better.

There is a strong school of thought which says that it is best to breed from a very lightly raced or even unraced mare. However, there are plenty of examples to discount this theory, and to find an ordinary winner it is best to stick to the golden rule above and leave the theorising to others.

If you want a horse who will eventually go jumping, look for some jumping blood somewhere in the bottom half of the pedigree.

Richard Hannon, a very shrewd judge of horses.

Again, when buying a yearling, you must make up your mind whether you want a two-year-old winner, or a horse who should be better over middle or long distances at three years old and upwards. The former should be by a stallion whose best racecourse performances were at a mile or under.

One word of warning – the old adage of 'speed to speed' is sound, but do not take the chance when it has been overdone; for example, the result of a sprint horse out of a sprint mare will probably fly for three furlongs, but unfortunately there are no three furlong races!

This is not a treatise on breeding, so let us look at the horse, bearing in mind that the sprinter type is usually chunky, while it is 'lean horses for long races'.

I am very lucky. I have always had a natural eye for a yearling.

It was nurtured and schooled by my father's friend Peter Thrale (great-uncle of champion jump jockey Richard Dunwoody), who became my first trainer, and by Atty Persse, whose last assistant I was. As a result, when I started training on my own and could only afford to buy cheap yearlings, I enjoyed remarkable success. Fortunately, both these great old judges liked the same type of animal as had always filled my mind. They seldom bought stayers deliberately because they expected their purchases to win as two-year-olds. Both bought horses not paper. 'Take the catalogues away from most of these modern trainers', grumbled Atty, 'and they wouldn't have a clue. They'd be lost.'

Peter, who watched every lot go through the ring at all the sales, would always start bidding on the animal he saw in front of him and would ignore his catalogue until it started to reach the price of his own valuation. Then, if the catalogue encouraged him, he might go higher. He was very kind to me. As a vet and trainer of vast experience, he would point out faults which I had missed. Then, if I obviously liked a yearling and he knew that my money was limited, he would say: 'Let me know when you can't go any further. If you haven't got him, I'll go on.' But on these occasions he would never bid against me.

So, when your catalogue arrives, whether you are buying in the top bracket or the bargain basement, you can use it not so much as a guide to what to buy but as help in elimination. For example, you would save time by scratching out all those lots with no recent winners on the dam's side of their pedigrees. If you're after two-year-old winners, you would draw a line through the wholly staying-bred lots. And, unless you have plenty of money to spend, you're better off forgetting all about the Dancing Braves, Sadlers Wells and the other produce of fashionable sires. Remember it's always better to buy the best produce of a lesser sire than the worst of the top ones.

Even if the youngster is not the progeny of a fashionable sire, you are entitled to take a chance on him if his dam has been a good winner herself or has produced winners. Almost any horse who is worth standing as a stallion is capable of siring winners, and this type of yearling is infinitely preferable to one by a fashionable sire out of a mare who has no credentials herself or who has not come from a good mare. It is a fact that really good mares nearly always reproduce themselves, although they may miss a generation or so. Moreover, experience shows that a good horse usually comes from a good tap-root on the dam's side. The same rule applies to sires. It is a mistake to use a stallion who comes from a badly bred mare on his dam's side, no matter how brilliant a racehorse he may have been, if you intend to breed a high class horse.

Before you discard your catalogue, there will be certain studs that you will particularly favour – those where the yearlings are regularly produced for sale in firm, hard condition. Many yearlings come to the sales so overloaded with fat and boosted by patent medicines or steroids that it is difficult to discover their true nature. In a couple of months, when the fat has been worked off, they are hardly recognisable as the sleek, fat animals who pranced around the sale ring so recently.

Before going to the sales, get your eye in. The real experts will have been looking at yearlings round the studs for some weeks, but even they must keep looking at lots of yearlings to attune their eye after seeing older horses every day.

At this stage you have clearly in your mind the type of animal you want for each owner and the amount that he is prepared to pay (an awkward item). Too many financial transactions are made by word of mouth in racing, stemming, presumably, from the fact that even the biggest bets are always struck in such a way. Today, unfortunately, this is not quite good enough in some cases. An acquaintance asks you, over a drink, to buy him a yearling for, say, up to 5,000 guineas. You take trouble and return with the right animal only to find that, for one reason or another, he doesn't want the horse. He may even deny having asked you to make the purchase in the first place. I have been landed like this and was only saved from a nasty situation by the typical generosity of a kind friend.

It was my first season as a trainer and I was delighted to be asked to buy a quick yearling. When I returned from the sales with a liver chestnut by The Solicitor out of Rue Royale, I thought I had done my new owner well. But, when I telephoned, he said that it had been wishful thinking; a joke really and he couldn't afford it! Nor could I and it was no joke for me to find myself heavily in debt to Tattersalls at the start of my career.

Naming your own horse has always been one of the beauties of buying yearlings. I deplore the French habit of naming them before they go to the sales. Abstractedly I registered one of my best names, Judgment of Paris, for this youngster. A good horse deserves a good name. The great showmen have always known this. What judge could fail to look at a show hack called

Liberty Light or a heavyweight hunter called Mighty Fine or Mighty Atom?

Blandford, Gainsborough, Sir Ivor, Mill Reef; these are the names of the good horses. Winagain never won and Passifyoucan was always being passed. There are, of course, exceptions to the rule, although Hard To Beat may not be pushing your luck too far. Perhaps only that great French breeder and wonderful lady, Elizabeth Couturie, could get away with calling a horse Right Royal. If most of us had done this, the colt would have smartly found his way to a selling hurdle at Bangor-on-Dee. But then, Mme Couturie was one of the few people with the gift, possessed by some old stud grooms, of being able to tell within the first twenty-four hours of a horse's life if he was destined to be a great horse. One morning when Tyrone Waterford was staying with her, she came in to breakfast after her usual morning visit to the stables. 'Tyrone,' she said, 'that colt who was foaled last night will not only be the best of this year's foals, he will be a really good horse. Do you mind if I call him Tyrone after you?' With foresight such as this she knew that Right Royal would be a champion worthy of his name just as surely as Dick Dawson saw a great horse in the tiny new-born colt he was to name Blandford.

Clearly, something had to be done quickly about Judgment of Paris, who was now broken and ridden away. I explained my predicament to an old friend of the family, our leading sausage manufacturer Colonel Peter Marsh, whose wealth was matched only by his generosity. Typically he never hesitated. Where so many rich men would have pleaded poverty, he said: 'I won't say I can't afford another horse in training because that would be ridiculous. Of course I can. Yes, I'll take him.'

As soon as I had the yearlings upsides in November, it was clear that his new purchase could go a bit. When I worked Judgment of Paris with older horses in March, I discovered he had exceptional speed. Peter had always liked a bet and we decided to run in the two-year-old seller at Liverpool's Grand National meeting during the first week of the Flat season. Unfortunately, word of his speed had leaked out and he opened at a short price. The owner, who had hoped for a big each-way bet at a long price, found himself faced with 6—4 and that only to very small sums.

Still, this was Judgment's day. On a normal course he would have won easily and would have expressed my gratitude to my friend. But this was Aintree, where the five furlong course ran towards the stands. A furlong out it looked all over bar the shouting. Our two-year-old was well clear of his field, streaking home. Then suddenly, finding himself galloping into a sea of shouting people, he threw up his head in fright and finished third.

It was the start of yet another chapter in one of the sport's oldest stories. All trainers have found over the years that the really good owner seldom receives his just rewards and seldom enjoys the luck of the bad owner.

Judgment of Paris went mad, slowly, inexorably through that season. His burst of speed lasted for shorter and shorter periods. After leading for three and later only two furlongs, he would drop his bit and trail in last at a hack canter. He did this one afternoon at Brighton, where in those days there was just a rail at the top of the pull-up hill past the winning post. He just cantered into this and turned a somersault over it. Fortunately the jockey, my apprentice Taffy Thomas, was unhurt. So, too, was Judgment. Bad horses seldom do themselves any harm. Good ones invariably seem to be badly injured or killed in this sort of situation. Finally, he ran in a maiden seller at Warwick ridden by that splendid veteran Davy Jones, who knew that the owner's business was making sausages. The two-year-old finished tailed off again and, as he dismounted, Davy said to me, 'His owner will know how to place him better than you!'

I learned several things from Judgment of Paris. First, get your orders in writing. Secondly, don't buy a yearling who has already been castrated. Similarly, don't buy a filly whose vagina has been stitched. In both cases the breeder has already had trouble; if you buy them, you're asking for more. Thirdly, don't buy yearlings with curly ears — they always seem a bit scatty. And lastly, avoid that rather dirty light liver chestnut, which also frequently characterises a nutty individual.

Colour is an important point. I will always avoid washy bays and washy chestnuts, particularly those with silver or flaxen manes and tails. They are usually soft. I like a rich hard bay, brown or grey. Many people hate black ('Isn't it the colour of the funeral horses?' say the Irish) and breeders will always try to describe horses of that colour as brown if possible. Certainly there have been some pretty vicious blacks of both sexes, but I don't mind the colour, provided that the horse has a good, generous head.

When I asked Atty Persse what he looked for in a yearling, the man who had bought The Tetrarch and so many other great horses said simply: 'The head.' He amplified: 'I never buy one with a bad head and especially small prick ears (pony ears). By a bad head I mean one with a small pig eye, a receding forehead or a bump between the eyes, the kind of characteristics you dislike in a man. I prefer a wide forehead; a good large, bold eye and good long, straight ears. Small ears may be all right on a Hollywood film star, but not on a racehorse. I have never trained a horse with short prick ears and a pig eye who was not a rogue.' A pretty conclusive verdict after more than fifty years at the very top of his profession.

The old man went on: 'If a horse has the courage that a genuine head indicates, I'll win with him, no matter how slow he may be. The other sort can be as brilliant as you like, but they'll always let you down when it matters.'

The only other point he would admit to looking for was a strong second thigh.

Before turning to detail, there are two general precepts governing the purchase of any horse. 'You can get enough trouble later on without buying it' and 'Never buy for the sake of buying'. You must really covet an animal and regret it bitterly if you are outbid. As Omar Sharif says, with such depth of feeling in those great liquid eyes, 'You must actually fall in love with a horse before you buy it.'

So first impressions are important. If you have been lucky, you will have had your card marked about several yearlings by their stud grooms. Atty always went round some of the big studs in August for this purpose, which was why he would sometimes buy unlikely yearlings who turned out to be wonderful bargains. Only the stud groom, who has cared for them from birth, knows which of the youngsters hates to be passed and, if left behind at the start of a gallop round the paddock, has the guts, the will and the ability to race between his fellows and win.

Try to see the yearling out of his box first, or you will develop a preconceived idea about him. This is a common British failing. When the English polo players some years ago were trying to sell some ponies to the members of that fabulous forty-goal American team, they had the animals all ready, beautifully turned out in their boxes at Hurlingham. But the Americans refused to look at them there. 'Have them galloped up and down that polo field,' they said, 'and then we'll pick out the ones we want to see in their boxes.'

You can't see them gallop at the sales. When a filly did get loose and galloped round the old Doncaster sales paddock, showing what a lovely mover she was, Atty and his pupil Cecil Boyd-Rochfort were the only two who took advantage of this unexpected bonus. In a spirited duel Cecil eventually won and she duly turned out to be a right good race mare.

However, you can see them walk. When Bob Colling retired, he asked his son Jack to buy him a yearling. Jack recalled:

> I was terrified of what my father would think of the one I bought him. We had just finished dinner when we were told that the horsebox had arrived back from the sales. In fear and trembling I accompanied the old man down to the yard to inspect my selection. He stood still, saying nothing at all, while the yearling was led round and round him. Eventually I could stand it no longer and blurted out, 'Well, at least you must admit he's a good walker Father.' He replied, 'They don't have walking races', turned on his heel and went back to the house.

Your yearling should be a free-going sort — not one who has to be pulled round the ring, but one who gives you the immediate impression that he is keen to get somewhere and will pull his lad along with him if necessary. Make sure that he walks straight in front and behind. You see so many yearlings nowadays who either wind a foreleg, knit (going so close that they knock their joints with the opposite foot) or paddle (going too wide in front). It's better to have one who paddles than one who knits. Peter Thrale used to say, 'They ought to throw in a pair of boots with that one' — but why take a chance on either? See that he has plenty of freedom for his elbow and that he uses his well laid back shoulder. He should use his quarters too, bringing his hind feet well forward so that he nearly or actually overtracks. If he brings his hind feet up in front of his forefeet, he will have great leverage. The best indication that he really uses his hind legs is his tail. It should swing wide from hock to hock as he walks. This is particularly important with potential jumpers. The late Lord Bicester, keenest of all National Hunt stalwarts and a great judge of jumpers, always insisted on a horse who 'walked as though he had just shat himself!' You don't need a Flat horse to go as wide as that behind, but the principle is the same. After all, that's where the drive comes from. Provided

*Atty Persse and Cecil Boyd-Rochford share a catalogue
at Doncaster Sales.*

that he is a straight walker with a good long stride, you can now inspect him standing still.

Before wasting any more time make sure that he's neither blind nor parrot-mouthed. Then, with a colt, satisfy yourself that he has two testicles. If in any doubt, ask a vet for help. It's better to take the trouble than find yourself landed with a rig.

Most of the old trainers always insisted on a large sheath, believing too small genitals a sign of ungenuineness and vice versa. Geoffrey Brooke, Atty's brother-in-law and assistant for thirty years before becoming a highly successful trainer on his own, held strongly to this view. There was one Persse apprentice who was an unmitigated rogue – a scrounging little crook who used to steal money from the other boys' letters and had nothing to recommend him. But Geoffrey wouldn't have it. 'He can't be all bad,' he said. 'He's got the biggest John Thomas I've ever seen! There must be some good in him somewhere.' I'm afraid Geoffrey was wrong and it is worth recording that Fortina, one of the finest jumping sires of all time, whose produce had unlimited guts, had one of the smallest sheaths I have ever seen. On the other hand, I have known a number of horses with large sheaths who were soft themselves and passed their lack of courage on to their offspring.

Now a great deal of nonsense is talked about the difference between thoroughbred and ordinary horses. If you are a good judge of any kind of horse, or indeed of a hound, you can be a good judge of a yearling because, of course, the basic conformation and mechanism must be the same. For example, a hunter who is back at the knee or too straight in front is even more useless than a Flat-race horse who has these faults, and what good is a hound who is tied in at the elbow, or a show jumper with round joints? So judge your yearling as you would a light-weight show hunter, bearing in mind that he is still growing up. However, one difference must be mentioned. As with any horse, it is important that the second thigh or gaskin should be well developed and pronounced, but in the case of a sprinter the hind leg itself need not be the purist's straight leg. If you think of the hind leg of a greyhound and compare it with that of a foxhound and consider their different uses you will see what I mean.

Another well known saying, 'Lean horses for long races', is not always true, but in the main you expect your sprinter to be the deep, powerful short-coupled type with a massive backside. 'The head of an angel and the farewell of a cook' is the old description of the ideal racehorse.

Nevertheless, the straighter the hind leg the better. Above all, it must be strong. I would never buy a horse with weak hind legs or sickle hocks.

Next you look for a good sloping shoulder and forelegs that are not back at the knee, as such a horse is difficult to train, the strain on the tendons being too severe. But a horse who stands over at the knee seldom breaks down.

Avoid small donkey feet, short upright pasterns and overlong sloping pasterns. Such a horse's value is immediately depressed because he could never be passed on to America, where the concrete is only just underneath the dirt and the jar on the joints would cause a swift breakdown. Furthermore, too many of our own courses are frequently hard enough to damage such an animal's legs. Look at the grass and dirt marks on the front joints of a horse with white socks after a race and you will see how hard they hit the ground at full gallop.

The fetlock joint should be clean, not rough or too round. The cannon bone should be short with as much bone as possible. If in doubt about a splint, ask a good racing vet. In principle you can ignore it if it is well forward and not too close to the knee or the joint.

The knees should be big, well formed and strong. The forearm should be strong and the elbow must have freedom. Far too many people who should know better buy horses who are tied in at the elbow.

With the notable exception of the fastest Flat horse and jumper ever seen, The Tetrarch and Arkle, who had extra long hind legs like a greyhound's or a hare's, a horse's withers will normally grow up to the level of his quarters. Another rough test of the height to which your yearling will grow was a favourite of the old trainers. Take a handkerchief or a piece of string and measure from the elbow down to the joint. Then, keeping the end of the handkerchief or string on the elbow, take the other end up to the withers. When the horse is full grown, the measurements from withers to elbow and elbow to joint should be about the same.

The head should be well set on a graceful, well made neck, which in turn should flow evenly back into the withers. See that he has freedom and is not too thick behind the jaw; even a yearling can go in the wind. Incidentally, this is a major point

Sea Bird II; a top class colt, despite being narrower framed than ideal.

frequently ignored by those intent on buying potential three day event horses. Unless a horse has complete freedom behind the jaw, he is physically incapable of flexing properly for dressage, but will inevitably become overbent.

Think where your saddle is going to sit. Your horse should have a good length of rein and your fast horse in particular should be close-coupled. A stayer can have a slightly longer back and it is usually argued that a chaser needs the extra length to balance him if he makes mistakes over big fences where a short-backed horse might topple over.

Although a stayer may be 'short of a rib', all horses should have plenty of heart room and a good spring of rib. It used to be said that you should be able to get your head between the forelegs of a good jumper, but that was in the days of the massive old-fashioned chaser, who has vanished with the disappearance of the Irish Draught mare and the discovery that the smaller, wiry quality chasers of today can do the same job even more successfully than their predecessors. Suffice it to say that your yearling should be neither too wide nor too narrow in front. Despite the brilliance of Sea Bird II and Santa Claus, I hate an animal whose forelegs seem to come out of the same hole.

Length from hip to croup — a rare quality these days — is just as important as length from hip to hock. Beware of ringbone, curbs and thoroughpins. Never take a chance. Let someone else have the problem. There are usually just as good fish in the sea and, even if the yearling grows into a Classic winner, you have done the job for which you are employed by your owner by not risking his money.

A few more points. Unless you are buying a well bred filly with the stud in mind, or a store horse, it is not worthwhile buying a late May or June foal. This has missed the spring grass and is usually too far behind to catch up. Many of the old trainers like Ossie Bell never ran a two-year-old until the animal was genuinely two.

Before you go to the sales make sure that your insurance company has any horse that you buy at any sale fully covered from the fall of the hammer! This is vitally important. I remember a very expensive yearling being killed at the old Doncaster sales on the way to the station and another being so badly injured when slipping up leaving the ring that he had to be put down. The first insurance should keep the yearling covered for three months — that is, over the breaking period.

Before leaving the sales paddock for the night see that your purchases are well bedded down, watered and fed and that they will be looked after again the next morning. The auctioneering firms are very good, but studs vary and all too often mistakes occur when the youngsters' own attendants have left, freed from responsibility now that their charges have been sold and anxious either for a night out or to get home.

It is hard to advise on bidding. I think some of the best bargains have been picked up either just before or, preferably, immediately after the sale of a big lot or of a very high class famous contingent, when everyone was talking, getting up and going out for a drink. I know that, as a vendor, I would much rather sell first lot in the morning than at one of those junctures.

The other times at which you can be lucky are on the Friday and Saturday of the week-long sales at Newmarket, in the calm after the drama of the first four days, and during one of those spells when a long series of poor lots are going through, frequently failing to fetch their unrealistic reserves. Then, occasionally, you will find among the depressing rubbish the offering of some good small stud. You just have to be alert for these opportunities. It's surprising how a sale can suddenly die, only to be resurrected equally unexpectedly. Some auctioneers have a particularly soporific effect, especially after lunch. As they drone on and people are nodding off round the ring, I have often wondered over the years why, just because a man is a director or a partner in a firm, he should assume that he is a top class professional auctioneer, fully qualified to sell the highest priced lots. It's all right for the purchaser, but bad selling can cost a vendor tens of thousands of pounds in a big sale.

Many rich men and women have spent fortunes trying to buy success on the Turf at the yearling sales. The failures have been plentiful and the disillusioned owners have been mortified to see the Classic successes of such bargains as Hard Ridden (270 guineas) and Hard to Beat (920 guineas).

It was not until David Robinson began to spread his wings that we saw how business methods and systematic buying can work with racehorses. David Robinson was a millionaire and in pre-Arab days the most successful owner in Turf history as regards the number of races won. He owned more horses than anyone in Britain and broke the all-time record of races won in a season. The organisation which he created in less than four years was bred from business efficiency out of countless cash flow. Racing's traditionalists sneered and called it a supermarket because Robinson did not breed horses. He bought and sold.

At the end of his record-breaking 1970 season he told me, 'They don't approve of me or my methods. They want everything done in the same old way. But my methods work. My horses have won £270,000 in prize money this season. My racing accounts show a profit of over £100,000 − that is deducting cost of keeping, training and racing from the prize money. My trading account − buying and selling horses − is also well in credit.'

When he gave me the first exclusive interview, his 5,000 guinea Ballsbridge yearling purchase, My Swallow, had beaten Mill Reef in the Prix Robert Papin at Maisons-Laffitte and had smashed all records by winning all the French two-year-old 'Classics', finishing with winnings of £88,000. The colt failed to train on, but his unbeaten two-year-old record stamps him as a truly outstanding buy as a racehorse and stallion for the future.

'They're all trying to buy the colt now,' said the tall, square-jawed television rental tycoon, whose love of racing stemmed from boyhood, when he used to bicycle from Cambridge to Newmarket fourteen miles away. 'They're talking in telephone numbers,' he added.

The interview, published in the *Daily Mail* of 16 October 1970, was a sensation. The Robinson methods were so revolutionary that they are worth recounting here.

How David Robinson came to buy My Swallow is an example of his working methods, which left the rest of the racing world a little disgruntled − and a long way behind. His scant regard for tradition and his commercial logic told him that success in racing comes via the same expertise that helped him build a multi-million pound television rental empire. So he surrounded himself with experts. With their knowledge and his money he bought the best.

In the catalogue for the Dublin sale in 1969, his breeding expert, Charlie Chute, saw My Swallow and wrote: 'Like the horse. Should win races.' But that was not enough. David Robinson then put his team of other experts to work. They compared the horse with every other animal in the catalogue. Robinson had picked well. His team included Lord Harrington, who advised and made bids; Jack Colling, a former top trainer; Jack Freeman, a veterinary surgeon; and his three private trainers, Paul Davey, Michael Jarvis and Bob Smart. On their advice, he

*David Robinson's highly successful purchase, My Swallow, winning
Kempton's Usher Stakes.*

bought My Swallow. That year, horses running in his green, scarlet and pale blue colours won 103 races worth £100,000.

Traditionally, successful owners were horse breeders, but Robinson saw no point in following the Derby, Rosebery, Aga Khan, Boussac and Astor tradition. For one thing, it would have taken too long.

'I feel sorry for owners who are landed with unsound horses, some of which never even see a racecourse,' he said. 'We eliminate chance as far as possible and never buy unsoundness. Any horse with an 'if' is struck out right away. We may have some who *won't* race — but virtually none who *can't*. They call my team Robinson's Rangers. They work hard and are worth their weight in gold.'

From an allotted amount of money, the team bought about fifty yearlings each autumn and a number of foals. But selection was not enough; the Robinson formula for planned improvement and success would take over. His three stables were adjacent and inter-linked, each trainer having about forty horses, new purchases being distributed as fairly as possible between the trainers. The animals were graded into three colours on their ability: red for outstanding, blue for good and green for fair. All the horses were graded red as two-year-olds and regraded after they had shown their ability on the racecourse. Therefore, they could earn colour promotion or relegation, but only on race performance.

Racecourses were similarly graded and only red horses ran at the ten red courses in Britain, blue at the twelve blue courses and the remainder at green courses. Even jockeys were graded. 'I change the system only if there is a big race, say, at a green meeting. Then a red horse might drop in class.'

The nerve centre was the Operations Room that linked the stables. Briefing took place every Sunday morning. Each trainer would study the *Racing Calendar*, list the races he considered suitable, and make his case at the weekly conference. Robinson and Roy Allen, an old business associate, would then make the decision. The Operations Room had a list of all meetings for the next two months. One wall had a list of all horses over the age of two. Another had a list of two-year-olds. Plaques denoted suggested entries; pegs were for definite runners. Each horse had his form figures attached to his name. Robinson and his team could tell, at a glance, the efficiency and progress of any animal.

David Robinson did not bet. In keeping with his business-like approach, he had some strong opinious on racing and its organisation:

> Our animals are always trying when they run. Apart from winners we have had one hundred seconds this year [1970].
>
> In France, they run racing very efficiently, but here, I am afraid it is a mess. The powers that be know that the answer is to get rid of the bookmarkers, but they won't do it.
>
> How can you run any business and get things done in the way the Jockey Club insists on perpetuating? I ask you!
>
> I wouldn't join the Jockey Club if they asked me. There would be just one almighty row and that would be the finish.'

Robert Sangster and Vincent O'Brien, taking a leaf out of David Robinson's book, exploited the international yearling sales with a different approach. Their aim, in which initially they were supremely successful, was to create international Classic stallions.

With Vincent's judgment, supported by a quorum of experts, like 'Robinson's Rangers', they selected the best-made colts with the finest stallion pedigrees in the world, laid out record sums to buy them and then proved their worth on the racecourses of Europe before selling them as stallions at a substantial profit or, in some cases, keeping them at stud in Ireland. Just one really good one would more than pay for the total outlay.

The Arab invasion, with jumbo jet loads of 'experts' and hangers-on virtually taking over the cream of the world's year-lings for the oil-rich sheiks, coupled with an apparent decline in available cash and some inferior selections halted the bonanza. But we still have to thank Sangster and his henchmen for the likes of The Minstrel, Alleged, El Gran Senor, Lomond, Caerleon, Sadlers Wells and others.

CHAPTER THREE
Breaking

While their guv'nor is at the sales, the stable lads have been sitting at home studying the reports and figures in *The Sporting Life* and *Racing Post*. The character, quality and ability of his purchases will affect their lives fundamentally throughout the next twelve months and frequently beyond.

Although stables nowadays run pools, so that every lad receives a bonus at Christmas, this and the additional authorised percentage of winning stakes depend upon winners. Moreover, where a lad does two or three horses, he will have a far better life mentally and financially if he is allotted charges who can run frequently and win. I have often marvelled at the philosophical way in which the average lad takes it when his horses turn out to be duds, and have thought it unfair that the initial allocation should carry so much weight for so long.

Running a small stable and having a reputation for buying bargains, I used to receive some old-fashioned looks sometimes when I returned from the sales.

I was very lucky; I had some of the best lads in the business and they were all my friends, but even they could be so wrong in their first impressions, which are apt to be influenced by the amount paid for each of the young entries.

So when I brought plain, lop-eared, gawky Paper Money back from Ireland, nobody wanted to do her. Apart from her looks, they knew that she had cost me only 80 guineas and I think they believed I had gone mad. The bay Pappageno filly turned out a great success: she won eight races, was placed a number of times and has produced good winners.

In fact, the 'ugly duckling' story is constantly being repeated in racing and is one of the excitements of most branches of horse sport.

At this stage the trainer must think about marrying up his lads and the new intake, although the actual allocation will probably not take place until they are ridden away or perhaps even later if, for example, a lad is still doing two horses, both of whom are going up for sale at Newmarket in November.

The temptation is always to give your most prized yearlings to the best lads. It should not wholly be resisted, certainly until a proper wage structure has been evolved rewarding ability, loyalty and length of service. The 1990 agreement between the National Trainers Federation and the Stable Lads Association is a welcome move in this respect, since it was formerly ridiculous that a smart, conscientious, efficient married lad of, say, thirty-five, who was a good quiet horseman and turned his charges out beautifully, should receive the same money as a scruffy, surly, ham-handed youth just out of his time.

However, I still believe that a scale should be drawn up with increments at least every four years, whereby a top class lad could be earning the maximum wage (and a good one, too, comparable with industry) by the time he is thirty. This would only be social justice. A stable lad is not only doing a strenuous and, at times, a dangerous job. He is also entrusted with highly-strung animals worth thousands and in some cases millions of pounds to their owners. Happy lads make happy, good horses and the opposite is equally true. The most valuable horse can be ruined by a rough, frightened or idle lad.

It doesn't make any kind of sense. As racehorse owners, the Jockey Club should know that it is absolutely vital to attract the best type of people into the industry and to keep them, otherwise disaster is not far away. The French have taken great steps in this direction and are already reaping the benefit, but then the French authorities look after staff from the time they come into the industry and pension them off when they leave. Furthermore, they help their trainers by laying down a minimum training fee, insisting that every owner must pay his share of the trainer's salary as well as the full cost of keeping his horse, which, of course, includes the lads' wages. In this country we have the unhealthy situation where the lads are paid far too little and some trainers are actually subsidising their owners. Yet, when I asked the Senior Steward why the Jockey Club did not follow the French example, I was given the historic reply: 'It would be impertinence to lay down a minimum training fee. I wouldn't tell Jeremy what to pay his butler.' God, how we have to fight for every commonsense reform.

Under my scale a Grade A lad would be worth his light weight in gold to his employers. A top class girl would be paid the wage of a Grade B lad because, whether she likes it or not, the trainer must necessarily think twice about the horses she rides and looks after. In the first place, she is just not physically strong enough to ride the big, hard-mouthed, pulling jumper. Secondly, all experience shows that we must accept the great Fred Darling's opinion that girls should not be allowed near colts for basic sex reasons which I shall deal with in the next chapter. But I like girls doing fillies. They mostly ride well and their light touch when strapping does not upset or overexcite the animals.

On the night when they arrive, after the strain of the sales, I like to settle the yearlings in with a small mash. Thereafter, until they have been ridden away, they will probably be fed only hay, which must be placed on the floor of the box, never in a haynet. There have been far too many tragedies caused by horses getting their feet or teeth caught in the mesh of the net.

At this stage all the young entries are usually left in the charge of the big strong lad, who will be responsible for breaking them, and of his assistants.

Remember that handling varies on different studs and even today you are dealing with a very nervous, untamed animal. It is more than ever important to obey the golden rule and never take a chance. Never stand in front of a yearling, be careful how you pick up his feet and don't tie him up at any time with anything but string or binder twine, which is easily broken. You won't use rack chains until well into his second year.

All your breaking tack and gear should by now be assembled after being thoroughly inspected. Nothing must go wrong or irreparable damage may be caused.

Basically, you will need:
1. *Breaking bridle* with easily operated buckles and breaking bit equipped with players.
2. *Two webbing lungeing reins.*
3. *Cavesson.*
4. *Side reins and saddle attachments.*

5. *Riding reins.*
6. *Roller* with side rein (breast girth) attachments and one-hand buckle crupper.
7. *Saddle* fully equipped, but with string girths (to prevent galling).
8. *Hunting whip*, with extra long thong, or *driving whip*.

I intend to describe two methods of breaking: (A) for the very small trainer, who is normally coping with older potential jumpers, either cannot afford or hasn't got an assistant and so has to do the job himself; and (B) for the professional trainer of horses on the Flat.

Both methods have worked satisfactorily for so many years that they would be worth following strictly. On the other hand, they are intended merely as guides, because there are, of course, many variations on the same theme.

METHOD (A)

1. Put the bridle on, with its keys (players) but with no reins, and leave it on all day, removing it before bedding down.

2. The following day put the bridle on again. Put a cavesson on, ensuring that the middle of the three straps is really tight.

3. Depending on the available facilities, lead the horse to an indoor school, enclosed barn (with non-slip floor), covering yard or large ordinary box.

4. With one lungeing rein on the near side ring of the cavesson, show the horse the roller, side reins (with spring clips) and crupper that you are about to put on him. Let him sniff them, nibble them and generally try to understand them.

5. With his head turned towards you, place the roller over his back and clip the side reins on to the rings of the bit. Then quickly fasten the girths up very loosely. All this time you should be talking to your horse, soothing him and showing him that he is not being hurt.

6. Still keeping his head firmly turned towards you and holding on tight with your left hand, use your right hand to place the crupper round under his tail and do up the buckle.

7. If there are going to be fireworks, they will start now, so be careful as you tighten the girth strap and the horse really feels the tack for the first time.

8. If the horse has been well handled (most Irish three- or four-year-olds will have had bits in their mouths to be led in

the show or sale ring as yearlings or two-year-olds), you can, after he has fought the tack and quietened down, transfer your rein to the bit on the near side. You would then slip your right hand down over his neck with the other rein and fasten on the off side.

It is better, however, to assume that, like most store horses bred and reared in this country, he has not been led on the bit but on a headcollar. In this case do the same thing, quietly fastening the second rein on to the offside ring of the cavesson.

Before this last stage you should, if you are still in a loose-box, have led out into a small, well fenced field or enclosure. If you are already in a covering yard or indoor school, all is well. In either case your driving whip should be lying handy on the floor.

9. Quietly slide the off side lunge rein over his quarters, allowing it to rest on his hocks and at the same time letting out the near side rein so that he can 'ring' around you to the left. Going this way you will not normally require the whip. The horse is in a very nervous, frightened state and inclined to jump forward in any case. Only if he is dead lazy should you pick it up in your right hand to give him a light tap.

At this stage your side reins should be fairly loose, just tight enough to prevent your horse from stretching his nose straight out.

If the animal has been handled a lot and is therefore well used to the bit, you may prefer to have the reins now on the rings of the bit instead of the cavesson for greater control. On the other hand, there is no doubt that the longer you use the cavesson, the more chance you have of producing a good mouth.

Lungeing to the left should present no problem. But now comes the crunch and this is when it is so much better to have an assistant. However, in this hypothetical case you are on your own. So when, after a good spell of trotting to the left, you decide to change the rein, you must make use of a well fenced corner of your paddock or the walls of the indoor school.

From the start you will have been talking to the horse, getting him used to simple words of command ('Walk on', 'Trot' and 'Whoa!') and to the different tone of voice associated with each. The cavalry teaching on this subject is the best. 'Walk on' is a flat, quiet order; 'Ter-ot' is higher pitched and sharper; 'Whoa!' is decisive, long drawn out and musical.

Pull him up, get his head into the corner, turn it quietly round to the right so that the left rein now rests on the near-side hock, and set him off as best you can. The one thing to remember is never to let him get his head straight.

After a good trot to the right, pull him up, make a fuss of him and take him back to his box. He must be rewarded immediately, so remove all the tack except the bridle and, with that still on, let him drink and eat a bowl of oats. Leave the bridle on until evening stables. This will, of course, mean leaving the crupper on as well, because an animal with no withers, as is frequently the case with a yearling, could pull the roller forward on to his neck. However, after giving him a quick brush over at evening stables, I prefer to remove the roller and breast girth for the night.

When you tie him up to brush him over, it is essential that you do not tie the rack chain direct to the headcollar. Either fasten the end of the chain to the headcollar with a piece of binder twine, or dispense with the chain altogether and plait up some binder twine to use instead. Over the years there have been an incredible number of horrible accidents caused by yearlings running back on an unbreakable chain. For the same reason, rack chains should never at any time in a horse's life be left hanging in the box when the horse has been let down and is loose. Colts in particular will play with the chain and it is all too easy to get it stuck in the teeth with the resultant broken back. One of Britain's finest stallion prospects was lost in just such a way. The lads must get into the habit of removing the chain with their grooming kit as they leave the box after letting their horse down.

There are those who like haynets. I know they are economical, but personally I'm dead against them. In a stable with strict discipline they may be all right for fillies and geldings, but a colt is far too handy with his forelegs and teeth and, if the temptation is there, he is likely to succumb sooner or later. For those who do use haynets, the head man on his final tour of inspection at midday and evening must ensure that they are pulled up and tightly fastened and twisted round. Those who employ apprentices must insist that the boys stand on buckets to tie up their haynets.

However, with yearlings in the breaking stage, haynets are obviously quite out of the question. No hard food at all should be given during the period and, while I don't agree with the old principle of starving them, I suggest a few pounds of hay in

Educating a young racehorse in long reins.

the corner of the box will be quite sufficient until at least a week after the yearlings have been ridden away. Nevertheless, on mash nights (I like three a week in the winter months), they can probably be allowed a small mash with a few salts as soon as they have been ridden away.

The single-handed breaker will now repeat the performance for several days, teaching the horse to drive in long reins and using his driving whip. After becoming thoroughly accustomed to the roller, the yearling will usually be quite ready to accept a saddle, provided that he is shown what is going on his back. The saddle should be equipped with breast girth and crupper and the side reins should fasten to the girth straps, while the other end should again have a spring clip on to the rings of the bit.

It is a matter of preference whether you start with the irons run up or hanging down. Personally, I prefer the latter. In this case, long reins can pass through the irons on either side.

The cavesson can be dispensed with after the first few days, as soon as the yearling has shown that he is sufficiently well mouthed to have both reins on the rings of the bit.

Believing as always that prevention is better than cure, and that it is fatal to take chances with horses, I suggest that even the most stubborn loner should recruit some help when it comes to backing the yearling, either with a human or with a dumb-jockey.

METHOD (B)

In direct contrast to the foregoing is the quick mass production method used by the big stables who cannot afford the time or the labour for more elaborate ways of breaking. The season is still not over; they will be having runners all the time and besides, they want to get on with the yearlings as quickly as possible.

Yearlings cost money and, however much owners know about horses, they are far better kept away from the stables during this period. Unless you are professional, living with the animals all the time and knowing the necessity for quick, efficient breaking, it can be an alarming procedure. The fact that the yearlings have automatically been insured for at least three months from the drop of the hammer, or have been insured by their owner-breeders from the moment that they went into training, may at times, in the heat of the moment, seem almost immaterial. Nevertheless, however much they may fight against the tack, throw themselves down and perform the most terrifying antics, they seldom seem to do themselves any harm, though at the time it may seem that they are going to injure themselves for life.

In describing the method employed by Atty Persse, who taught me my job, I realise that there are, of course, many variations. The breaker will doubtless compromise between the two extremes, depending on all the factors involved, particularly time, labour, resources and the temperament of the individual animals.

For each yearling you need two strong men, one of whom is equipped with the 'Long Tom', a hunting whip with an extra long thong, such as is used by hunt servants.

Atty preferred to make a ring, either in a lightly-ploughed field or more usually at this time of year, in burnt stubble. Be careful in the latter case to keep an eye open for cracked heels.

With the same gear as before, the breaking bit in the mouth and the cavesson, get the yearling running both ways, keeping him on the go until he is sufficiently tired to stand while the tack is being put on. Next, the man who is holding the reins stands close to the yearling's head — never in front of him — being ready to dodge if the animal swings his head. A horse's head with a cavesson is a heavy weapon. He shades the near eye with his right hand, while his helper carefully puts on the roller and crupper and clips on the side reins.

The yearling will almost certainly start when he feels the roller. Gingerly tighten it before letting out the reins. Now at all costs he must be kept going forward, round to the left. This is the time when he is likely to indulge in his most ferocious antics. Most trainers prefer a yearling to have a real go at the tack. They believe that if he doesn't do so and 'get it out of his system' at this stage, he is likely to be a difficult customer later on. Whatever I think of this theory, it is certain that a brave, young, untamed thoroughbred is entitled to resent this first real attempt to control him.

Once he has settled going round to the left, pull him in to the centre of the ring (never go to him), quietly tighten the roller and start him off to the right. After a good trot in both directions he should be thoroughly tired from his exertions. Take him back to his box, remove the cavesson, check the fastenings of the roller, crupper and bridle and side reins, and leave him with the tack on until evening stables. Then remove all the tack except the roller crupper and breast girth, which should be left on all night.

On the second morning, after the yearling has been settled and tired, it should be possible to place a saddle equipped with crupper and side reins on his back instead of the roller. At this point I prefer to drop one lunge rein over the offside, allowing at least a measure of driving. But the Persse method excluded any driving. When the yearling is back in his box, one man should hold the head firmly, covering his near eye, and the other man should carefully leg up a light lad to lie on his stomach over the saddle, ready to slip off at a moment's notice. This should be done several times before the tack is removed. Roller and breast girth should be put on before the horse is let down. Repeat the process on the third morning, although now the saddle, with its leathers and irons hanging down, should be placed on the horse's back before he goes out, and on his return the light lad should be able to swing a leg carefully over, so that he is half sitting and half lying in the saddle, gradually sitting up. This should be repeated several times in preparation for the fourth and final day.

At this stage you will need to have a hack ready, or a sensible older horse. After repeating the performance of the two previous days, the light lad should carefully put his feet in the irons and the yearling should be led out of the box behind the older horse. If it is possible to find a hill for this first occasion when he is to be ridden away loose, so much the better. In Upper Lambourn there is an ideal steep little hill called Hobbs' Lane, after that great horseman and jumping trainer who turned out so many winners from his yard at the bottom of the lane. It was from this little yard that the American stallion, Battleship, was sent to Aintree to triumph in the Grand National, ridden by Reg's seventeen-year-old son, Bruce.

Hobbs' Lane runs between high banks with trees covering its full length on either side, so that the young horse had no distractions. This is the ideal place. You can lead the yearling to the bottom and loose him off as the older horse starts trotting. By the time he gets to the top he will have got his back down. A couple more times up the lane and the yearling is said to be 'ridden away'.

Of course, if you have no Hobbs' Lane, you will have to make do with the next best thing, but in any case this method normally guarantees to have the yearling ridden away from scratch in four days.

The light boy riding the youngster must ride with long leathers and must be told never to hang on to the horse's mouth, but to keep a finger constantly in the neck strap so that when his mount darts forward, or to either side, his young unformed mouth is not hurt.

This is, of course, one of the many arguments for prolonging the driving period, for a man with good hands on the long reins can do much to make a horse's mouth and in the long run this is usually helpful.

I believe that two of the most important factors in horse-mastership are impulsion and the constant practice of never taking a chance. During the breaking period all movements around the horse must be even more gentle and even less hurried than usual. A few extra minutes spent soothing a puzzled, frightened youngster and in adjusting the tack correctly must inevitably pay dividends. In the quick method the man holding the reins is almost less important than the man with the 'Long Tom', except, of course, that he must ensure that the horse never gets his head straight and it is he whose words and whose feel on the reins will inspire confidence. However, his safety and the impulsion imparted to the animal depend entirely on the man with the whip. Although his friend holding the reins may be quick on his feet, he has little chance if the yearling decides to charge him in frenzied resentment. The man with the whip must keep close to the other in the centre of the ring and keep the animal on the move.

Either way, the yearling must receive no oats until he is ready to joint the string. During the breaking period, condition will fall away if the horse has been readied for sale on patent medicines. On the other hand, it is wonderful to see how the products of the best run studs, who have been well exercised and fed on first class natural food, maintain their condition even through the physical and nervous strain of this period.

It is important to remember that a yearling does not require more than an hour's exercise and initially, providing that you have some good hills to trot up, three-quarters of an hour will probably suffice.

Remembering that they have never had anything round their legs, and therefore taking the necessary precautions, you should always fit knee boots if you intend using the roads for your walking and trotting exercise. It is surprising how many modern trainers ignore this elementary safeguard against broken knees which can, after all, wreck the chances of a valuable animal. Talk about spoiling a ship for a ha'po'rth of tar!

In the hands of good lads the yearling will soon learn to go kindly in the string and keep a horse's length behind the tail of the one in front. However, at this stage a kick should not do much harm unless you are really unlucky, because you will have no shoes behind and probably, following the old trainers' practice, just tips in front, allowing the young foot to grow.

Provided that he keeps a hold of his neck strap, do not worry if the lad on top waves his hands to and fro and side to side in his attempts to keep the animal up into the bit. Count Robert Orssich, probably the finest producer of a show horse ever known, told me: 'I always like to buy my potential show horses out of training. Instead of frigging about behind their bits messed around by silly girls, they have been ridden by stable lads "rowing a boat" and they can all walk properly. This is vital in the training of a show horse.'

Nevertheless, it is essential, with all horses in training, to walk, trot and canter very steadily at all times. The widely held theory that a horse should walk out at exercise is quite wrong. Atty Persse taught, 'You can take condition off a horse quicker by walking and trotting fast than by any amount of galloping.'

Moreover, in string work, if the leading horse is allowed to trot at more than a very slow hound-jog, those at the rear will inevitably be cantering. Atty always insisted on the lead horse being ridden by a responsible man who could be trusted to obey this precept. The lads behind hated it, particularly on Monday mornings, because their mounts, restrained to a slow pace, were liable to mess about, jump, kick and duck out, but the end product was the envy of all; the unmistakable Persse horse, carrying enormous condition when in full training throughout the season.

Since you are dealing with a soft unused article, keep a close watch for galling with the saddle, girths or bit. In every case, prevention is better than cure. The last thing you want is to be forced to start all over again after a lay-off due to injury.

After a short while, when a youngster is going really kindly in the string, it will be possible to remove the side reins and in most cases the crupper. However, bear in mind that although a horse's withers will always grow up to the height of his quarters by the time he is full grown, at this stage the withers of many are still low enough for the saddle to slip forward, so the removal of the crupper must depend on the conformation of the individual animal. Incidentally, Atty had some splendid old cruppers with a long strap hanging down on either side a little behind the saddle, which prepared the yearling for the feel of the clothing which he would shortly be wearing. I have not seen any of these since, but I'm sure that they should be reintroduced.

One of the best examples of a yearling who needed a crupper throughout his breaking period — in fact until he was almost ready to run — was the little chestnut colt by Ballyogan out of Damians, whom Atty bought for a fair price at Dublin sales for Jack Olding.

We could not believe our eyes when the new draft from Ballsbridge arrived in Upper Lambourn and the yearlings were paraded. Someone looked at the tiny chestnut and said boldly, 'I didn't know you bought donkeys, Mr Persse!' The old man turned those steely blue eyes and I thought for a moment that there would be an explosion. Instead, he took the cigar out of his mouth and chuckled somewhat ruefully, 'Neither did I,' he said. 'I can't think how the hell I ever came to buy him. I was perfectly sober, but it doesn't look like it!'

There was always a shortage of boxes and the guv'nor had to turn away would-be patrons. The chestnut colt was so small that Atty ordered the pan to be removed and a manger to be fitted in the lads' lavatory, next to the feed house in the main yard. Ballydam, as he was called, stayed there throughout his highly successful racing career in England, after which he went to America to win more races and become a useful sire of fast horses.

'A lot of nonsense is talked about the advantages of big boxes,' said the old man. 'They can lose a lot of condition by walking about. Some of the greatest horses I ever trained spent their lives in stalls.'

As soon as the trainer is satisfied that the yearlings are sufficiently tractable, the next stage begins. Accompanied by the hack or lead horse, they should first have a good trot and get their backs down, and then go into a paddock, field or whatever open space is available to learn about going 'upsides' and for their first canters. The easiest way of accomplishing the former is that practiced by Atty Persse. It was almost like cavalry riding school training, trotting round in figures of eight and coming upsides in fours on the straight strokes of the figure. This is a very important exercise. Those who attempt to hang back must be forced to go up between other horses and must be accustomed to having their sides bumped by other horses without worrying.

The cantering at this stage should be very steady for not more than two and a half furlongs with a good distance between each horse. This will teach them a measure of independence. Inevitably there will be some loose ones during this period, so, if possible, the yearlings should be exercised in completely enclosed paddocks. This safeguards the animals from injury, which could so easily occur if one escaped and galloped into the road or wire. But it can be an unnerving experience for the rider of the horse as he frolics loose in and out of his companions, taunting them and tempting them to come and play with him.

Bryan Marshall, subsequently champion jump jockey, who was with Atty at Stockbridge said, 'It was a standing joke. If you wanted to put the fear of God into the other lads in the paddock, you'd shout, "Look out! Grab your neckstraps fellahs! There's a loose one!"'

Paddy Prendergast, whose two-year-olds always knew their job first time out as well as Atty's, varied this procedure. The entire string would canter round very slowly, upsides or in any order, getting used to the idea of horses in front, behind and on all sides, chopping and changing position at random.

By the middle of November, the yearlings should be sufficiently forward to start the final stage of their breaking. This will have come considerably earlier at Newmarket where, lacking the hill, and training so much on the open Heath, many trainers have their yearlings cantering within a week from scratch.

I will now describe the method employed by Atty Persse with such success that he remained at the top of his profession for fifty years and in 1930 was champion trainer with two-year-olds alone. I have used this method myself and know it works, but it can be argued that, with a slow-maturing type of animal, it is better not to make him so free. On the other hand, Atty, a great horseman and horsemaster, leading amateur rider at one time in five different countries, was just starting training at the turn of the century and had to evolve a method which would create the maximum impulsion at a time when the jockeys were all following the lead of the American import, Tod Sloan, and riding with short stirrup leathers 'like monkeys up a stick'. Since that day, stirrup leathers have been shortened still further so that we have reached a ludicrous position. Fortunately, there is a tendency for the pendulum to swing back a bit the other way and I hope that, with the help of some of our fine riders like Willie Carson and Steve Cauthen, jockeys will settle down once again to the classic length adopted by such great riders as Steve Donoghue and, in recent years, by Jimmy Lindley and the Australians, George Moore and Bill Williamson. With this length of leathers a man can use his legs for the purpose for which they were designed — to guide and, to a certain extent, to drive.

But it is, of course, impossible to achieve the same measure of impulsion as if you were riding long like the old time jockeys, including Fred Archer and, for that matter, Atty himself.

Atty would have the yearlings parading round after a preliminary canter, either in the big paddock, or on the downs. By now the breaking bridles would have been replaced by ordinary exercise bridles. Side reins and all other impediments would have long since been removed and each yearling equipped with a running martingale — not the usual type with the straps running up to the rings; straps which are all too tempting for the colt to play with and get caught in his teeth, causing a horrible accident — but a bib martingale which is the same except that the two straps are bridged and held together by a solid bib of leather.

As they circled round him, Atty would select three, or four, or five yearlings and send them down to gallop up two and a half furlongs, with the orders, 'Jump off and come the whole way.'

There are always some naturals who have done it all in a previous existence and gallop up the first time as straight as a gun barrel. But the average yearling, when he is turned around and asked to gallop flat out, has no idea what it is about. They will duck and dive, stop and start until, eventually, they reach the trainer in a fair amount of disorder.

'Go down and do it again,' Atty would order. This time they would come upsides a little better. 'And again,' said the old man. Now they were beginning to get the idea.

The following day he would do the same thing. 'My word, that Persse overworks his horses,' was the usual verdict. Of course, this was not true. Atty, who had been a highly successful jumping trainer, was merely schooling them. The short gallop took nothing out of them physically, but educated them mentally so that by the end of a week they would be bowling along upsides, catching hold of their bits and thoroughly enjoying themselves like older horses.

Atty's owners and he himself had always liked a bet. Very few people, even those closest to him, realised the astute brain was working towards that end from the very first time the yearlings worked upsides. 'The only time to have a bet is first time out,' he would say. 'If you are a jumping trainer, the phrase means that you can train your horses to jump. If they fall, you are falling down on your job. On the Flat, the same thing applies; a trainer means a man who can train the horses in his charge to do their very best the first time that they appear in public.' And any jockey who rode for him discovered that every Persse two-year-old knew his business from the word go. They were racing, straight into their stride from the moment they broke from the starting gates, so it was imperative that he alone should know the strength of the young entries. 'If you play your cards properly, only you know the true strength,' he said. 'If you give them an introductory race first time out like most trainers do nowadays, a whole host of other people

Australian jockey George Moore, seen here on Royal Palace, one of the big race winners he rode during his visit to Britain in the late 'sixties.

Top jockeys from different places and generations.

Steve Donaghue winning the Woodcote Stakes on The Tetrarch.

American Steve Cauthen (left) typically stylish in a tight finish, rides a winner at Sandown.

will know the strength or have a damn good idea of it, including your jockey, who, with all his friends, will have a darn great bet and you'll be lucky to get a price at all for yourself and your owner, to whom you have a duty in this respect.'

When, in these initial little training spins, the yearlings were instructed to go down again and gallop up, nobody paid any attention to the fact that they had been regrouped. They imagined, not unnaturally at this stage, that the selection of the raw yearlings when galloping up together was haphazard. They were so wrong. From the very beginning, as soon as his all-seeing eye noticed one going better than his fellows, that one was quickly transferred to a group containing the others who had shown precocious ability. The slow ones were quietly, seemingly accidentally, grouped together so that even the riders did not realize the strength of their mounts.

As the season approached in March, the system would still be enforced. At the first Liverpool meeting, Atty would always run two or three of the middle division, never the best or the worst. By the way they performed he would then be able to gauge the strength of the remainder and have a pretty shrewd idea about the type of season he was going to have.

When the yearlings are galloping freely and straight, it is time to ease off. From the December sales until the third week of January, Atty liked to have them, like the remainder of his string, walking and trotting in the paddocks or on the roads. At Christmas the horses would be physicked (unfair on them at this festive time of the year, I always think, but it gives the lads a break) and then we got them accustomed to wearing a standing rug, starting off with a sack under an ordinary light roller and breast girth. The fillet string was always a bit of binder twine. In this way they were not costing money if they started tearing their clothing!

The Persse system of breaking works with at least ninety per cent of horses, even though they may not be the best rides in later years. The exceptions, of course, include the genuinely lazy animals. These break normally and are perfectly tractable, but they show nothing at all at home and only wake up when they appear on a racecourse, so that even the best laid plans cannot prevent the trainer from being surprised. Ballydam was one such. He not only looked, but worked like a very slow donkey at home and was completely transformed when he ran in a race.

That is at least a pleasant surprise, even if the betting trainer has not been able to have a bet. The worst kind are the villains who are frequently classified as unbreakable. The old trainers had a number of ways of coping with this kind of horse. One was to fit 'blinds' which come down over a horse's eyes so that he can only see his knees, and then drive him in long reins. Another was to harness the stubborn animal between two enormous cart horses. He had no choice. He just had to go, or be dragged along protesting.

That great horsemaster, Ryan Price, said, 'In all my life I have had only one horse whom I could not break. I was going to shoot him, but someone from the West Country persuaded me to let him have him. He said that he would guarantee to succeed where I had failed. When I went down to his place sometime later to see the horse, I wished that I had shot him. He asked me if I would like to see how he achieved his results. We went to a field where there was a huge bank. The horse was trussed up just like a chicken for roasting and rolled repeatedly down this bank. He broke that horse all right. In that he was as good as his word, but the poor creature was utterly useless and had to be destroyed. All his spirit was broken and he had nothing left.'

As I noted earlier, there are inevitably some horses who take longer to break in than the majority. These are the ones who should be driven skilfully for perhaps several weeks before being ridden away. As a result, those who are the most difficult to break may well become the best mannered in the long run.

CHAPTER FOUR
Staff and Routine

Winter work for all Flat-race horses will necessarily depend on the terrain in which individual training establishments are situated. The two extremes between which compromises will, of course, be made are the flat Heath at Newmarket and the hilly Berkshire country.

At Newmarket, horses need more work, both slow and fast, to build them up and keep them in trim.

After his start at Hambleton and Middleham high on the Yorkshire moors, Sir Noel Murless took over from Fred Darling at 'cold, damp' Beckhampton in Wiltshire, which, with his dicky lungs, he hated, and then made his final move to Warren Place on its little hill above Newmarket.

Just as he had done at Beckhampton, the Guv'nor took no time at all to acclimatise himself to Newmarket and to adjust to its gallops. He discovered that horses need more work at Newmarket, not so much because of the flat terrain compared with the hills of Yorkshire and Wiltshire, but because of the texture of the gallops. The grass turf of the Heath takes far less out of a galloping horse than the matted moorland of Hambleton or the springy virgin downland of Beckhampton. But, cautioned the Guv'nor, 'In the hottest, hardest weather you could work two-year-olds up that summer gallop at Hambleton, getting them really fit, so that when you brought them out on to the hard ground at the racecourse, they would win first time out. But the next time that they met hard ground they did not like it so much!'

So much is heard nowadays about watered racecourses, watered

The late Sir Noel Murless smiles in the winner's enclosure. His career was proof that a top class trainer can train in varying environments.

gallops and all-weather surfaces that Sir Noel's views are relevant and interesting. He loved Newmarket's traditional summer gallop, The Limekilns, where for many, many years racehorses of the highest calibre have galloped in the hottest summer droughts. He explained:

> The Limekilns is right on chalk, and in sunny weather the chalk comes to the top so that you get an almost powdery surface there. That only happens in the summer heat. It's an ideal surface. A horse coming off The Limekilns onto a hard racecourse is quite happy. I have always been against watering. It makes the ground so false. The grass grows up instead of down to look for moisture. What's more, with the watering systems they have in this country, one spot will get fifty gallons and ten yards away the course will be lucky to get five.

As soon as a horse leaves his stable in Berkshire, he is automatically working. Training yards were usually built in the valleys between the succession of downland ridges. One was that stretch from East Ilsley right across to Marlborough – those watersheds which have for years boasted the finest natural going in the world. Around Ogbourne Downs and White Horse Hill, which rises in the triangle between Wantage, Ashbury and Upper Lambourn, there are innumerable hills for horses to trot up steadily, slowly putting on muscle in the right places; building vital condition which should stay with them through the long season ahead.

These hills are equally good for jumpers when they come in from grass; and some of them, like Hungerford Hill, the long, steep climb out of Lambourn village, are exceptionally good for very slow cantering of bad-legged horses who are being prepared for hurdling and chasing.

The tarmac surface should not deter the trainer of such animals from cantering. A rough, hard surface does far more harm to the legs. When readying his jumpers, Fulke Walwyn, consistently the greatest National Hunt trainer of recent times, believed in fitting cheek martingales (with the straps fastened to the rings of the bit) during this building-up process so that the horse cannot help but develop muscle as he works against himself.

The old trainers believed that during the off season you should feed your horses really well. The only governing factor, which in those days of expendable labour worried them little, was that the animals should be just rideable. Winter exercise on roads which were frequently icy and slippery could be a nightmare for Atty Persse's lads. The long string resembled a mad chorus line of horses jumping, kicking, rearing and whipping round while Archie Hughes, the head man, shouted ironically to lads in terrible difficulties, 'Don't get off now, Belfast! Well rode, Dublin!'

Nearly all the Persse boys were known only by nicknames. One first class lad, when he first arrived as an apprentice, was considered to resemble the old time jockey Billy Higgs. His own name was forgotten and he remained Billy Higgs throughout his long service with Atty. I believe his name was Wilson, but we all called him Billy and letters used to arrive addressed to Mr W. Higgs.

The staff holidays must be arranged during the winter months in a Flat stable. Half will probably go away for the fortnight including Christmas, returning for the New Year when the remainder can go on leave for the same period.

Depending on the weather, slow cantering in the Berkshire-Wiltshire area can normally be expected to start towards the end of January when all have returned from their holidays.

As far as possible it should be organised so that the older horses go out first lot and the two-year-olds (as they have been since New Year's Day) pull out second lot when the weather is likely to be a bit milder. The first lot should ideally be out for not less than one and a quarter hours and the two-year-olds not more than an hour. Big, strong jumpers will probably do with two hours; providing that the trainer has a full staff of one lad to two horses, he should not, during this period, have to get out more than two lots. Even though financial necessity may now require each lad to look after three horses, third lot is necessarily shorter, comprising recent runners, backward animals and those that are off-colour or convalescing from sickness or injury.

The staff of a normal middle-sized stable will probably consist of a head man, a travelling head man, a yard man, a number of paid lads who are out of their apprenticeship, doing two horses each, and a fair number of apprentices, of whom the newest recruits will probably be restricted to one horse for a while, until they are more practised stable men. For many years trainers exploited apprentices as cheap labour. Atty was one of the worst offenders and was still paying his best boys half-a-crown (12½ p) a week in 1953. He had various methods of recruiting, but the chief source of supply was his native Ireland. Looking like Churchill, smoking his cigar in Dublin's famous Kildare Street Club, he would summon the little page boy, smiling with deceptive charm: 'Would you like to be a jockey, boy?' Immensely flattered by the invitation from the trainer whose name was a legend in a country where bloodstock is the main industry, the fourteen-year-old would stammer, 'Oh yes please Mr Persse.'

'Then bring your father along tomorrow and we'll sign the forms.' Atty always used the totally binding formal indentures which had been employed for over a hundred years by the time I joined him in 1948.

Below are extracts from the most famous indenture of all time drawn up when Fred Archer was apprenticed to Mat Dawson in 1868. Of course, the wage had changed slightly, but only slightly, eighty years later. The last paragraph was modified in the matter of clothing; Atty's boys undertook to provide their own clothing the first year and thereafter the trainer was supposed to supply them. In practice they often arrived almost in rags and were seldom much better clothed right up to the end of their time.

> Frederick Archer now or late of Prestbury near Cheltenham of the age of eleven years or thereabouts doth put himself apprentice to Mathew Dawson of Newmarket All Saints in the County of Cambridge training groom to learn his Art.... to serve from the day of the date hereof until the full end and term of Five Years from thence next following to be fully completed and ended.
>
> During which term the said apprentice his Master faithfully shall serve his secrets keep his lawful commands everywhere gladly obey.... he shall not commit fornication nor contract matrimony during the said term he shall not play at cards or dice tables or any other unlawful games whereby his Master shall have any loss..... he shall not haunt taverns nor playhouses nor absent himself from his said Master's service day or night unlawfully..... He the said Mathew Dawson will pay unto the said Fred Archer the undermentioned wages that is to say seven guineas for the first year, nine guineas for the second year, eleven guineas for the third year and thirteen guineas for the Fourth and Fifth year respectively and his said apprentice in the Art of a Jockey and Trainer of racehorses which he uses by the best means that he can and shall teach and instruct or cause to be taught and instructed finding unto the said Apprentice sufficient meat drink and also hat coat and waistcoat each year and lodging during the said term.....

The indentures were completely binding. If a homesick boy, badly shaken by discipline which was at times deliberately cruel, ran away, Atty immediately sued the parents for breaking the indentures. As they were not normally able to pay the £25 penalty, their son would be returned to the stable in disgrace.

Times have changed and now apprentices are not only well looked after, but also comparatively well paid. They cost a lot to keep and, although a good boy will more than repay the money spent on him during the last years of his apprenticeship, he is usually more of a liability than an asset at the beginning.

As for fulfilling his side of the bargain in training the boys to be jockeys, I don't think Atty ever gave the matter a second thought. They never got a real chance. Even the great Michael Beary would never have been heard of if the old man had had his way. Steve Donoghue, who was then the stable jockey, realised the Irish boy's immense potential and one day, unbeknown to Atty, picked Michael up from Chattis Hill, drove him to Salisbury and put him on a winner.

Atty invariably ignored the fundamental principles in selecting boys who could turn out to be jockeys. There are mighty few exceptions to the rule that a son will end up taller than his mother. So a conscientious trainer must inspect both parents, for however small the father may be, the minute, poorly fed boy will surely grow too big for racing if he has a big, buxom mother.

It is terribly important that boys should be kept happy from the start, because horses respond so much to atmosphere, and they should be trained in the right way by a top class paid lad in all aspects of horsemanship and horsemastership. Only if he understands why he performs his various duties in a certain way will any apprentice who has never been associated with horses grow up to love them and treat them properly. It is a bold trainer who decides to make apprentices into jockeys, because he will inevitably lose a number of races which he would otherwise have won. Therefore it is only fair that during this period the apprentice should receive no fee for riding horses trained by his employer and that the employer should receive half the jockey's fees and presents when his pupil rides horses for outside stables. Top class, conscientious trainers of boys, like Sam Armstrong and Frenchy Nicholson, richly deserved the rewards which they received when their apprentices blossomed into leading jockeys. Unfortunately, such men are few and far between.

Of course, boys can be a nuisance. By virtue of their youth they are apt to fool about with high spirits and a head man looking after a lot of valuable horses will have to enforce strict discipline.

It is remarkable how the same bad habits appear in succeeding generations of stable lads. Two such habits stand out. It is vital that a head man should know whether his horses have licked out their mangers. Even a dirty manger can be a sign of approaching sickness or, at best, of something slightly amiss. An amazing number of lads have the ingrained idea that if their horse leaves, it is somehow a reflection on themselves and so, if they can get to the manger before the head man, they scoop the leavings out into the straw and, when asked, reply that their horses have eaten up. This is one of the chief reasons, in my opinion, for breakfasts and standing feeds, even if each consists of not more than half a bowl of oats. In each case, the breakfast

The late 'Frenchy' Nicholson, widely respected as mentor and producer of good young jockeys.

before morning exercise and the standing feed before evening stables, the head man must have visited each horse at least half an hour before his lad arrives to tie him up. The other bad habit, which can be even more harmful, is the deep-rooted desire always to win the gallop. This ignorant practice is surprisingly to be found among some well known jockeys who should know better. It is a subconscious characteristic which must be checked before it develops; a trainer gives instructions for his horses to work at a nice training gallop − a good three-parts speed on the bridle − or tells the stable jockey to work at this speed and instructs the lads or apprentices taking part to lay with him. All too often, some lads will disobey orders and surreptitiously make their horses win the gallop. Even if the orders have been strict, they have their own ways of doing it unseen. If, at the finish of the gallop, they are due to pass the 'Guv'nor' on the near side, the hands and legs on that side will be deceptively still while the off side hands and legs will be hard at work scrubbing.

Old Frank Hartigan at Weyhill always followed his orders for work with the instructions 'And no f−−−−g blind heeling either!'

One of the truest sayings in the sport is that more races are lost on the gallops than on the racecourse. The late Peter Thrale was wont to say, 'The reason we Epsom trainers win so many races is that we've got no proper gallops.'

So the danger of winning a gallop and blind heeling is all too obvious.

From the start it is essential to insist on the highest standard both in and out of the yard, so that, even if he does not make the grade as a jockey, the apprentice will become a first class stable man and a competent horseman able to get a job with horses for the rest of his life. All too few trainers take sufficient trouble and are apt to keep boys on who will clearly never make the grade. One of the most common failings is fear. A nervous lad will quickly communicate his fear to the horse, not only 'down the reins', but also in the box, with the worst possible consequences. I have always believed that the brilliant Nasrullah filly, Nassau, would not have been such an evil-tempered creature if she had not been originally given to a nervous apprentice. I shall always remember him strapping her quarters with a lead rein tied to her headcollar so that he could keep her head pulled round to him constantly, to prevent her kicking. As a result she became quite impossible and one of the most expert deliberate kickers I have ever known. She could run backwards nearly as fast as she went forwards, once she had selected her target. This was the first time I have ever seen blinkers used on a yearling. However, she appeared to work so well that she was given her first run at Kempton without them. Although Atty had all the boys locked up in their Nissen hut quarters until after the time of the race, word had got about so that the trainer, Jack Olding and the filly's owner Lord Sefton got a very short price to their big bet. Today, with starting stalls, they would have collected. As it was, Nassau was so intent on kicking her rivals that she whipped round when the gate went up and was left.

Atty put her under the starting gate in blinkers just once and ran her in them at Salisbury. They doubled their bets and the issue was never in doubt. She won six races that season and would also have won the One Thousand Guineas instead of finishing fourth, if her owner had not insisted on having her home and turned out to grass during the winter, against his trainer's advice. After that first victory Nassau wore blinkers every time she left the stable, whether to go on exercise or to be loaded into a horsebox for a race. She had tremendous guts but resented people and other horses. After she had finished third in the Queen Mary Stakes at Royal Ascot and the blinkers had naturally been removed by the jockey to weigh in, she was being led back to the stable through the crowd in the paddock when a female admirer stupidly got too close and received an almighty kick in the jaw. This led to a court case for which Atty and Sefton briefed Fernley-Whittingstall, who knew his subject too well for the opposing counsel. The case cost a lot of money and taught several lessons. First, a trainer must see that he is full covered by insurance against any eventualities of this kind − a child can easily be injured if, for example, he finds his way into a paddock where horses are turned out to grass. Secondly, recalling the case, Atty always insisted that the woman would have received immediate satisfaction with a fair sum of money if she had sued the Ascot authorities instead of picking on the owner and trainer. The Ascot authorities are fully covered and, he said, would have simply turned to their insurance company and instructed them to recompense her.

The nervous lad is inclined to raise his voice to his horse and also to knock him about in the box. Several of our finest trainers, notably Ryan Price, invariably treated such behaviour as grounds for immediate dismissal. So it is kinder all round if an unduly nervous apprentice is sent out of racing to find himself some other occupation while he is still young enough to learn.

A good trainer of apprentices will naturally study the boys' diet. Atty's youngsters were appallingly fed, as cheaply as possible, which inevitably meant starchy, stodgy food; the worst

The late Capt. Ryan Price (left) with Fred Winter at Newmarket Sales in 1963. Renowned for the affection in which he held his charges, Price would not tolerate rough handling of horses.

possible thing for budding jockeys.

Poor little devils, they were dreadfully treated for their half-crown a week. Paddock days, during the winter months and the early part of the spring, were sheer purgatory. Although I was always given some good older colt to ride, I can still remember the sinking feeling when the paddock gates shut behind us, as soon as the horses felt the grass under their feet. Before long they knew every blade of grass and would seize on the slightest chance to duck out and create a scene. After all, it was in just such paddocks that they had romped, frolicked and fought from birth on the stud until not so long ago.

Lads were liable to be fired off in all directions and, as there was no escape from those well fenced enclosures, the loose horses would gallop in and out of the string, jinking and kicking, tempting their fellows to get rid of their encumbrances and join in the fun. It could be a very frightening performance, particularly if you were riding an older colt with savage ideas, as I usually was. I've known the time when there were as many as six loose ones at the same time, out of a string of twenty-five.

There was the morning when that great jockey Neville Sellwood arrived, young and handsome, from Australia to take over the job of first jockey to Atty's stable. Neville was unfit after a long and luxurious sea voyage from Sydney and in any case, great horseman that he was, he was totally unaccustomed to anything like the Persse paddocks. There was quite a gathering of owners to watch the newcomer as he turned up looking so smart in his superbly tailored jodhpurs. They were well rewarded.

We put him up on Lord Sefton's magnificent, powerful chestnut, Bob Cherry, a very useful son of Bobsleigh, who was eventually to find his way to Australia as a stallion. They made a lovely picture in the fitful early spring sunshine.

'Trot on,' ordered Archie Hughes, the head man.

Bob Cherry took two strides, put his head between his forelegs and catapulted Neville a good twenty yards. The lads, of course, were delighted. So were Bob Cherry and Atty. Sefton looked worried. We caught the colt and I put his jockey up again. Within five minutes those beautiful jodhpurs had been soiled even more. This time the Australian was hurled still further. Perhaps Bob Cherry was after an Olympic record. I have never seen anyone propelled in a bigger parabola than Neville when he sampled the Berkshire turf for the third time. Even the jockey, albeit somewhat ruefully, saw the funny side of that little fracas. But it was not always so amusing.

Bob Cherry's little sister, a tiny chestnut filly by Hyperion, had all the waywardness of her sire's female offspring. One day, in the lower paddock at Kingsdown, his lordship's pretty chestnut suddenly flipped onto her back with lightning speed, leaving our best work and riding apprentice no chance.

The filly got up and galloped off, causing havoc with the rest of the string, flirting madly with the snorting colts and kicking slyly at the fillies.

The boy lay still on the sodden turf, a small pathetic bundle of shabby clothes, blood seeping from his mouth. He was quite unconscious. He had taken the full weight of the filly.

Hughes and I started forward to help. Atty Persse shouted, 'Stand back! Leave him alone!' As tough as ever at eighty, the great trainer, looking like a benevolent Churchill except for those wide, icy blue eyes, hobbled over on his two sticks, the cigar clenched firmly between his teeth. Deliberately he kicked the little bundle on the wet grass. 'Get up,' he said. 'You lily-livered little bastard!' Then, the incident forgotten, he turned away to give orders to the string.

We got the ambulance. The boy didn't regain consciousness until he had been in hospital for some time. Fortunately, he escaped with nothing worse than a bad shaking. He could so easily have been killed.

There are many conflicting ideas on the best way to combat bad weather conditions in the winter. It is now accepted that an indoor school or covered yard is the best way of keeping the horses exercised and on the go however much snow and ice there is outside. But only the bigger trainers can afford such rides, so the majority will still have to use the old methods. Most sensible Flat trainers will keep their horses in if it is raining, unless they are due to run in the immediate future. If you are caught in the rain when out at exercise, there is one essential rule that applies to all horses. Instead of leading or walking home, you should always trot for at least the last ten minutes, so that the horses are warm when they arrive in their boxes. If you dry off the ears and loins, you will find that the rest of the horse dries very quickly, and you will have no danger of chills. It is inviting trouble if you walk them home, cold, wet and miserable.

Some horses loathe rain. I used to ride a big brown Blue Peter colt at Atty's. He was called Sailor's Knot and won the Blue Riband Trial Stakes at Epsom. He was rather a nasty individual, but he was a good ride, except when it rained. Then there would be delighted yells from the back of the string, 'Watch out Major! Here it comes!' Even though equipped with an old-fashioned hood covering his entire neck, and a good big sheet, Sailor's Knot would go mad when he felt the first drops. It was a most unnerving experience. He would try to throw himself on the ground and I believe if there had been a rabbit hole he would have gone down it!

Most trainers still prefer to use straw beds when the roads are too slippery and the ground is snow- or frost-bound. Atty hated them. He pointed out that for a straw ring to be any good it must be very wide and very deep. This becomes extremely expensive. Moreover, nervous, skittish horses, ridden by shivering lads with frozen hands, are liable to jump off the straw bed on to the frozen ground and you might just as well not have had one in the first place.

The old man kept his horses in their boxes, warm and comfortable, during these bad spells. You must naturally cut down a bit on their food and give them salts in their mashes, but they will come to no harm.

One winter the cold snap continued right through January and February, only breaking a week before the start of racing at Lincoln. Atty kept his string in their boxes through this spell. As was his custom, he had three two-year-olds entered for the Liverpool Grand National Meeting and, though he was able to give them only a few sharp canters and put them under the starting gate, he had no intention of altering his plans.

Dermot McCalmont's grey filly, Fly's Eye, was one of the trio. Michael Beary was ordered to give her a nice race and to ease her up when she started to run out of steam. She flew out of the gate like a true Persse two-year-old, going as straight as a die after all that pre-Christmas tuition, and at half-way Michael was amazed to find that she was going better than any of her rivals. He moved his hands and she flew to the front to win comfortably. I have proved the benefits of this method myself and can also vouch for the fact that it is a mistake to attempt to force two-year-olds by taking them to the sands during bad spells. They may, if you are lucky, win one good race against their unfit rivals, but they will probably be ruined for the rest of the year. Sands, like straw beds, take a tremendous amount out of most horses and have to be used sparingly for short periods. Incidentally, if you are using sands for older horses and jumpers it is essential to have the hard surface broken up with a harrow every day before use.

After the preliminary canter in the home paddock, Atty would always seek out a steep hill — the steeper the better — so that other Lambourn trainers used to say, 'He must be mad to canter his horses up that going like a side of a house,' and he would have the horses cantering steadily up it. It did not matter if the surface was a bit rough because they were going so slowly on the collar the whole time. The two-year-olds would canter only half-way up the hill. This was the first stage of building preparation before, as they say in Ireland, 'stealing them into their fast work'. Here begins the most exciting stage of a trainer's life, when he will learn whether any of his geese are likely to be swans. For a few weeks, until he has the chance of testing them against other people's horses, he can dream, and dreams are the stuff of which racing is made – 'They all go fast past posts and bushes', is the cynical old phrase, but, while they are doing so, it can be immensely exciting.

When I see American tracks carefully harrowed after each race, I wonder about these new all-weather gallops which, at vast cost, appear to have become regarded as an essential feature of every modern training establishment in this country. Without wishing to decry 'progress', one is tempted to ask how the old masters managed so well without.

However, they are here to stay and, for a lone trainer, who can harrow it after each lot's work, an all-weather gallop can obviously be an asset, provided that, first, he uses it sparingly, that is only when the turf is definitely too hard; secondly, he realizes that, with even the best product, this is a false surface; and, thirdly, whatever any new-fangled pundits may insist, even though not as bad as sand, work on an all-weather takes more out of a horse than galloping on good sound turf. Trial and error: adjust accordingly.

However, in a large centre, where it is used by a number of trainers and hundreds of horses, an all-weather gallop can be disastrous. Whereas it should be harrowed after, at most, every fifty horses (two hundred hooves), it never is and you may be sure that many hundreds of gallopers and thousands of flashing feet will quickly turn it into a veterinary nightmare. Although usually not immediately apparent, initial minor strain, sprain and damage will be inflicted on joints, tendons, ligaments, knees, shoulders – damage which will result in breakdown later on. Beware overused, unharrowed all-weather gallops. If you know how to use it, like the French trainers at Chantilly, I'd much rather have sand.

Some three-year-olds will have improved out of all recognition since their two-year-old days. The backward horse, whom you did not hurry last season, will reward your patience by revelling in work over a longer distance. The cheapest yearling, who you suspected might go a bit, now confirms your hope.

Atty used to have three work days a week: Tuesday, Thursday and Saturday, with Wednesday as 'easy day'. Most trainers prefer to work on Wednesday and Saturday, having Thursday as 'easy day'.

The week might go something like this. Sunday a day of rest for all, except for the following day's runners, who will need to be cleared out, and the runners for the remainder of the week, who should be led out to stretch their legs. On Monday, one or two steady canters, depending on the conformation and condition of the individual animals. On Tuesday, a steady canter and a sharp canter. On Wednesday, a steady canter followed by half or three-parts speed work. Thursday, led out for an hour each lot. Friday as Tuesday. Saturday, a preliminary canter followed by good work.

It is not advisable to work the two-year-olds over more than three-and-a-half to four furlongs at this stage. In any case, horses should normally be worked at a distance shorter than that over which they will be asked to race. As far as possible, horses should normally be kept on the bridle, working well within themselves at home. After galloping they should be trotted straight back to the trainer so that he can listen to their breathing.

Many foreigners consider that we waste a lot of time in the preliminaries before work. The old trainers used to insist that an old horse must be out walking or trotting for at least three-quarters of an hour before he did his preliminary canter. There is a great deal of sense in this. All too many horses suffer from varying degrees of muscular rheumatism and are liable to be stiff when they first pull out. It stands to reason that, if they are to work well, they must have had sufficient time to limber up and loosen their muscles like a human athlete. Although in summer the weather may come too hot, so that it is an advantage to get the first lot out early, the normal English climate favours a start at about 7.30 a.m. Except for the most yappy colts who may have to be ridden by light boys, horses should normally be led back after work. For this reason it is usually advisable to issue each lad with a leading rein. This, as I noted earlier, does not apply if you are caught out in the rain.

It is usually advisable on work days to send horses home as soon as they have galloped, or at least as soon as you have a responsible lad free to take back a batch of those who have worked. The guiding principle in ordinary work is always to keep horses as much as possible with others of the same ability and, in all work on the bridle, to ensure that they gallop at the pace of the slowest so that not even the worst horse is unduly extended.

There is further description of a day's work in a later chapter. First lot will normally be back in the yard by about 9.15 a.m. The horses will immediately be strapped over, with particular attention paid to the sponging out of the girth and saddle sweat marks, set fair, fed, watered and let down. The lads should then have a reasonable time to eat their 'lunch'. When working two horses you will usually aim to pull second lot out at 10.30 a.m. The drill is the same. The lad goes to his second horse, ties him up, mucks out and leaves the box clean and ready for re-occupation on his return. Once all have been fed, the head man will normally ensure that the lads look in at their first lot horses to see that they have sufficient water and will insist on the yard being swept spotlessly clean before the staff are dismissed for their meal. The yard must now be kept quiet until the head man makes his tour of inspection with standing feeds before evening stables. This is particularly important as it gives horses a chance to lie down and rest, which the best ones will nearly always do. Some trainers employ a feeder, but I prefer to have the head man feeding the horses because it is undoubtedly a help to have seen the work which each of his charges performed and how they did it. In a few big yards the evening stables inspection is still the ceremonial parade that it always was. Nowadays, however, in the great majority of stables the trainer just goes round and inspects each horse as he is being done.

Although they can be extremely useful, girls can be an embarrassment to those stables which are not equipped to cope with both sexes. Moreover, however good they are, girls are inevitably governed by some restrictions. Their light touch when strapping a filly is beneficial, but they should never be allowed near colts. The late Fred Darling was particularly insistent on this point. He would never allow women owners to visit their horses until he was present and always instructed them not to use scent.

As most expensive scents are manufactured from the sex glands of animals, he was right to assume that the smell is exciting to a colt. In fact, there are many old stud grooms who still cover their arms with scent when holding a mare to be covered by a nervous stallion. The great Beckhampton trainer also believed that colts are affected by women who are having their monthly period.

Furthermore, when a colt yaps (playful bites) and when he draws (gets an erection), he will receive a firm corrective slap from a man, but most girls, even the best of them, cannot bring themselves to do this with the same severity. Their taps are like play to a colt. He enjoys them and becomes spoilt as a result.

A well known trainer's wife, a superb horsewoman, used to ride one of the stable's chief Classic hopes in his exercise and work, throughout his two-year-old career and during the winter preceding his Classic season. When she had to stop riding to have a baby, the horse became quite impossible and would not allow the lads to go near him, so that eventually he had to be castrated and, of course, was unable to run in any of the Classic events.

Another worrying aspect of employing girls in racing stables is that the normal trainer somehow feels he has to pick and choose their rides rather than putting them on anything. As he already has a number of green apprentices on his staff, it is apt to make the nightly preparation of the next morning's lists too much of a headache. In passing, however, it is worth recording that Fred Darling used Norah Wilmot to ride his colts in their Classic trials!

I have long held that stable lads should be graded according to their ability and length of service and that they should be paid accordingly. A 'Grade A' lad is surely entitled to a wage as high or higher than he could get outside racing. He is an expert, performing a fairly dangerous job involving the care of animals worth many thousands, and sometimes millions, of pounds. But this will only come in Britain when all owners pay the full cost of keeping their horses, including their trainer's salaries, and I cannot see this happening until we get a Tote monopoly, at least for all off-course betting.

It was sad indeed to see the Ministry coaches arriving in Lambourn each morning to take top class stable lads off to Harwell and Aldermaston to use vacuum cleaners and frequently to be paid more for this unskilled labour than the budding young scientists in the same establishments. However much he loves horses and racing, a married lad who has not risen to the happy position of travelling head man or head man inevitably finds it hard to make ends meet.

I will deal with grooming and the other details of stable management routine in Chapter Nine.

CHAPTER
FIVE
Owners

Owners can be a great worry to trainers. I don't suppose there is anyone in the profession who has not said, at one time or another, that he wished to heaven he could train his horses without owners. And there is a great deal of truth in the old saying that it is easier to train horses than their owners. Nevertheless, as they pay the bills, they must be studied.

Owners come in four main categories. There are those who really know and understand horses. They seldom interfere but always discuss plans with their trainers. They never say, 'My trainer says...but I think....', but always include him in the word 'we': 'We plan to run at Ascot', or 'We have decided to send the filly to stud'. They can take the ups and downs which are a part of the sport with complete sympathy, because they genuinely love and understand animals. Unhappily their number is becoming smaller all the time.

The second category can be nearly as good to train for. They are successful businessmen and their wives, often living in the neighbourhood of Sunningdale or Stratford-upon-Avon. In many cases they are honest enough to admit that vanity was one of the chief reasons why they became owners. This can sometimes create difficulties for the trainer who wants to place his horses so that, however moderate they may be, they will win races.

I trained for one such man, a charming millionaire motor manufacturer. He was very enthusiastic about his horses but said quite openly, 'I would rather run down the course at Ascot or Sandown than win at Warwick or Worcester.' As he was not prepared to pay a great deal for his horses, I used to follow his instructions in the main, but in order to make them winners I had to take them to the smaller courses where he would only sometimes, and then reluctantly, come to watch them. He never grumbled when they finished unplaced at the big meetings, but, of course, it was not good for his horses to be outclassed. There is nothing that the average horse likes better than winning. Watch yearlings galloping in a paddock and you will see what I mean. These owners are loyal and genuine and, frequently admitting that they know little about horses, are prepared to trust their trainers through thick and thin, once they have made their original selections. Many of them bet quite heavily, but they are good losers.

The third group of owners has much in common with the second as far as business and means are concerned, but there the resemblance ends. Whenever you see an owner constantly changing his trainer, you can be sure that the fault is with the former. It is so easy to throw mud at a trainer when things are not going too well and these men will always listen to the mudslingers in their clubs, the know-alls who know nothing and have never owned a racehorse, but who are so free with their comments and advice on every aspect of the game. For example, although the trainer may warn against undue optimism, living with the horse and knowing his ability as well as he does, some owners make up their minds that they are sure to win a certain race and tell all their friends to support the animal. When he gets beaten these sporting experts, talking through their emptier pockets, must find a scapegoat. The jockey either wasn't trying, or rode a bad race. The going didn't suit the horse and the trainer should have known this – and in any case he hadn't turned the unfortunate creature out as straight in condition as he should have been. Everybody and everything are blamed except the horse who was not good enough, as the trainer had originally warned the owner.

This sort of talk will always be heeded by such owners. They will distrust their trainers and jockeys and interfere with the most honest and capable men in a manner which would have bankrupted them had they used it in business.

It is a funny thing about owners. They trust their trainer to use his expert judgment to buy them a yearling. If, as frequently happens, the animal turns out no good, they will never believe this fact and rather than take their trainer's advice to cut their losses, they will send the horse to another stable where he will be just as bad as before. These owners would much rather you insulted their wives than that you told them, in their own interests, that their horses are no good.

If they have beginner's luck, they become particularly nasty when the luck changes, as it surely will in racing. When their horses go sick, or take time coming to hand, they become impatient. They usually pretend to bet in much larger sums than they actually do and are exceptionally bad losers. Of such a man it was once said, 'He is as despicable when winning as he is odious in defeat!'

After a few months as owners they are confident that they know everything about racing, although the nearest that they have previously come to a horse has been when their daughter performed in the local pony club. Moreover, they behave as though they owned their trainers. They think it is their right to visit your stables in their opulent cars at any time and on any day, expecting to be shown their horses, even on a Sunday afternoon, and then regally entertained. They will telephone by day or night, whenever it suits them, and become pompously righteous unless their trainers behave socially like paragons of virtue, even though they themselves fall a long way below this standard. One of the chief reasons why these people have horses is to obtain information about the other inmates of the stable, and to do this they will often try to bribe your lads. Even when dealing with his patron's own horses, a trainer naturally likes all information to come from him and not from members of his staff. A good lad always answers such requests with, 'You'd better ask the Guv'nor, Sir.' The cliché which has to be repeated to these owners all too often is that their horses are not machines. It has little effect, the owners being convinced otherwise.

Oddly enough, even people who should know better may fall into this category when they become racehorse owners; it seems to go to their heads. I once trained a very useful filly for a vet. Even though I had won races with her, he was furious when I refused to run her because she was coughing. So furious that he immediately removed the filly and sent her to another trainer.

Jockeys can be the bane of a trainer's life when dealing with this kind of owner. However young and inexperienced a jockey may be, he is apt to think that he knows more about the animal whom he has sat on for a few minutes than the man who has been looking after him since his yearling days. This type of owner is invariably attracted by the 'glamour of the silks' so that he listens eagerly to the jockey and takes his word for everything, even if it is completely contrary to his trainer's opinion. There are few Lester Piggotts. Would that there were more, because their advice is worth anything to a trainer. Most jockeys' stories after a race are, consciously or subconsciously, affected by their desire to excuse themselves. This frequently leads them into downright lies. Few owners are skilled race riders. One of the commonest faults occurs when the horse is left several lengths at the start. The jockey will ride him flat out in order to catch up in the first half-furlong and on his return will say, 'Left? Me? You must have been looking at another horse, Sir. I was one of the first out of the gate.' You can be sure the owner will believe him even though you know that the reason he lost was because of that early unbalanced burst. If the jockey had accepted his poor break and sat into the horse until he had time to get balanced, he would probably have won.

The Tetrarch nearly suffered defeat only once. This was in the National Breeders' Produce Stakes at Sandown. There is a picture of the 'Spotted Wonder' on his knees with the tapes of the starting gate caught in his mouth. He was actually left twenty lengths in the season's top two-year-old race. Steve Donoghue knew his colt and knew the Sandown five furlong track, which is the stiffest in the world, on the collar the whole way. He sat quite still behind his field. At the distance they started to come back to him and the great horse shot through them to gain a narrow victory. It could not have happened on any other course, but it was a wonderful lesson in race riding by one of the greatest exponents of the art.

The Tetrarch's trainer, Atty Persse, never listened to jockeys, however famous and great they might be. When they started their gesticulating stories he would glare at them, take the cigar out of his mouth and say, 'Go on in. I've got a pair of eyes!' You cannot always blame the jockeys. Those below the leading division are probably making excuses and overpraising the horse for fear that they will not be asked to ride him again.

A combination of conceit, interference, and listening to gossip and to jockeys, often makes the type of owner under discussion unbearable and, provided that he has sufficient means to do without the horses, a trainer is better off without him. Furthermore, a large number of them are not quite as rich as they would have you believe. Owning a racehorse is an expensive pastime.

When there are more than one, the bills can be enormous even when the owner is not paying the full cost. Although no one forces a man to own racehorses, any more than he is forced to buy a Rolls-Royce, his vanity frequently leads him to overstep the mark when he poses as the great sportsman. Although the younger generation of owners have improved on their predecessors, there is an unfortunate tendency to believe that the one person who can be kept waiting for his bills to be paid is the racehorse trainer. Of course, the opposite is in fact the truth. With his inadequate training fees and enormous overheads in forage, transport and wages, he is the man who should be paid first. The ideal is for the owner to pay all his bills through Weatherbys, who reimburse the trainer from the owner's account with them as soon as they receive the monthly bill. For some reason which I will never understand, the Jockey Club has constantly refused to announce a minimum training fee and to help trainers collect bad debts of this kind. In France, all training accounts are paid through the Societe d'Encouragement; if an owner is three months in arrears, his horses are debarred from running until he has paid his training fees. It is high time that this system was introduced over here. There is all hell to pay if a trainer is slow in paying his jockey's retaining fee and expense account (even though some owners have probably not paid their share of these items) and Weatherbys are particularly punctilious about collecting for jockeys. However, they do nothing to protect the trainer from unscrupulous owners.

By an old law, you are not allowed to impound an owner's horse against payment of his debt unless you have a little plate somewhere in your yard bearing the legend 'Livery and Bait Stable'! If you have such a plate, you can take this unpleasant but sometimes necessary action. You don't want to have it displayed in a prominent position, however, or you will have people queueing up to hire horses for rides!

One of the main disadvantages of a trainer's life is that the social and business aspects are almost inextricably merged. Your profession is your owner's luxury, hobby and recreation. This type of owner usually insists on you drinking with him whether you want to or not. As far as possible, I think that a trainer should try to keep things on a business footing when dealing with these people, although it is often hard to maintain this attitude throughout your association. As I have said, the greatest service which the Jockey Club could do for trainers is to follow the French example and introduce a minimum training fee which would cover the cost of a horse's keep and the trainer's livelihood, reviewing it every year and increasing it with the rise in the cost of living. This would rid the Turf of undesirable owners, who would find that they were living beyond their means and would therefore be forced out of the game which they had no right to be in.

The last category of owners is as welcome as the first or second. It includes most jumping owners and those who only have one horse, or frequently just a share in a horse. These are the real enthusiasts, the genuine sportsmen and women who have learned to love racing for no other reason than for the fun they can get out of it. Although it may entail more clerical work looking after their interests, they are in general a joy to train for. Fortunately, the big trainer who shamefully neglects the small owner, in favour of those with large numbers of horses, is becoming a thing of the past.

Many horses are now owned by syndicates and by companies. The Rules of Racing on this subject are clear and precise. If in doubt, trainers should consult Weatherbys.

One of the saddest facts of racing life is that a trainer so seldom seems to be able to win for the best owners. Anyone in the profession will tell you 'It's nearly always the shits, the real bastards, who have all the luck!' One of the most delightful owners I have ever known was Ronnie Basset. His father, Arthur, one of Atty's original owners, enjoyed considerable good fortune, but Ronnie had horses in training with Atty for twenty-five years before he had a winner. Yet all the time he was the most generous patron any trainer has ever been blessed with and the lads literally loved him and his wife, Lady Elizabeth, Lady-in-Waiting to Queen Elizabeth, the Queen Mother.

Even when he did have his first winner, the little horse Baloo was sold for a low price and proceeded to win some first class races in other colours before being sold on at a large profit to America where he won enough dollars to qualify as a stallion.

I had the Bassets' home-bred Sunny Brae in my stable, which contained most of the backward Persse two-year-olds. Atty advised his sale because he had little patience with animals of this type. Running in the Rothschild colours, Sunny Brae developed into a top class handicapper and won two City and Suburban Handicaps, carrying 9 st. 3 lb. on the second occasion in 1954.

That is the luck of racing. A trainer is really happy on the all too rare occasions when the best horses belong to the best patrons, as in the case of Arkle and Anne, Duchess of Westminster.

I think that trainers, though some are burdened by ever-increasing paper work, should go out of their way to keep their owners informed at all times. I do not quite visualise a system like the regular cards sent out by the greyhound trainers: 'Your dog....is sick/injured/resting/in season', etc., with the alternatives which do not apply deleted. But I do think that every owner deserves a brief monthly communiqué and should always be told as far in advance as possible when or where his horse is going to run, so that he can make plans accordingly.

I remember meeting a famous woman owner at the Maisons-Lafitte Spring Meeting, at which her classic hope for that year was engaged in the Guineas Trial, the Prix Djébel. She was in tears and told me, 'I have just met my trainer. He was very rude. I had always understood that my colt was to run here and have come all the way from the South of France and he has just said, "What are you doing here? Your horse is not running. Go back at once!"' Nevertheless that owner-trainer association remained an enormous success. Another of this trainer's well known owners, however, left the great man. She told me, 'I had a special lunch put up by my hotel in London to take down to the Derby and we stopped in an attractive place to eat it. My trainer got back into the car and said, "I do not care for this sort of thing. The car will come back for you." He ordered my chauffeur to drive him to Epsom and left me crying by the side of the road with the lunch!' Some people can get away with anything, provided they produce results, which this trainer consistently did. But I believe that the owners of today who pay the huge prices for horses and pay their bills deserve kind treatment. The smallest things are greatly appreciated. Most owners derive pleasure from naming their own horses. In this department a trainer, who has so much more practice, can often assist. He should certainly help in the registration of colours, which now have to be re-registered every year. There are so many different combinations of colours in existence that it is hard to pick one that is not rather messy. Certain guiding rules apply here. Try, both for your own and the owner's sake, to select colours that are easily visible. Most people find that green is easy to see, particularly in combination with white, and that striped sleeves can be picked out from a distance because the one part of a jockey, crouched on a horse, that you can normally spot are his arms.

Some trainers hate green. Racing people are apt to be superstitious. For instance, you should never wish a trainer 'Good luck' before a race. A loose horse at exercise in the morning is said to portend a winner for the stable in the afternoon. It is very lucky to pass a funeral, or that now rare sight, a sweep, on the way to the races. And the number of trainers who have nearly killed themselves, trying to drive under a railway bridge as a train is passing over, must be countless. It's especially lucky if you go underneath just as the last coach, or guard's van is crossing.

The late Ossie Bell was one of those trainers with a hatred of green. One day on the way to the races his assistant trainer's wife produced a green comb. In a fury of rage he seized it from her and threw it out of the window. And yet Ossie's luckiest colours, those of Sir Hugo Cunliffe-Owen, were green and white and were carried on his Classic winners Felstead and Rockfel. So much for the inconsistency of a superstitious trainer's mind.

Probably the most important qualities which a trainer should try to instil in his owners are trust and patience. Trust in the trainer himself, his staff and the jockeys he employs. It is so easy in racing to believe the worst of people. Every day we hear someone saying that a jockey stopped a horse, or that a beaten favourite wasn't trying. Whenever a well-fancied Persse horse was defeated in a race, Atty used to receive bunches of abusive letters. One, which pleased him enormously, began, 'Dear Mr Bloody Persse....'! These people are, of course, talking through their pockets, but it is easy for an owner who knows little of the game to develop this type of thinking.

In jumping it is not the morals of the jockeys that are called in question so much as their courage. Let the finest and bravest jockey in the world be beaten a few times on well-fancied horses and the ever fickle racing public will start insisting that he has lost his nerve. This is a most insidious claim that can snowball alarmingly, so that owners will instruct their trainers not to employ certain riders. When a man has been riding for some time and strikes a patch of bad luck, he is a sitting target for allegations that he is too old, past it, punch drunk or generally windy. I can hardly think of one great jockey about whom these cruel lies have not been spread. Even Terry Biddlecome was virtually written off at the end of the 1971–72 season. His list of injuries, which I published in *Steeplechase Jockeys: The Great Ones*, was terrifying. It was not his fault that he suffered nosebleeds and blackouts through excessive wasting to make weights that were ridiculously low for such a big, powerful man. Even when he rode his beloved Gay Trip so brilliantly into second place in the Grand National, beaten only by the weight, they still said that Terry had 'gone'. Happily he threw the lie back in their teeth the following season, forgetting about wasting and riding with all the brilliant, brave, power-packed skill which made him indubitably one of the greatest horseman-jockeys of all time.

The finest contemporary example of trust and loyalty was that between Neville Crump and his jockeys, expressed by Gerry Scott on his retirement in the most moving letter of gratitude which was published by *The Sporting Life*.

Patience is a virtue which most owners believe they possess. They would be most indignant if you told them that they do not, but in fact they are deceiving themselves. Ninety per cent of owners have to be taught to be patient: many never learn.

A typical example was the keen hunting businessman who asked me to buy him two yearlings who would train on to make three-year-olds and, later, jumpers. He said that he hated two-year-old racing and had no interest in it whatsoever. He had given me little to spend, but I fulfilled his order. Unfortunately one of the pair, although a big horse, showed me sufficient speed to warrant a run in a maiden two-year-old race. As soon as the owner heard this he insisted on my running the animal, who made matters worse by finishing third. After this, my life was purgatory. He wanted both these big, backward two-year-olds to run frequently and it was all I could do to persuade him otherwise. Eventually, disgusted, he sold them both. One became a first class performer, first over hurdles and then over fences, winning a large number of races, and the other won some big staying events on the Flat before being converted into a successful chaser. If only this owner had had the patience that he professed, he would have enjoyed everything that he most wanted out of racing. Unhappily, he is all too typical. Even some of the best and nicest owners tend to become impatient unless they have been born and bred with horses. Even those who should know better can be a terrible headache, particularly when a horse gets a leg, for example, and has to be fired. A good vet, knowing that rest is the best cure of all, will prescribe a lay-off of eighteen months. If he gets a year, he is very lucky. The animal goes back into racing far too soon and inevitably breaks down again.

One of the most patient trainers was Fulke Walwyn. If, at exercise, you admired a splendid four- or five-year-old, he would say, 'Yes, nice horse. But he'll be much better next year and the following year he could be a really good horse.' Unfortunately, this true horseman's patience is all too rare even in trainers.

Fulke developed one particularly sensible rule when training for that strange character, The Honourable Dorothy Paget, who lived at night while others slept. After enduring a succession of long telephone calls well after midnight, Fulke decided that, even if he lost all those wonderful horses, he just could not stand any more of this abominable interference with his private life and the fatigue which it entailed. So he put his foot down and informed his owner that under no circumstances would any calls be accepted after eleven at night. It worked like a charm. Even 'D.P.' respected his wishes and did not try again.

Partnerships and syndicates in particular are a great help to racing. The only difficulty about partnerships between two people is that, sooner or later, they seem to fall out unless they are extremely good friends from the outset. This can result in the trainer losing the horse which he badly wants to keep. But, on the whole, a partnership is a help because it reduces the cost of ownership by so much. One of the happiest associations I had as a trainer was with two doctors, one farmer and one businessman who owned a very useful filly. When she won at Newmarket, I managed to get all four of them and their wives into that holy-of-holies, the winner's enclosure. Believe me, that was quite a feat at the time.

In all partnerships and syndicates there must be a definite leader and spokesman, one who can carry all responsibility attached to the horse. A partnership can have as many discussions as they like, but the trainers and, indeed, the authorities must have one man to deal with. Today, even though the names of both partners of a horse appear on the race card, the rules insist that the colours can no longer be alternated each time the horse runs. Some trainers, therefore, will stipulate that the horse runs in one partner's colours for one year (minimum period), and in the other's the following year.

Owners' whims and fads must be studied by the trainer to a certain extent, but a successful trainer knows where to draw the line. One of Atty Persse's favourite stories concerned the brief period when he trained for Colonel Hall-Walker, who later became Lord Wavertree, the donor of the National Stud to Britain. Although he had only just started training, Atty was confident that one of Hall-Walker's animals would win at Royal Ascot. He told the owner so, but it had no effect because Hall-Walker believed implicitly in the stars and was convinced that nothing good could happen without a favourable horoscope. Recounting the tale; Atty said:

'I think he told me that Jupiter had been interfering with Venus, or something like that! Anyway, he said that his horse had no chance at all. I thought otherwise and had a good bet at a decent price. Unluckily for him, Hall-Walker met the King, Edward VII, who asked him whether he should back his horse. 'No, Sir, under no circumstances. It has no chance,' he said. As I had foretold, the horse won very comfortably. The King was not best pleased. 'I'll never ask you again!' he told Hall-Walker, who promptly left the meeting very upset by the whole performance, with his faith in the stars at least temporarily shaken.

CHAPTER
SIX
Feeding

Horses, like human beings, cannot do themselves justice unless they are feeling well. If they are to be built up to stand the test of racing and the rigours of a season, they should eat well.

Thus feeding has always been one of the most important factors in training the racehorse. Some trainers prefer to employ a man as a feeder pure and simple. I prefer to have the head man feeding the horses in his care because, as I remarked in an earlier chapter, he watches them work and, on the strength of what he sees on the gallops, can gauge their feeds accordingly. On the other hand, there is no doubt that feeding is an art in itself and, if you cannot find a head man who is gifted in this respect, then it is better to employ a feeder.

It is quite possible that before long this chapter will be out of date. Over the past few years, research into concentrated food has progressed apace, having been largely instigated in France by Dr. Edouard Pouret, former President of the French Veterinary Association and in Ireland by the late Maxie Cosgrove. Both men decided that the first essential was to discover exactly what the horse needs in the way of food, starting from scratch. Until this had been fully established it was obviously impossible to go further. Experimenting with his own horses both in training and on his Normandy stud, Dr Pouret was soon an advocate of feeding nuts to horses. He said, however, that it is no good treating them like oats, buying them in bulk and using them over a period until they are finished: 'The vitamins and proteins that you put in deteriorate so rapidly that you must make new nuts three times a week if the horses are to gain the full benefit from them.'

76

One of the features of nuts which it is hard for an Englishman to understand is that, ideally, a horse should have no other food at all. Since time began, we in this country have laboured under the misapprehension that animals, particularly dogs and horses, think like human beings. As a result, far too many horses and dogs are left entire when they would have much happier lives were they castrated.

This muddled thinking has long applied to feeding horses. Even the Army, which in most other respects had brought horsemanship to a very high standard indeed, preached the principle that a horse is liable to become bored unless he has some hay to nibble. This is just not true. The same people insist on large, loose boxes to keep their horses happy, whereas, as we have seen, some of Atty Persse's best horses, including Bachelor's Double, spent their entire racing careers tied up in stalls.

Although he has considerable memory a horse has little capacity for abstract thought, and is not a human being. He will be perfectly happy if he receives a sufficient quantity of the food that his body needs for the functions which it performs. Only man can be happy when he is unhealthy. The quantity of hard food will necessarily be varied according to the work which the animal is doing. Obviously, an injured horse resting in his box will require less than the same horse in hard training.

I think that there is a greater measure of ignorance in matters of feeding than in any other aspect of horse training. How often will you hear someone say, 'Such and such a horse is a tremendous doer. He eats nearly 30 lb. of oats a day.'

Atty Persse told me that, in all his fifty years as a trainer, the horses he had known who could be worked up to 21 lb. per day, just over the period of a race, could be counted on the fingers of one hand. We had one such when I was with him, Lord Sefton's beautiful dark brown Britannia Stakes winner, Marconi. The average young racehorse will normally eat about 12 lb. of oats per day and the good feeder will quickly gauge the amount that the horse needs, feeding him accordingly so that if he leaves anything in his manger it is clear that there is something wrong. Since they cannot talk and tell you when they are feeling off-colour, it is important to have such a guide. Nowadays a great many animals in training are apt to leave food after they have done a strong gallop. You have to go easy with them until they come back to their food. Of course it takes all sorts. One of the best point-to-point horses I ever owned or rode was trained for me by a splendid West Country farmer whose only idea of feeding was to fill the manger to the brim with black seed oats and leave them there until the horse had finished them before filling up again. It seemed to work with this particular horse, but I would not advise it as a general principle!

It was riding this horse which first started my dislike of bookmakers and their influence on the Turf. Deprived as we are now of all our little jumping meetings in the West Country, except for Newton Abbot and Devon and Exeter, the point-to-points have, since the war, assumed a far greater importance than before. Local shopkeepers in Devon and Cornwall keep their own form books cutting the results out of *Horse and Hound*. Although they are not in the same league as some of the Irish point-to-points and little race meetings like Killarney, there is often quite a good betting market, invariably better than at any point-to-point fixture up country.

On this occasion the race was the biggest of the West Country season, the King's Cup at the Dartmoor point-to-point. It was an Open race which had attracted runners from all over the country and I was a hot favourite. After jumping the first few fences I found that another runner was crossing me at each obstacle. At first I thought that the rider could not control his mount; I shouted at him to keep straight and tried to avoid him. It made no difference which side of him I was. He came at me the more purposefully at every fence, trying to push me through the wing, bumping and boring the whole time, and I realised that it was deliberate. After the last fence the course wound up in a letter 'S' round the cars and temporarily out of sight of the crowd in a dip before swinging into a short straight to the winning post. Thanks to the guts of my horse and a fair bit of rough riding, I thought that I had finally shaken off my assailant, but as I was galloping out of that dip he made one last despairing effort which caught me completely unawares. He galloped at me sideways so that if I had kept on riding we would both have smashed into the line of cars and come to a sticky end. At the last moment, realising that I had no option, I had to pull out. He kept me out until the second favourite, who had been well behind, galloped by to win. As I rode back, almost in tears, the bookmakers shouted delightedly, 'Thank you Captain!' I dismounted and went straight to the Stewards, who were friends of mine and included the last of the great Corinthians, Lord Mildmay. They immediately called for the unknown rider and began a quick search which revealed that he had galloped straight to a waiting horsebox, loaded up the horse with the saddle still on, and driven away. They were never traced. To judge from my horse's previous and subsequent form, my opponent had been no ordinary point-to-pointer and his rider was certainly not the amateur he had professed to be. Anthony Mildmay was convinced that they had been hired for the express purpose of knocking the favourite out of the race. As long as there are bookmakers and a beaten favourite can make money for wrong-doers, there will always be crime on the Turf.

To return to feeding. Until the current research has discovered the right answer, it is obviously better to keep away from nuts, accepting Dr Pouret's statement that they deteriorate, and to use the foods that have stood the test of time.

The most important factor in choosing forage is consistency. If you vary your oats in the middle of a season, you will find that your horses are likely to lose their form. For this reason the big trainers now buy their oats from Canada and Australia. On the other hand, I have used plenty of Scotch or English oats with considerable success. It is vitally important to use only the best oats, hay and bran. Despite many views to the contrary, Atty Persse taught me to avoid food that is two or three years old. As long as they are good and well saved, new oats and hay can be used any time after January, but they must be in first class condition or they may cause the horses to scour.

Atty preferred English oats, like winter oats at 42 lb. to the bushel, or black tartars at about 40 lb., or the thick-skinned Scotch white oats at 46 lb. to the bushel. In his heyday he liked a mixture of English winter and black tartar. But even he had to bow to the changing times and when I was with him he relied on well known corn merchants to produce the best English oats available. Although, when he was at Stockbridge, he had preferred to buy from the local farmers whom he knew, at Lambourn he advised me to use a middle man despite the extra cost. 'It is far too risky nowadays to rely on farmers you know,' he said, 'If they have a bad year, you can find yourself in the soup. If the middle man sends you a bad sample at any time during the season, you can always send it back.'

I don't think that the size of the oat matters. Some of the best oats that I have ever known, and which won me a lot of races, came from Scotland. They were small, but they really weighed.

The test of good oats is that if you take a handful of the sample and squeeze them hard they will bounce back against your fingers. They should be fed lightly bruised, not crushed. It is important not to have too large a quantity in the bins at any one time. Between refills the bins should be cleaned thoroughly. Screenings can cause excessive urination or 'diabetes', to use the misnomer common among racing people.

For a long time after the war it was impossible to get good samples of bran. That situation has happily changed. If you put your hand into a sack of good bran it will come out white, covered in flour.

The quality of hay must be the very best. A great deal depends upon the land which produces it and it is better to have hay grown on rich alluvial soil. The ideal is to buy a rick and have it hand cut in trusses. Unfortunately, this has become virtually a thing of the past. Therefore, the best type of hay should be string baled. This allows the hay to breathe, whereas wire baling compresses it too much and you can have serious trouble inside the bales, particularly if, as so often happens in England, it is still a little moist when it is baled. Once again, to avoid this possibility, a number of the big trainers buy their hay from abroad with the guarantee that it has been made with the sun on it. Norwegian hay has become very popular. It is a pity that almost all farmers have stopped making sainfoin hay; for horses in hard work this was invaluable provided that the trainer knew how to feed it. It was very rich and heated the blood so that, when given to animals not in hard training, it was liable to make the legs fill.

Rye grass with a little clover is probably the best and, for a change, some old meadow hay, as long as it has a really good nose. The head man should keep an eye on the bales as they are broken. You can never be quite certain what the inside is like and a young, inexperienced apprentice, feeding hay from a bale which is not quite right, could so easily cause 'diabetes' which would set the horses' training back for quite a while.

As I said in an earlier chapter, I prefer hay to be fed on the ground, not in nets, even though the latter are far more economical. Anyone who insists on using nets must ensure that they are pulled right up to the limit, tied firmly and twisted round so that there is no chance of a horse striking his foot and getting it caught. It seems that there will continue to be fatal accidents caused by nets and which could so easily have been prevented. Boys don't like being made to stand on their buckets, but unless they are genuinely tall enough to tie their nets, they must be made to do so. I think that the army scale of 10 lb. of hay a day is quite sufficient for a horse in training. A normal day's feeding will start with breakfast — anything from a double handful to a bowl of oats, depending on the individual — for the good doers who have licked out their mangers, given at least half an hour before the lads come to their horses. After morning exercise the feed, which will normally be given to each lad by the head man, into a feed sack on the ground, will consist of oats, a double handful of bran, a little chaff or chop and probably some 'green meat' to make it more attractive. Trainers will find that it pays them to grow a patch of lucerne in a plot near to the yard and have the necessary amount cut each day for this purpose. Before the lad folds up his sack to take the feed to his horse, the head man will lightly damp it with water. Lads must be instructed to mix the feed well in the manger. If you have one of those tiresome horses who either gobble their food in a way guaranteed to give them indigestion (I had one such who used to eat up in record time and then lie down groaning from his greed), or who, in their excitement, throw the food out of the manger on to the floor of the box, you should put large stones or lumps of rock salt in the manger.

Standing feed in the evening is like breakfast, but will only be given to the really good doers in hard work. The evening feed will be similar to that given after morning exercise, but will normally be slightly larger.

During the winter I like to give three bran mashes a week to Flat horses, cutting this to two a week when they start fast work. You should have two boilers on the go, one for barley and the other for linseed. Both should be allowed to boil for eight to ten hours before use. A good mash tub on wheels is an essential piece of equipment. Empty an equal quantity of oats and bran into the tub before evening stables, add the boiled linseed and barley and stir up thoroughly, cover with sacks and allow to stand until the time of feeding. Each lad brings his bucket, which you fill from the tub with a shovel. You will soon discover the quantities of forage you require to give each horse a full bucket of mash. There are a number of general aids to health which can be given in the mash, such as salts when needed and some form of cod liver oil. The easiest way of feeding this is in little brick-shaped things called Codolettes.

Some horses eat up well during the day and not so well at

night, or vice versa. A good feeder will quickly discover what a horse likes best and how much he eats, and will keep him to that as far as possible. Some animals will do really well on as little as 7lb. of oats a day, while others will eat considerably more and never get into good condition. It is perhaps worth noting that the horse still recognised as the fastest of all time, The Tetrarch, was also one of the best doers that his trainer ever handled and was one of the few, as I mentioned earlier, who would eat 21 lb. of oats a day.

On easy days, and sometimes after light work, I like to let a horse pick a bit of grass, which in the spring has definite medicinal properties. There is nothing better for settling a horse mentally than being allowed to pick grass for a while.

I am not a great believer in patent medicines and any trainer who wishes to use some of the many tonics available would do well to study their contents and ensure that they do not contravene the rules of racing on doping – 'other than a normal nutrient'. A good feeder, knowing when a horse is due to run, will build his food up to the maximum that he can happily take over a period of five days. The race will normally be on the fourth day and he will be allowed one more day at this peak before being let down to his normal ration.

I am sure that not enough attention is paid nowadays to water. Nearly all trainers give their horses the mains water of the area in which they live. This has invariably been treated and I have no doubt that the animals would thrive from a change to more natural water, such as rain. When Atty trained at Stockbridge, all his horses drank rainwater which was stored in huge tanks specially built for the purpose. The effect on horses who had previously been drinking normal water was, he said, quite remarkable: they acquired a new bloom on their coats and their form improved. The old man used to claim that the water was the reason why Irish horses took so long to acclimatise to England. In those days there was very little mains water in Ireland, where they drank the soft peat water in the countryside. When they came to England and changed to our water, they would usually keep their form for up to six weeks. After that, they would start going back in performance and condition, a state of affairs which could last for up to eighteen months in some exceptional cases. Reg Hobbs, who trained so many American horses with such success and won the Grand National with one of them, Battleship, told me that horses from

The Tetrarch; an explosively fast horse, and a great 'doer'.

the United States, a civilised country where the water was more like ours, acclimatised far quicker in England than those from Ireland. It would be an interesting experiment to put a string of high class horses on to rainwater. I am convinced that, as long as you could take their water with them when they travelled to race meetings, they would show a marked improvement.

But this seems to be one of the details that tend to be ignored by trainers of today, like the provision of a large sand pit filled with silver sand for horses to roll in after work. There is nothing better for drying off a sweating horse, and the mental relaxation which a good roll produces in an animal who has been keyed up by a strenuous gallop has a wonderful effect on him.

CHAPTER SEVEN

Reams of Bumf

All trainers must have up-to-date copies of *The Rules of Racing*, a first class booklet produced by Weatherbys, which explains all they need to know about the rules and regulations governing their profession. They should learn it by heart and keep abreast of all additions/amendments; this today, is more important than ever.

Over the last forty-five years I have watched the trainer's job become more complicated until even the smallest trainer is forced to employ a secretary to cope with the vast amount of paper which racing today seems to demand. Now, more than thirty years after the introduction of overnight declarations, the teething troubles of which caused so much heartache and in many cases damaged the careers of horses whose entries were not accepted for one reason or another, we are used to the routine and, except on rare occasions, everything seems to go smoothly enough.

Racing is an expensive luxury and trainers must always try to keep costs down for their owners. This involves much thought and care in making entries, although, particularly during the months of January and February in a normal English winter, it usually pays to enter jumpers fairly widely in view of possible cancellations through bad weather.

Until a few years ago, many races on the Flat closed before a horse was sold as a yearling, and some even closed before potential entries were born! These sales with engagements involved the purchaser in a great deal of unnecessary expense. The trainer was faced with the problem not which races to enter his new purchases in, but from which engagements they must be scratched. Unless you were careful, you could buy a yearling with forfeits standing at, say, £100 and in a short while your unfortunate owner could be presented with an astronomical bill as they mounted up to a huge sum. Fortunately, this practice has now ceased. Even the English Classics which, until recently, closed while the animals were still yearlings, now close much later, so that you should be able to decide whether the horse is worth leaving in the race. Racing is founded on optimism and, although the eventual rewards for success in the Classics are fabulous nowadays, the cost of the original entries alone is sufficiently large to warrant a great deal of thought.

Apart from the fact that it is dangerous to have a lot of no-hopers cluttering up the Derby field on that tricky Epsom circuit, when the bad horses start dropping back just as the good ones are trying on the pace, as we saw in the tragic Tattenham fall of 1962, a horse's entire career can so easily be jeopardised by this run. Wherever he finishes, he will inevitably be overrated by the handicapper and will thus be prevented from winning the class of events for which he is suited and in which he should have been running all the time.

Early one year, before the Two Thousand Guineas, I sought the help of that splendid old trainer and delightful man, the late Noel Cannon, to find out whether it was worth running a useful three-year-old in the Newmarket Classic. With typical kindness Noel arranged a gallop for me at Druid's Lodge, in which my colt performed very well indeed. So well that I was excited and full of hope at the thought of the future. Noel congratulated me on my colt's work, but when I asked him whether I should let him take a chance in the Guineas, he hesitated and then said kindly, 'When I have the same problem, I always say to myself that, although admittedly someone has to win each Classic race, that someone isn't usually me!'

The same principle should really be applied to entry in the Classics. Atty used to quote one of his favourite owners, who, when asked if he wanted a yearling filly entered for the One Thousand Guineas and the Oaks, answered, 'I don't think so. For her to win one of them would be too much like a miracle.' Of all the racing maxims, one of the soundest is 'Keep yourself in the best company and your horse in the worst'. Nevertheless there are trainers who overdo this golden rule and, as a result, never win decent races for their patrons. Certainly it does horses good, particularly as two-year-olds, to enjoy comfortable success in their first outings. But it should not be necessary to run in sellers when you are capable of winning at Royal Ascot, or, like Rockfel in 1938, of winning the fillies' Classics.

To apply for your training licence you will have to be able to show a fair quota of horses. The Jockey Club are fortunately becoming stricter about issuing licences. A member of the security staff will usually come down and inspect the training establishment of the applicant, who should also have good gallops and the use of training starting stalls, or adequate schooling facilities for jumpers. The best way of ensuring against disappointment is to serve a period as pupil/assistant to a top class trainer who has established an enviable reputation in his profession and whose recommendations will carry weight.

Things have changed since 1950, when I applied for my licence under both rules with a reference from Atty, who was now my next-door neighbour, and I was sure of my Flat licence because I had ten horses (the mystic figure at that time was eight) of which six were yearlings. But three of my friends who were my new owners had jumpers, which naturally I did not want to see trained by someone else. Two of them were dual purpose Flat and hurdle horses. As it was now the jumping season, I applied for a licence to train under National Hunt Rules and was surprised to receive a terse refusal from Weatherbys stating 'The Stewards regret. . . . . .' I applied again with all my credentials, only to receive the same reply. Of course, as I discovered later, the Stewards had no cognizance of the matter. In those days it always appeared that the tail wagged the dog.

So, in desperation, I went up to London and in the offices, then at 15, Cavendish Square, I saw the boss, Sir Francis ('Gugs') Weatherby. By now I had learnt that the necessary number of jumpers for a licence was five. I put this to him saying that, although the three animals on my form were the only horses who I should be runnng under National Hunt Rules, I did have two old point-to-pointers, one of whom was now my hack, but that neither of them had ever run under N. H. Rules, nor was there any conceivable chance of their ever doing so in the future. I said 'If I put these two on my form, it will make up five which I'm told is the number which you require, but I shall be signing my name to a lie.'

He replied, 'Well, my boy, it is up to you.' So I wrote down those two names, signed the form and handed it to him. He went straight upstairs and returned with my National Hunt licence!

Once a licensed trainer, you have to obtain permission to train for each owner, and each new owner must be registered with Weatherbys. In addition, all partnerships must be registered and also any contingencies to any one of the horses belonging to these owners. For example, if one of these horses has been bought for a certain sum with an additional, say, £1,000 if he wins the Grand National, this contingency, however small, must be notified.

You will need an Authority to Act for each owner. This will cost him £26 plus VAT at the time of writing. Incredible to think that, thirty years ago that fee was half a crown! Moreover the Authority must be renewed every year.

This authorises you to act for your owner in every way on the Turf. It is also necessary for the trainer to register 'Authority to Act' forms for his wife, his head man and his travelling head man. These are most necessary precautions against accidents. Furthermore, the travelling head man, at least, will be using his every time you have a runner, when he makes the final declaration at least three-quarters of an hour before the race. The same, of course, will apply to your wife, if you have runners at different meetings, or if you are sick. One of the most important lessons I learnt from Atty was that the trainer should not make this declaration himself, although he will naturally check it on his arrival, but whoever is travelling with the horse should be responsible for doing it so that, if the horse arrives, so does the declaration, and vice versa. Quite apart from the fact that the trainer's car may break down, or he may be held up in some other way (no flying in fog, for instance), there is no danger of a non-arrival being declared. One of the worst rockets I have ever received from the Stewards was when, riding in every race at the meeting, I declared my own horse for the major event for which he was favourite, never realising that my horsebox had got lost on the way.

Once you have registered your list of horses with Weatherbys, they will send you a list, pre-typed, every month and it is up to you to delete any horses who have departed and add any new arrivals. All deaths must be reported to the Registry Office at once.

One of the easiest ways for a trainer who is just starting to acquire owners is to lease horses. Normally this is only worth doing when the owner of a stud wishes to retain fillies as brood mares, but does not want the expense of keeping them in training.

This can frequently be an ideal arrangement for both sides. The lessor has the chance of owning a useful racehorse to run in his name, win him prize money and land bets for him, without the enormous initial outlay involved in buying a yearling or a horse in training. The breeder will have his produce tested on the racecourse and stipulate for which seasons he would like to lease the animal. Normally he will arrange to lease for the two- and three-year-old seasons so that he can have the filly back to be covered as a four-year-old. The lots submitted by an owner-breeder are always apt to be suspect. It is only natural to wonder why they are being sold at all, and to assume that the best are being kept. Hard as it may be, the only solution is for the breeder to make it known that he sells all his colts annually without exception even though he may be convinced that he is parting with a Derby winner. The fillies are different. It is understandable that he should keep his best bloodlines. So he can either submit them for sale, with a substantial reserve, and lease them if they fail to make it, or lease them in any case. The trainer who is trying to attract owners will often find a fair selection of animals who can be leased among those that are led out unsold at various auctions. When leasing, you must insist, in your owner's interest, that an option to purchase is agreed between the lessor and the lessee and that this is entered on the lease form, which has to be signed by both parties and registered at Weatherbys. As a rough guide, the breeder should be asked to work out the sum at which the animal stands him in, including keep of the mare, covering fee, keep up to the time of lease, transport, etc., and should then add sufficient profit to make him happy, without being greedy. Once an option-to-purchase price has been agreed it can be exercised at any time throughout the lease. The breeder may feel a little disgruntled if the animal wins several races and is obviously worth considerably more than this price, but he has been asked to stipulate a figure which would have made him happy at the time. The scales are in fact loaded heavily on his side. It is the lessor who has to foot the monthly training bills, jockeys fees, entries, transport, etc., and who is taking by far the greater risk. When I started, I leased a number of horses to attract owners into the game, but the option to purchase was exercised on only a very few occasions.

The termination of leases, partnership-leases and contingencies must be notified at once to the Registry Office on special forms provided for this purpose.

With regard to the naming of horses, Weatherbys' computer now produces a book containing the names which are registered and therefore cannot be used. Naming your own horse is part of the fun of ownership and it has always surprised me how many horses are given bad names when there are so many good ones available which would be eminently suitable. We cannot all be epigrammatic, but there is a lot of truth in the old saying that a good horse deserves a good name.

If in doubt, I strongly recommend the hound list which contains an alphabetical record of splendid, dignified names with the accent on the first syllable for calling. It is advisable to get your owners to register names as soon as they acquire a horse. Under a new rule a name, once registered, cannot be changed after the horse has run under rules in any country. This can lead to complications when horses are sold. Bob Boucher, one of the luckiest owner-breeders in the game (Wilwyn, Fleet, Realm, etc.) bought back a brother to the useful Padlocked. To Bob's horror, he found that the colt who he had bred and of whom he was now, once again, the owner, had been named Lovelace Watkins. 'I gather this is some pop singer', he told me. 'So I wanted the name changed. But Weatherbys informed me that, as the colt had run in this name, he must keep it, under a new rule. I wrote to Feilden, but he replied that, as the name was apparently not obscene, nothing could be done about it!'

If the trainer has a stable jockey, even though he may have only third claim, the retaining fee will be divided between his owners, depending on the number of horses which they have in the yard. This fee must be registered with and paid to Weatherbys; the first half is paid at the beginning of the season and the remainder at the end. You can also expect to receive a bill for travelling expenses from Weatherbys twice in the year for all jockeys who have ridden for the stable during that season. If a jockey has three rides in an afternoon, he will charge each owner a third of the expenses and so on. But of course, if he goes to the meeting for just the one ride, the owner of that horse will be required to pay the full amount.

Some trainers do still employ their own jockey who is paid a retainer and expenses, but nowadays a big owner may retain a jockey to ride his horses no matter where or by whom they are trained. Whether a horse is owned in partnership (of not more than four partners), by a syndicate (of not more than twelve members), or a 'recognised club', the Jockey Club will not sanction more than four trustees who will be responsible for the animal. In the case of a recognised company, one nominee must be registered in whose name the horse will run as though he were the absolute owner.

Each stable employee must be registered at Weatherbys. In recent years, with the chronic labour shortage in many parts, the Jockey Club have been very lax in their enforcement of rule 54 (i), which states; 'no trainer shall employ any person to work in his stable who has previously been in a racing stable without referring to his last employer, and receiving a satisfactory report in writing.' I find that a number of trainers are particularly blameworthy in this respect. Good security is not possible unless the rule is observed.

No trainer is allowed to engage or employ any stable lad, or stable girl who does not have a current Identity Card, issued by the Stewards of the Jockey Club. The trainer and the proposed employee must apply jointly for an Identity Card to the Registry Office. Two passport photographs will be required. The trainer is expected to keep the Identity Cards except when they are required for the employee to go racing. Once he or she receives the ID card, the stable employee is covered by insurance.

Every trainer must necessarily take the *Racing Calendar*, which is no longer the unwieldy publication we always knew. It contains the conditions of races and each race has a number. You no longer send off the entry forms, but keep them as copies.

Under the five-day entry system nearly all entries are made by telephone to Weatherbys five days before the day of the race. Read the conditions carefully and call the Registry Office by, at the latest, 12 noon, but preferably much earlier, first thing in the morning. The trainer and his secretary will have been given a security code. When Weatherbys answer − they have umpteen lines − give your name, security code, race number and name of horse. Your will receive an entry reference number for that race, which you can quote when you declare. Weatherbys, who, incidentally, tape all telephone conversations, will come back and confirm. Any queries can be double checked.

If a trainer wishes to strike his entry out of a race, he must do so by the stated declaration time on the morning of the previous day − overnight declaration − otherwise it is a declared runner. Although it varies according to the time of year, if declarations close at 10 a.m., the declared runner will be on Prestel by 11 a.m. and on Channel 4 Cefax by 12.30 p.m. Under the new rule you must now declare your jockey by declaration time the previous day. The table below shows the days for entries and declarations. On Sundays Weatherbys are closed for entries but open for overnight declaration. If a horse who has been declared is cast in his box, or suffers some other sort of injury which necessitates his withdrawal after the time of cancellation, such withdrawal must be notified by telephone, but a veterinary certificate must be produced at the meeting to substantiate it, or the trainer is liable to be fined.

Day:	*Sun.*	*Mon.*	*Tues.*	*Wed.*	*Thurs.*	*Fri.*	*Sat.*
Five-day entry for race on:	–	Sat.	–	Mon.	Tues.	Wed.	Thurs./ Fri.
Overnight declaration for race on:	Mon.	Tues.	Wed.	Thurs.	Fri.	Sat.	–

Some premier races have an early entry system. After making the initial entry, there are forfeit stages whereby you can withdraw your horse on or before a particular date so that you do not pay the next entry fee stage. Five days before the big race you confirm your entries and then declare overnight as usual.

It should be noted here that, in view of the comparatively long period between forfeits in some cases, it is safer to scratch the animal on the spot, rather than wait until the forfeit day before striking him out, if for some reason he will definitely not be running in the big race in question.

Many owners who are businessmen object to having to keep fairly large sums of money in their accounts at Weatherbys, who must make enormous profits out of the interest. Nevertheless, if the trainer does not persuade his owners to keep their accounts in credit, he is liable to arrive at the race meeting to find that Weatherbys' representative has advised the Clerk of the Scales that the horse cannot run until his entry has been paid. This can be extremely awkward, particularly if the owner is not at the meeting and if the trainer himself is delayed for one reason or another, so that the only person responsible is the head man who is unlikely to have sufficient money on him at the time. The only solution therefore is for all owners and trainers to keep their accounts at Weatherbys adequately stocked. However, in these days of high bank interest it is worth keeping a close eye on these accounts, otherwise it will be the Jockey Club secretaries and not the owners who will benefit. In fact, vast sums must accrue to them during every year from the interest on the prize money won or from sums lodged with them. This has always been a cause of grievance, not only against Weatherbys, but also against the world's most admirable auctioneers, Tattersalls. Both are quick to demand money owing to them, but, when the boot's on the other foot, you have to ask for it before they will send it to you. This is certainly the only fault I have to find with Tattersalls nowadays. In the war and immediate post-war years they are said to have accumulated a fortune in interest. When somebody is killed, probably the last thing his relations will think of is that several years earlier he had a horse, or horses, in training. It is quite likely that he might have been a partner in one or two animals unbeknown to his family. Or, when hostilities threatened, he might well have instructed his trainer to sell his horse or horses at auction. So, apparently, the sums just lay there accumulating interest until eventually someone thought of asking.

Depending on the number of horses the owner has in training, I think it is wise to have a standing order with Weatherbys that any money over, say, £500 in his account should be transferred to his bank and that Weatherbys should inform him as soon as his account is down to £200 to give him a chance to replenish in good time. Of course, owners of high class horses with Classic engagements and forfeits will need considerably more than this in their accounts, but I think the principle still applies and for the good of the game, so as not to discourage new owners, trainers must obviously keep a close eye on such matters and keep the costs down as much as possible.

If a person is on the Forfeit List, which is published by Weatherbys at regular intervals, this means that he has not paid his account and is therefore declared a 'disqualified person' until Weatherbys receive the money due to them. Before taking on any new horses, or owners, the trainer should make a routine check of the current Forfeit List, although Weatherbys will be quick enough to tell him when he applies!

If there is any chance that an owner will be absent when his horse wins a big race involving a cup or trophy, the trainer should ascertain beforehand whether the owner would rather have the value money of the trophy instead. Some of the big old challenge cups can be a nuisance to clean.

The normal practice now is for the trainer to receive ten per cent of all prize money, win and place. You must make your own arrangements with your owners and potential owners in advance concerning your commission on sales and purchases, both of which have, of course, involved your professional skill. I suggest ten per cent on sales and five per cent on purchases.

The Rules of Racing will inform you and Weatherbys will administer the other percentages deducted from prize money — lads (so much for the stable of winner, second and third), jockeys, etc. and you should ensure that your owners know their commitments. Weatherbys will send you the lads' money quarterly and you must divide it as you think fit from your stable 'pool'.

Incidentally, in addition, you must have a recognised scale of presents for winners. Current rate in a well known successful National Hunt stable is £20 each for the head lad, travelling head lad and the lad who does the winner.

These days it's almost as profitable to be a vet in a training centre as to be an estate agent, solicitor or accountant! The introduction of inoculations as a compulsory measure involves nuisance to the trainer and expense to the owner, and has frequently been resented because certain forms of vaccination used have been suspect and are wrongly believed by some trainers to have done more harm to their horses than would have happened had they contracted the virus. However, inoculations are here to stay.

Every named horse, that is to say, every horse foaled from 1965 onwards, must be provided with a passport containing all his details and description. In the back of each passport must be inserted two certificates signed by a vet to show that the animal has been inoculated against equine 'flu and tetanus. This passport and the certificates must be produced on demand and whenever the horse is to travel abroad. They must also be produced at the port or airport of re-entry to this country and again on the course when the horse has his first race in Britain after his return from a foreign country. Keep them up to date.

The passport has nothing to do with each horse's identification card, which is lodged with Weatherbys at the start of his racing career and contains all his physical details, including an accurate diagram showing his individual markings.

The other form required for a travelling horse is a landing

permit issued by the Ministry of Agriculture, Fisheries and Food. Fortunately, there are now some excellent agencies who transport horses by air or sea, who will give any information and will help in procuring the necessary forms.

Although the trainer's own lads will accompany the horse, the transporting agency will, of course, ensure that the animal has a comfortable flight and have the necessary equipment to deal with any emergencies in the air. Some horses travel badly by air. Unfortunately this is impossible to foresee, and the only safeguard, taken occasionally by the richest trainers, is to have a trial flight. I arrived at The Curragh one day to find that the splendidly fit colt I had flown over for the Irish St Leger had lost about 3 st. and was a shadow of himself.

One important point to remember when dealing with all forms of horse registration is that, as soon as a colt is 'added to the list', Weatherbys must be informed and the passport must be returned for alteration from colt to gelding.

Nowadays it is not usually necessary to book stabling when horses are running in Britain. The obvious exceptions are small meetings, on Bank Holidays, and the really big fixtures such as Cheltenham National Hunt Festival and Royal Ascot. In the latter case, trainers of horses engaged are sent forms on which to state their requirements by the executive.

The same applies to lads' accommodation. Trainers will usually work this satisfactorily with their travelling head men and will only ask their secretaries to book accommodation if the lads are not happy.

The motorways are a great boon to trainers. Until they were opened up there were so many meetings for which you not only had to send your horses overnight but also, frequently, had to leave them in the racecourse stables another night after the race. This was an added expense and it meant you were without at least two lads for morning exercise.

Unless you have a nervous horse who is better arriving only a short time before his race, you should always aim at arriving several hours in advance so that he can be let down for a brief spell of relaxation after his journey, wearing a muzzle, of course, to prevent him from eating his bedding. Nowadays I find that few horses are given the luxury, which I was brought up to believe was essential, of at least two hours' rest before being loaded up to go home after the race. It is short-sighted not to allow your runners this break, because without it so many animals are apt to break out in a sweat on the way back.

Reverting briefly to the subject of winning presents, let me give you some food for thought. In the 1930s, when you could buy a car for £100 and a packet of Players for $11\frac{1}{2}$d, lads received £5 a winner. For this sum in those days, I'm told, 'You could buy a new pair of jodhpur boots and a new cap and still have enough to get roaring drunk at the pub!' The trainer is, of course, responsible for his staff's P.A.Y.E. and National Insurance contributions. These records must be kept as meticulously as those for the horses.

Of the latter the most important is probably the engagements book, which should be an exact record of every race in which each horse has been entered, its value and distance, details of how he performed on each outing and the trainer's remarks. Unless this book is accurately kept up to date, there is bound to be trouble because so many races at home and abroad are either confined to horses who have not won a certain amount of money, or are framed on conditions based on the amount of money won.

Each trainer has his own way of preparing the monthly bill for his owners. Most stipulate a comparatively low fee and add on innumerable extras − for chemist and saddler, gallops, farrier, etc. While this may encourage a few owners, I am convinced that the system adopted by many top class trainers is the best. They charge a realistic all-in figure so that the owner knows exactly the extent of his liabilities and has no reason to query the account. Veterinary and racing expenses are always, of course, separate items. The latter will include lads' board, wages and also, depending on his arrangement with his owners, the trainer's personal expenses for race days.

As the majority of trainers will not be able to afford more than one secretary, it is vital that he or she should be extra efficient. It is an all too common error to employ the sort of part-trained horsy girl who just wants a job that is glamorous and different. Such women may be all right working for the average small or medium farmer, but they have no place in a modern training stable where the responsibility is as enormous as the money that is usually involved. Certainly it is a great help if the secretary has a knowledge of horses and is keen on racing, but that must be a secondary consideration; ultra-efficiency should come first. I remember Atty paying hundreds of pounds out of his own pocket after one Royal Ascot because his secretary, dreamy about her impending marriage, left a fleet of horses in at the big meeting. That was more than thirty years ago: there is ten times as much paperwork today. If you can justify computerising your office, do so. By mastering the use of these wonderful instruments to make them serve your own requirements, you will save yourselves an immense amount of work, lifting the headaches and, at the same time, ensuring accuracy. Certain leading trainers have become enthusiastic experts in computers and may be kind enough to spare time putting you on the right lines. You will never regret it.

The trainer must always check that each owner's colours are registered every year on the form provided for this purpose.

Either his wife, or his secretary, or, in the case of a big stable, a special person employed for the purpose, must be responsible for the apprentices' administration: indentures, clothing, catering, accommodation, recreation, application for licences to ride, bookings, transport to and from meetings where they have mounts, checking the record of riding fees, winning presents, etc. (The trainer himself and his head man will normally be responsible for discipline and instruction in horsemanship and horsemastership.) Altogether quite a job, but it is one in which most women can fulfil themselves, and trainers' marriages very seldom seem to go wrong.

CHAPTER
EIGHT
Stables and Transport

During the first half of Atty Persse's training career, he preached and practised that horses, like fruit trees, needed plenty of fresh air. When I joined him in 1948, he believed in keeping them warm behind closed box doors.

Both methods seem to work perfectly well, provided that you are consistent. To have top doors open in all weathers, you must have plenty of clothing on the horses. Even with the second method you will have your top doors open during the hot days of summer, so that one essential is a good cage on the doors. I think that the most effective cage is that which goes the full length of the doors from top to bottom. Sam Armstrong fitted these at St Gatien in Newmarket. They have the immense advantage that a horse cannot chew the door, as he can with the usual cage fitted to the top of the bottom door; in normal English weather he can still look out over the half door; and on really hot days both sections of the main door can be left open, so that the entire horse is exposed to the air outside. The disadvantage of this type is that if (as is sadly so frequent nowadays) you have empty boxes, you either have to keep those doors shut, pretending that there are sick horses inside, or leave them open like the others, declaring to all visitors the extent of your dilemma!

Brick boxes are unquestionably the best. And I mean brick, not those built with breeze blocks which are nothing but an invitation to a horse to rub his tail. Wooden boxes have increased so much in price that they are no longer very good value. Unless you can afford to have really substantial wooden boxes built like those in the sales paddocks at Newmarket by Tattersalls, it is better to spend that bit more on brick.

One thing is certain. Wooden boxes must be lined with wood all round from top to bottom. There is no compromise such as lining half way up. A horse does not have to be a crib-biter to enjoy biting wood and experience shows that he will always have a go at the struts in the side of the box and at the top of the wooden lining. Always keep a supply of creosote and a brush to paint it on with, even if this is no deterrent to the really determined animal.

If you do not line wooden boxes at all, there will always be the danger that a horse will be cast and get his leg caught and wedged in between the struts. In the early days of wooden boxes a great many accidents happened in this way. Personally, I prefer solid brick with the walls smooth under paint. A lining of coconut matting half way up from the floor prevents injury through kicking.

Floors have always created a problem for the trainer. Concrete is easy to keep clean, but it is undoubtedly cold and in these days when it is becoming increasingly difficult to buy long straw a horse will inevitably find these floors hard and cold. Many people believe in tightly packed cork flooring, which certainly cuts slipping to a minimum. But, encouraged by Atty Persse, I favour chalk floors provided that they are repaired and levelled every year. A horse likes nothing better than to paw at his floor, making irritating holes. The chalk floors may not be quite as slip-proof as the cork ones, but they do have this advantage.

Mangers must be made from pottery, well rounded. There is really no substitute. I prefer them to be encased down to the ground so that there is no ledge on the bottom against which a pawing colt is liable to damage his knee.

That great old favourite, Brown Jack, used to rest sitting against his manger. In order to make it more comfortable for him, they fixed a leather covering to the edge of the manger, but he promptly tore it off. It was the cold that he liked. Horses who do this are, of course, a nuisance because they tend to dung in their mangers. This, of course, puts them off their feed and will present a strong case for keeping a horse confirmed in the habit in a stall rather than a loose box. I like salt licks in boxes, but they should be placed sensibly so that a horse when feeding is not likely to knock his eye out if some sudden noise makes him lift his head violently. Furthermore, the salt licks should be kept full. The edges of an empty one are always a danger.

The rings should be well up on the wall. I have no objection to old-fashioned hay racks and would not remove them if I took over a stable where they were installed. I like a bucket to be placed inside the door. In this position it is easy for the head lad to check that the horses have enough water without disturbing them too much. Horses have been known to get caught up on bucket hooks in the corner of the box. It is initially more expensive to use wooden buckets rather than zinc ones but, when empty, the latter provide handy playthings and, apart from being bashed about themselves, are obviously a possible hazard. However strongly made, the box doors must have three fastenings and, when the lads leave their horses, the head man must check that all the fastenings, particularly the bottom one, are done up. At this time he will also look in through the windows of each box to make certain that the rack chains have been removed.

I like cage boxes. Although it is argued that any epidemic spreads more quickly when the horses are all sharing the same air, this can be an advantage. They will catch it anyway and so you might as well get it over with. Horses seem to do well in cage boxes, where they can hear and see their fellows and the body warmth spreads throughout the building.

Most big trainers now have some boxes fitted with infra-red lamps and, to judge from those used by Sir Noel Murless at Warren Place, they can be particularly successful with animals who may be a trifle delicate and for bringing horses forward in their coats and general condition, particularly in the early part of the season. So many animals nowadays suffer from rheumatic conditions that the infra-red warmth can do nothing but good.

In every yard there should be some boxes designed for the fastidious bad feeders. The best way is to have the mangers of the adjoining boxes placed together with a grill in between, so that the inmates become jealous of each other and eat up that much better.

From time to time trainers see fit to provide a bad doer with a companion in the form of a goat or a sheep. Although it undoubtedly settles horses who are inclined to fret, this is not always as successful as it might be. I gave a goat to a particularly bad doer, only to find that horse continued to get thinner while nanny grew noticeably fatter. Careful observation showed that as soon as the horse had been fed and the lads had left the yard, nanny would leap up on to the manger. Although at first we were delighted to think that the horse was eating up at last, all the grub had been going into the goat!

Fulke Walwyn's brilliant chaser, Prince of Denmark, was very fond of his goat. After one close finish he was so excited and tensed up when he came back to his box that he snapped at the first thing he saw, which was his goat's ear. Thereafter he had a one-eared companion. Ryan Price's old favourite Canardeau, winner of twenty-five races, whom he gave to me as a ten-year-old when he had run in and won his hundredth contest, always had a sheep. When he came to me and was deprived of his friend I wished he had never been given one in the first place. He adopted the childrens' pony and if, on a misty day, he could not see the pony from his box looking out across the fields, he would create a rumpus which could be heard miles away.

When Canardeau left Ryan's yard, his friend the sheep was given to Ryan's brilliant entire horse, Nuage Doree. All went well for some months and horse and sheep seemed to be getting on famously together. One morning, when the head man came to the box, tragedy had struck. 'It looked like a butcher's shop,' said Ryan. 'The horse had not just killed the sheep, but had torn it into tiny bits and had plastered them all over the box.'

One of the main difficulties besetting a trainer today is that it is becoming increasingly difficult to find long straw now that combine harvesters hold sway nearly everywhere. Alternative forms of bedding are never quite as satisfactory and the majority of trainers use any straw that they can get. Incredible to remember that it is not all that long ago that mushroom growers would not only exchange the best straw for your dung, but would also pay you a fair sum on top. Today the price of straw is far in excess of what you receive for your dung. Peat moss is widely used as a substitute, but it is inclined to be cold. Provided you 'middle' it well every time you muck out, it lasts well and, well heaped up against the sides, makes a fair bed. But never fall into the trap of using peat moss from your yard on the gallops. It is inevitably full of seeds from the hay and you will find weeds growing in abundance in the one place you least want them. Their softness will undermine even the tough durability of a grass like Kentucky Blue. Instead of having an even, matted surface, you'll soon have a gallop which is patchy and treacherous.

I think it is always advisable to have a roof with a good overhang so that the area immediately outside the box is kept dry in most weathers. Moreover, the walk outside the box door should be as near non-slip as possible, since during the winter months frost can cause nasty accidents. In this connection, no yard should be without a large sack of industrial salt to melt any ice and remove the dangers in the yard, both on concrete and gravel.

Returning to the subject of box doors, some horses develop an irresistible urge to dive out. This can result in one of the most tiresome — though not always totally incapacitating — injuries, dropped hip. Stand behind a horse who has one and you will see the meaning of the term. The horse should respond to direct restraint, but if he is slightly scatty about it, you may have to resort to pads, or better still a roller on the pillars of the box door. That great sprint stallion, Whistler, had two doors on his box at Cloghran Stud: one from the yard and the other leading to his paddock. When the latter was opened he would hurtle through it with his tremendous speed undiminished. The only way to prevent him from injuring himself badly was to fit a roller which went with his hip as he struck the door.

When building a new yard, it is obviously an advantage to have as many boxes as possible facing south, facilitating easy control by the head man. The plan usually adopted is an 'L' or an 'E' without the middle stroke and with the long side facing south.

Dung pits should be easily accessible both for the lads with their muck sacks or skeps and also for the dung lorries, which must be able to drive up to load without going through the yard. A loading ramp may appear unnecessary nowadays with so many low-loading horseboxes, but you never know when you may be required to load a horse into an old-fashioned cattle truck type of box. The ramp must have strong fencing on either side or nasty injuries can result from an excited horse slipping over the edge.

As I noted earlier, I believe that a sand pit, large, safe and full of the best silver sand, is an essential part of any training establishment.

Ideally the head man's house or cottage should be at the entrance to the yard, where he can hear any untoward noise, such as a cast horse thrashing about, and be right on the spot to guard against intruders. It is extremely difficult to make most old British stable yards thoroughly secure. After taking every possible precaution as regards walls, fences, etc., the answer to the problem is probably some form of burglar alarm and guard dogs on the prowl at night. There are obvious disadvantages here, however, as when horses arrive back from meetings very late, but these can usually be overcome even though the head man who controls the dogs has to lose some sleep.

I always liked the famous big yard at Chantilly bearing the sign on the gates, '*Attention! Chiens méchants!*' As you entered trembling, expecting a ferocious Alsatian or Doberman, you were greeted by two minute dachshunds!

Apart from the loose boxes, a yard would ideally contain a large tack room and a small, best tack room, both with stoves, a feed room equipped with large forage bins or bunkers, and chaff cutter, adjacent to a boiler room with two boilers, a drying room and a lads' lavatory, if the temptation is not too strong to use it for little horses like Ballydam!

Incidentally, this practice of Atty's had some rather obvious but nonetheless unfortunate results. The boys, deprived of their lavatory in the yard, were apt to relieve themselves haphazardly around the premises. On one such occasion the head man, Archie Hughes, reported the matter to Atty's brother-in-law, Geoffrey Brooke, suggesting that, in his opinion, the culprit was a certain tiny, villainous new apprentice. Geoffrey dismissed his suspicions. 'You're quite wrong Hughes, it's far too large bore!'

Over the feed room with chutes down into the bins, there should be a loft where the forage for use in the near future is stored. The oat crusher will be needed in the preparation of the feed and may be kept in the loft. Again, the lorries should unload outside the yard and for this purpose a small hoist should be attached to the opening on the far side. Hay storage is obviously up to the individual trainer, but clearly he will want a fair quantity handy for the yard.

The amount of tack required naturally depends on the number of horses. Each lad will have his own set of tack and there may be up to half a dozen spare sets. The lad will use his tack on both his horses, but each animal will require a headcollar, rack chain, and a jute standing rug with blankets when necessary. It is vitally important that the standing rug should be properly fitted to avoid the horse getting sore withers. It should always have a breast strap and two straps, fore and aft. The strap round the girth should be kept comfortably tight and the other one may be left a little loose. Between them they will normally stop any rug from slipping, but in rare cases it may be found necessary to fit a tail string. When first introducing yearlings to rugs, it is advisable to use sacks with binder twine strings, held by the breaking roller and a breast girth. Then, if they bite them, they can do no harm. It is a common practice outside racing, and even in some racing stables, to use rollers without breast girths. Sooner or later this will result in a nasty accident, if not a tragedy, when the roller slips back; the reactions of the thoroughbred are so much quicker and more violent than those of the common horse.

Each lad will be issued with an exercise saddle, fully equipped with webbing girths, leathers and irons, a snaffle bridle with or without a noseband, depending on the whim of the trainer, a bib martingale and, during the summer, an exercise sheet; during the winter, an exercise rug (the cheapest and best are the striped variety).

When I joined Atty Persse's stable, many of the standing rugs, sheets and exercise rugs had been in use for the best part of fifty years. They had been patched so many times that some of them weighed far more than any horse should reasonably be expected to carry. The penny-pinching of the old trainers did not end there. Remember – and this is always important because we are so likely to lose sight of it – that to them the horse was as much a servant of man as the cow is today and was never placed on a pedestal. At least the horses were kept warm. But the little apprentices who had to care for them were often in trouble.

Now here I think the Guv'nor was at fault. He economised on saddlery, as indeed he economised on everything in his old age. Saddles with broken trees, stirrup leathers that were on the verge of breaking, irons that were too small for the size of the boy's feet, girths that were so stiff with years of sweat that eventually they were bound to gall, bridles just holding their own and even (heaven be praised!) nickel bits.

Although the price of exercise saddles today is prohibitive, they must be bought and, contrary to the practice adopted in 'civvy street', they cannot be fitted to the individual horse; because a lad is going to use his saddle on any horse he rides, they must be well padded. In case a horse is hopelessly unsuited to the lad's saddle, the head man must be ready to issue a pad to protect the horse's back. The pad will normally be the knitted kind, or alternatively the lad can use the cavalry method and fold a piece of blanket. You will always have to keep an eye on the modern light exercise saddle. Unless it is carefully watched, sore backs will inevitably result, through either the front or rear arches.

One of the worst falls I ever had was when, after I had jumped the last fence well in the lead, the straps to which the girths were fastened came away from the tree of the saddle. This is a fault which is seldom suspected and should be checked regularly.

It is too much to expect that every lad will know enough about tack to check his own, so this must be done by the head man and periodically by the trainer himself. There should be ample supply of saddle soap and leather dressing in the tack room and, for preservation as much as for safety, lads must be made to keep all leather in a good, supple condition. Repairs must be carried out as soon as they are necessary, or the damage will quickly spread. Girths should be scrubbed in a disinfectant solution at least once a week. As the season progresses, however strict the authorities are, girth pox and ringworm are likely to be encountered and they spread like wildfire through a yard. This is as bad as a minor injury to a horse who is ready to run, because the Stewards quite rightly ban such horses from competing and so, until the trouble is cleared up, the animal is a non-starter and may miss important races.

In view of the cost of saddles today, few trainers can afford to provide each lad with rawhide stirrup leathers, although in the end this will prove a definite economy. In pre-war days the jodhpurs of every lad in a good training stable bore the red mark of rawhide leathers. These will gradually stretch, but never break.

Similarly, it is an economy in the long run to have stainless steel irons and bits (never nickel), although there are some good strong metal substitutes on the market such as the alloy, kangaroo. Hand-forged steel is better chromed. It is too much to expect the average stable lad of today to spend time with a burnisher.

It may sound stupid, but little boys are apt to be stupid and have to be safeguarded against themselves. The head man must ensure that all lads and apprentices wear proper, narrow jodhpur boots with leather soles and that the stirrup irons used by each lad are roomy enough to prevent any danger of his being hung up and dragged. The same remarks regarding condition apply to the bridle and bib martingale as to the saddle. Here small details are important. For example, if the little keepers on the bridle straps break, they should always be replaced and any damaged stitching or broken buckles should be repaired at once.

Each lad will be issued with a nightcap and exercise sheet, which in the winter will be supplemented with an exercise rug (usually the striped blanket variety). Both sheet and rug will probably bear the trainer's initials and will always be equipped with a fillet string or tail string.

It is seldom necessary to sweat the racehorse of today in the way that his forebears were frequently treated. But, every now and again, you may have a particularly gross animal and for this purpose you should have at least one full-length hood in the yard.

Each lad should have his own peg in the tack room, where communal saddle horses will be provided for cleaning. The travelling head man is in charge of the best tack room, which will always be kept locked. Here he keeps the racing bridles, paddock sheets, rugs and rollers (some of which will be in the colours of the individual owners), all the different sets of colours, the colour bags and the hampers or boxes containing all the gear required when horses go to the races or the sales. In addition to the normal paddock clothing he will probably have some form of 'cooler' for use on horses immediately after a race, leading reins which he will keep as spotlessly clean as the rest of the racing tack, and at least two Chifneys in addition to those which will be kept by the head man in the main tack room for use on powerful colts who are difficult to lead. Moreover, in both the main and best tack rooms, there should be an assortment of the type of bridles which may be needed in particular cases: for example, there should always be at least one rubber snaffle, hackamore, drop noseband (preferably the cross-over type), tongue bit (which is infinitely better than the tongue strap), Citation bridle, etc. Most trainers and the travelling head men take particular pride in keeping their best tack room as clean and smart as in a good cavalry regiment and with just as much 'bull'. Just as we are always taught that a clean ship is a good ship, so a smartly turned out horse on the racecourse is indicative of a well run training stable. Each individual horse's plates are best kept by the head man in the main tack room. If a horse is to be plated at a race meeting rather than at home, the travelling head man can draw them before he leaves. In each box or hamper for the races, the travelling head man will have an equine first-aid kit and all the boots and bandages which could be required when 'out in the country'. Most head men will insist on doing all bandaging themselves, unless they are lucky enough to have some really good, responsible and experienced lads who are capable of doing this. They will keep a plentiful supply of ankle boots, brushing boots and probably a pair or two of polo boots. In a jumping stable there will be many more boots fore and aft for schooling. Until not so long ago, if you saw a jumper with boots all round it was an indication that he was 'not off'.

There will always be a large can of hoof oil and a brush in the main tack room; if the travelling head man wants to take some to the races, he will have to have his own supply. Some trainers insist on brand new bridles as a precaution for horses running in important events. They cannot then be blamed if something breaks and a vital race is lost. This happened on that agonising, but finally triumphant day of emotion at Auteuil, when Mandarin's rubber bit broke and Fred Winter achieved the impossible by riding the little horse round that hazardous figure-of-eight course, over all those unfamiliar obstacles, to win the Grand Steeplechase de Paris with no bit in his mouth. Inside each of those rubber bits is a piece of bicycle chain; although Fulke Walwyn had provided his champion with a brand new bridle and bit, it was this that broke. Among all the many telegrams of congratulation, the one Fulke liked best came from his old friend Neville Crump. 'Why can't you buy yourself some decent tack? — Crump'!

From a security point of view, many trainers consider it an advantage to have their own horseboxes, because the travelling head man can drive the box and be entirely responsible. The trainer can also travel his owners' horses at a cheaper rate than by public transport services and can still show a good profit to himself. In fact, it is often said that the horsebox is the best horse in the yard. On the other hand, if he has runners at different meetings he is liable to find difficulties if he has only one box — this applies especially on Bank Holidays when runners are likely to be scattered. It is then that the trainer in a centre like Newmarket or Lambourn gains by using the public transport service. Even if he has to share with other trainers, his horses will always get to the meetings with no trouble. More and more of the Lambourn, facing-forward type of box, with its well balanced body, low loading ramps and powerful engine, are being used. It gives a horse a good ride and the lads sitting in front with the driver are especially comfortable. A lot has been written about the advantages of horses facing forward, but in my opinion this has not been proved. Indeed, I am inclined to think that a horse may even be better off travelling backwards, particularly at night when, in a facing-forward box, he is constantly forced to stare at the approaching headlights of other vehicles.

Nevertheless, road transport of horses is so good that any modern box does the job comfortably and efficiently. The travelling head man and his understudies will quickly develop a satisfactory method so that they will not forget anything when they take a horse out into the country. Before loading, they will normally bandage him all round and put on knee boots. A tail bandage is necessary only if there is a rough surface against which the horse may rub his tail; it is usually not necessary in the modern, well padded boxes. The transport companies are punctilious about the cleanliness and hygiene of their boxes and scrub them down with disinfectant after each journey. This is particularly important to prevent the spread of any disease. All forage necessary for the stay away will be carried in the box and, if the horse has been on specially soft or rainwater, it is advisable to take some with him.

CHAPTER NINE
Shoeing and the Day's Work

Horses, like children, are creatures of routine. It is therefore just as necessary for the trainer to establish the schedule which suits his horses, his staff, and himself and to stick to it, as it is for a mother or nanny to accustom children to a timetable in the nursery.

Before examining the routine in the training stable, however, we had better look at the grooming kit that is issued to each lad.

First, he will have two stable rubbers, one for use under his saddle at exercise and another for polishing off his horse. The remaining kit is usually as follows, keeping strictly to modern utility requirements: headcollars, rack chains, one body brush, one dandy brush, one curry comb, one sponge (usually a piece of sacking nowadays), one dry sacking rubber, one hoof pick, one muck sack, one pitch fork. There should be a fair supply of communal hard brooms.

Luxury stables, particularly those in Chantilly, issue skeps like the old-fashioned stables and the sponges will probably be proper sponge instead of sacking. They will probably also issue extra rubbers. Individual lads who are proud of their jobs will collect extra items, but the head man will only allow the most experienced to use combs on manes and tails. He will usually insist that either he, or the travelling head man, is responsible for these.

The lad will normally keep his kit tied up in his stable rubber.

Timing depends so much on the number of horses in training and the number of staff available to look after them. Therefore, in detailing the old-fashioned routine, I am merely establishing

108

an ideal which will be modified by individual circumstances but which has stood the test of time, as long as the trainer has not more than two horses to every lad. Moreover, the timing of the first lot is liable to be varied at the height of hot summer and when the mornings become really dark in the winter.

Let us say that we pull out at 7.30 a.m. As we have seen, the first person to open up a sleeping yard is the head man, who visits each horse with his bucket of oats and his bowl. He must have given the last horse breakfast half an hour before the lads arrive at 6.30 a.m. He will at this time have noted the horses who have left any of their feeds, will be busy with his thermometer, taking the temperature of every leaver, and will have a list ready for the trainer. He will use his own initiative in keeping in any animals who are clearly off-colour or sickening.

The lad, on arrival, goes straight to his first lot horse — the list will usually be pinned up in the tack room — with his grooming kit. He ties the horse up on the headcollar and rack chain, remembering that, with a lately-broken yearling, or a two-year-old, he will use binder twine as described in the chapter on breaking. He removes the bucket, placing it outside the door, and proceeds to muck out, piling the clean straw to one side and removing the wet and dungy straw to the dung pit in his muck sack.

At all times the head man must ensure that when a lad leaves his horse, even for a few seconds, he closes the door behind him. Failure to do this has caused so many accidents.

Returning to his horse, the lad will have collected in his muck sack the necessary extra straw and the horse's ration of hay. He places this on one side before quickly sweeping out the box floor and laying down a rough carpet of straw. Then he picks out the hooves, keeping an eye open for loose shoes or for clenches which need hammering down.

Unfastening the rug sectionally, as we shall see at evening stables, he quickly grooms his horse over, sponging out the eyes and nostrils, taking care to sponge out, dry and brush all straw marks remaining from the night's rest. Then, collecting his tack, he puts the bridle, saddle, sheet and knee boots on his horse; if there is no chance of the horse doing fast work that morning, the exercise sheet or exercise rug will probably be put under the saddle. If it is a working day, the sheet will go on top, held on by a surcingle. There is nothing worse than sheets badly put on; lads must be trained to place them so that the rear end of the sheet is between two and three inches behind the hip bone. At most times of the year in England it is usually better to use night caps and frequently to have a light sheet under the saddle and an exercise rug on top, if you are one of those trainers who believes in warmth at all times.

Horses' heads vary in size; an experienced lad will learn to adjust his bridle accordingly, so that the bit just wrinkles the corners of the mouth. Similarly, it may be necessary to ask for extra long or extra short girths for particular horses. It is essential that the head man, or someone he can really trust, puts bandages on those horses who need them for exercise. Even over the cotton wool pad, they must be tight enough to give support and stay on and at the same time not too tight, or they might cause serious damage to the tendons. As a rough guide, you should be able to get your finger behind the knot, which should always be on the outside.

Now the lad quickly 'sets him fair'; lays out a proper bed with the straw piled up well round the sides, and places the hay, well shaken out, in the corner. At about 7.20 a.m. the head man will start telling the lads to pull out. They will jump up, or be given a leg up, and will start walking round the yard, ready for the trainer's appearance at 7.30.

The point is often argued whether a trainer should ride a racehorse or a hack in the string, and whether he is wrong to travel to the gallops in a vehicle. Personally I have no doubt on this issue. Even if he is an ex-champion jockey, the trainer can always change to a racehorse to ride work on the gallops. It will sometimes be necessary, either through age, or because he has to leave for a distant meeting, for him to go in a Land Rover. But I am convinced that normally the trainer should ride a hack, and preferably one who can be left unattended when his rider dismounts to deal with any emergency. By threading the buckle end of the reins through the stirrup leather and then back round the iron, a rider can leave such a horse unattended, contentedly picking at grass for an indefinite time without coming to harm.

On a hack, riding alongside his string, a trainer has an ideal opportunity of looking at each of his horses and, at the same time, talking to the lads. Only in this way will he learn the little intimate details which can make all the difference between winning and losing races. A horse's peculiarities, either in the box or when ridden, may seem insignificant; sometimes annoying, sometimes amusing, but they can help a sympathetic

Riding work at Newmarket.

A trainer should always value the comments of his staff; William Haggas talks to his lads after work.

Mounted on his hack, trainer Henry Cecil confers with Lester Piggott.

horsemaster to discover the key to his character and they can only be learnt from the lads who ride and look after the horses, not just in their fast work or races, but at all times.

I believe that it is also essential, even with the smallest string, to have someone dismounted who can catch loose horses, help with accidents and changing riders from horse to horse on the gallops.

Indeed, as we are dealing with the ideal top class string, I think that a Land Rover should come up to the gallops, possibly driven by the head man, or by a yard man. It can pick up the discarded boots and can be invaluable if it always contains a spare bridle, girths and leathers, in case of emergency breakages, and a first aid kit. If it also carries a spare lad, he will be able to take over and lead back home the horse of any jockey who may have been riding work and needs to return quickly, or of any lad who has been the victim of an accident.

The trainer's hack should be a gelding and preferably an ordinary-coloured horse – a bay, brown or chestnut. Some colts loathe greys and part-coloured horses, and will do their best to kill them. Strange, this business of colts and hacks. My best point-to-pointer, as well bred as most racehorses, became my hack in latter years, occasionally emerging from semi-retirement to win a nice race. But although he was bay and thoroughbred, some of the older colts in Atty's string clearly decided that he had the smell of a hack and treated him accordingly. They would try to savage him, and if I met the string coming in the opposite direction in a narrow lane, they would get up on their hind legs and attempt to strike him down with their forelegs. It was most alarming. Some years ago the late Sam Armstrong, sitting on his hack surveying the Heath as he awaited his string, was startled by a scream, 'Get out the bloody way!' Indignantly and loudly he rebuked the stable lad who had yelled so impudently, only to receive the desperate answer, 'I don't care who the hell you are. You'll be bloody well dead if you don't get out of the way, now!' Just in time the trainer realised that the shouting lad was hopelessly out of control on a huge colt, who was bearing down on him at a rate of knots, with the obvious intention of destroying his hack and, incidentally, himself. He got out of the way. (The colt was Derby winner, Never Say Die.)

At the back of the string should be a responsible lad (the head man, unless he is in a vehicle), followed by any recruit apprentices on their ponies. As was mentioned during road work, the leader should be ridden by another senior lad who can be trusted to go slowly at all paces. It is hardly necessary to add that the colts should be in front and the fillies behind, preferably divided by a few geldings, and that, as before, the lads must keep at least a horse's length between each other when walking and trotting to the gallops.

We have seen that the old trainers insisted on at least three-quarters of an hour before three-year-olds and upwards were asked to do their first canters. I see no reason for this practice to be altered, however persuasive modern arguments to the contrary may be.

Whether the gallops are his own, or public ones, the trainer will know which are open for cantering and which are for fast work. Gallops must be rested in strict rotation. This is done by the gallop man closing strips with the aid of chains and dolls. Summer gallops must be strictly preserved. Nowadays few people are as lucky as Henry Candy, who owns the world-famous gallops which climb smoothly from the Lambourn downs to the top of the hill from the other side of which the ancient White Horse looks across the Vale that bears his name.

Henry guards his unique gallops with justifiable jealousy. He opens them only in the hardest summer when others are forced to use dirt, tan, cinders, peat moss or all-weather, and closes them at the first spot of rain. They are covered with virgin downland turf untouched, as its name implies, by plough, spade or furrow. The grass, of a similar consistency to that found above some seaside cliffs, is quite different in depth. You can burrow with your finger eight inches down through this closely-knit mat, before you ever come to soil. During blazing summer months, when hooves are ringing out and legs are being jarred on racecourses and gallops throughout the land, you can work six horses upsides at full stretch on White Horse Hill and never hear them coming. Watch a man, or a horse, walking on that turf: it sinks under his feet and rises up like resilient sponge.

It is really important to know your gallops. When the trainer moves his yard, his annual quota of winners drops because he does not yet fully understand how to use his new gallops. They may be too easy so that he under-works his horses, or they may be too severe like the Faringdon Road gallop out of Lambourn which is on the collar the whole way, so that four furlongs is the equivalent of five on a level surface.

When a string arrives on the gallops, the trainer will normally canter on to a vantage point where all the horses will pass him. This will normally be a furlong from the finish during the first part of the season when, although the older horses will canter five furlongs, the two-year-olds out in the first lot will only cover four furlongs. There are trainers who like to do their first canter with the horses close behind each other, but normally in England we canter with between fifteen and twenty lengths separating horses. The first horse must canter very slowly. The system has a decided advantage in teaching horsemanship because, even if at first he is fearful of 'going for the papers', a boy will quickly learn that if he gives a horse his head at the bottom of the canter he will quickly be able to bring him back. On the other hand, if he catches a tight hold, the horse is much more likely to run away.

The trainer will watch each horse's action. If he is happy that they have been nice and free when trotting and cantering and they have a clean bill of health, then they will be fit to work. If, on the other hand, they have been scratching along with an unusually short stride, or there is anything else amiss, it should by now be apparent. On cantering days he may now order the more robust horses to come up again at a sharp canter, leaving some of the others to canter steadily once more, or sometimes to do nothing further except, perhaps, pick a bit of grass.

On work days the horses will circle the trainer on the walking ground at the top of the gallops. Heavy lads in particular will have dismounted to get the weight off their horses' backs. The Guv'nor, who will already have organised the morning's work before he set out, will now detail the first animals which he wishes to gallop together and will see that they are ridden by the jockeys who suit them and who are of the correct weight.

As a general principle, he will work his horses over a distance shorter than that which they will be required to cover in a race. Noel Murless's Derby candidates normally galloped over one and a quarter miles instead of the one and a half of the Epsom Classic. As we noted earlier, it is better in normal gallops to have every horse working happily on his bit. Only when training big, gross sprinters are the usual Persse instructions valid: 'Come the whole way, Michael. You boys lie with him!' Many of the old trainers liked to have their horses galloping hard-held, unless they themselves waved them on over the last furlong. Then, as soon as they saw the Guv'nor's arm waving, the lads would ride their horses out to the finish, once again producing the right response at the right time. If a horse is being trained over longer distances, it is always a help to have some turns. Horses go much better round bends. As most experienced riders know, this is when they are liable to catch hold and try to run away with you. It is no accident that horses like Bald Eagle only find their best form when they are repatriated from the staring straights of Newmarket to the sharp left-handed turns of the United States; although those with their minds firmly rooted in the past still maintain that Britain's wide, straight tracks are a test of courage and that those horses which resent them are *ipso facto* rogues, modern experience proves that the exact opposite is true. After all, so many recent Derby winners have been bred on the other side of the Atlantic from sires and dams raced on those same sharp circuits, where they prove their international worthiness to be regarded as leading international stallions and brood mares.

Mill Reef, a tough and brilliant American-bred horse, trounces his field in the King George VI and Queen Elizabeth Stakes at Ascot.

After each batch of horses has galloped and the work riders have been changed to their fresh mounts, the trainer will probably send them home, normally led and in the care of a responsible lad. Each lad will have a six-foot leading rein in his pocket which he will now use for this purpose, although light apprentices may have to be put on a few colts who are difficult to lead even after work.

It is normally possible for a trainer to gallop his horses in what amounts to a rough trial for his own satisfaction, foxing the touts by slipping it in amongst the other work. A real trial, however, needs some organising and it is not all that long ago since trials at Newmarket were run officially under the supervision of the Jockey Club. Atty, when training, at least in his latter years, used to gallop his horses away from prying eyes and send the entire string away down to the bottom of a hill so that no one should witness the gallop that was taking place along the top. He forgot that Lambourn touts had power-ful telescopes!

The procedure is normally this. The previous day the head man will weigh each of the work riders and insist that they wear exactly the same clothes the following morning. The trainer will tell him alone what weights he wishes the horses to carry in the gallop. Armed with knowledge of the lads' weights, the head man will then be able to adjust the weights secretly by adding weight cloths made up with the necessary amounts of lead. The big betting trainers, of whom Atty was one, had a set of indistinguishable cloths already made up at every different weight so that there was no need to open pockets and so that it was impossible for an inquisitive lad to feel and guess at the impost which his horse was carrying under the saddle; the head man, of course, saddles the horses entirely by himself on these occasions.

In English weather conditions a stopwatch can be most mis-leading, but it is advisable to use one in trials just to make sure that the gallop has been true. Despite all precautions, however, even the best laid-on gallops at home can lead you astray. There are all too many 'morning glories' − brilliant at home, but useless on the racecourse.

Although none of the lads had seen one of Atty's trials and even the work jockeys had no idea of the weights that were being carried, there was always an air of suppressed excitement round the yard afterwards. This continued until the great day dawned when the horse or horses in question were due to run. Then all the lads would be locked up until after the race and the fancied animal would be given to the press as running at a different meeting and the horsebox would set out for the false course, only to be turned round after a few miles and redirected by the travelling head man. If, after this elaborate performance, the horse opened up at 6−4 and started at odds-on first time out, the old man always blamed the work jockeys and stopped their half-a-crown a week pocket money, which was nonsense, as Geoffrey Brooke used to say on these occasions: 'It's Olding's and Sefton's money that makes them odds-on. You are not telling me that people are going to bet in thousands on the word of poor little Joe Snooks!' (naming one of the apprentice work jockeys).

Some trainers never really try their horses. I watched a number of Noel Murless's gallops and I was always impressed by the way in which he satisfied himself as to their worthiness and fitness to compete in their selected races, and at the same time did not ask too much of them. In his Derby gallops on Racecourse Side, Noel's horses galloped in single file until the last three furlongs, when the Classic candidate and probably his counterpart of the previous year were given plenty to do to overhaul and beat the lightly-weighted leaders, who were nevertheless four-year-olds of some consequence.

Either at this stage or in subsequent sharp work, a trainer will hope to receive that sudden inspired thrill when his horse shouts out, 'I will win!'. It is hard to describe these moments which come all too seldom to the average trainer. As he gallops up to you and passes you, you can scarcely recognise him as the same animal you have watched working. His entire action and his outrageous confidence and well-being give him a sort of star quality, so that he seems to flash. If he gives you this sign when you clear him out on the day before his race, you cannot wait to get back to breakfast and telephone the owner so that he can have a good bet. Of course, many horses will win for you without it, but it is only this flashing action that inspires that real confidence beforehand.

The head man will usually have been one of the first to leave the gallops so that he is ready to receive his charges, in the yard, as they return. The lad will now unsaddle, sponge out sweat marks, particularly under the saddle and girths, with a wet sponge, then dry them, brush his horse over, rug him up and wash out his feet, leaving them and the legs wet. Contrary to an opinion expressed in some circles, you will not get cracked heels if you leave them wet, but this is quite likely to happen if you dry them. After setting fair his box and giving his horse a clean bucket of water, he will turn him loose, removing headcollar and rack chains, and will collect his feed from the head man before closing all fastenings on the door and hurrying off to his 'lunch'. As I wrote earlier, it is a tremendous advantage, particularly in a hot summer, if horses can be given a roll in a sand pit after fast work.

The second lot, which will probably pull out at about 10.30 a.m., is likely to be a more leisurely affair because the trainer may have to go racing, the horses in serious training for races in the immediate future will have gone out first lot, and backward two-year-olds now being exercised require no more than about an hour out of their boxes. When they have returned and have been done up, set fair, fed and watered, the head man will have the yard swept spotlessly clean while he goes round ensuring that the first lot horses have sufficient water to last them through the afternoon. Then away go all the lads to their meals and afternoon's rest. This is one of the strange things about the stable lad's life. He is free from about 12.30 p.m. until 4.30 p.m., a period when his wife probably doesn't want him in the house and when all the races in which he is interested, and which are the breath of life to him, are being contested. So he is liable to spend his afternoons in and out of the betting shop. I think it was George Beeby who said that Lambourn in the afternoon reminded him of nothing so much as a mining town on strike!

It is perhaps worth mentioning that, unless a horse is particularly thick in the wind, it is normal nowadays to clear him out over three or four furlongs on the day before a race; only the grossest horses need the old-fashioned pipe opener on the morning before the event. Then, and indeed at all times after fast work, they should trot straight back to the trainer so that he can listen to their wind. But this doesn't mean that they should pull up quickly. The opposite is extremely important at all paces, even a steady canter; the lad must slow down gradually and gently, trotting his horse right out to a walk in a straight line. Pulling up or turning sharply can jar or wrench ligaments and cause endless trouble in the future. It is surprising how many leading jockeys on the Flat yank their mounts up sharply after passing the post in a race, with so little sensitivity that one wonders whether they are horsemen at all. Jumping jockeys, coming mostly from families whose livelihood has depended on horses in one way or another, and riding so many animals who have already suffered leg trouble, are seldom guilty of this crime. Too much depends on keeping good horses sound.

The ritual at evening stables has changed in the last fifteen years. Owing to the labour shortage, few trainers feel that they can insist on the old routine. Those who can, however, undoubtedly enjoy the benefits. As with so many practices outlined in this book, I will therefore describe the way that evening stables were always conducted by the great trainers of the past.

By 4 p.m. at the latest the head man will have done his rounds and distributed small standing feeds to the best doers in hard training. The lads should all be in the yard before 4.30 p.m., ready to start work sharp on the half-hour. This will give them about forty minutes for each horse, allowing ten minutes to tidy up before the Guv'nor's inspection at 6 p.m.

The drill for a fully trained experienced lad is usually as follows. He ties up his first horse, mucks out, picking up the clean litter and heaping it in a smart rectangular pile against the long front wall of the box. As before, he spreads a thick carpet of straw over the floor and twists in the edge by the door, brushing the remainder of the sill clean. Twisting in used to be one of the good stable man's little skills. In the best cavalry regiments it used to be done with an edging of raffia in the regimental colours. Leaving his first horse tied up, he hastens to the second and repeats the process. Now he gets the necessary hay and new straw for each animal and piles it neatly on the end of the litter. He will have to take his turn with the hoof oil and will use it on the hooves of both of his horses, as and when the chance occurs during the evening. This means that he should pick the hooves out immediately so that he is ready for the oil. Some trainers now use a sophisticated mixture containing Stockholm tar, but most of the old trainers, recognising the need to save money on all but essentials, used sump oil. The real reason for oiling hooves above and below is not so much for smartness, as to ensure that the lads pick clean and inspect the hooves, looking for risen clenches and loose shoes, and for any sign of thrush or cracked heels. Then, of course, it will be necessary to treat with medicaments such as Stockholm tar.

Now, going to his first horse with the bucket half full of water, he sponges out the eyes, nose and dock, in that order ('How would you like your hair brush, etc., on the breakfast table?' the old cavalry instructors used to preach). He will now undo the rugs in the reverse order from that in which he did them up, starting with the rear strap, then the girth and the breast strap, and will proceed to groom his horse in quarters, starting on the near side and always using the hand nearer the horse's head to do the sponging, rubbing or brushing, having rolled the rug back to that it rests over the animal's loins and quarters. First he sponges the whole area from the head down the neck to the point where the rug is resting, paying particular attention to sponging out any remaining sweat marks, or dung marks which the horse may have collected while he has been lying down. Once he has damped the whole area, including the near foreleg, he proceeds to dry it briskly with his dry sacking rubber and then, with body brush in the left hand and curry comb in the right, scraping out dirt from the brush at regular intervals, he brushes firmly with a circular motion and then sleeks the coat down before throwing the rug forward, so that it covers the part that he has just strapped, and repeats the performance with the near side hindquarter. Putting his horse over, he repeats the performance on the off side. The good stable man, when strapping a colt or a gelding, will remove the rug for a few minutes to wisp him thoroughly with a hay wisp, which undoubtedly helps the circulation. He can afford to get his full weight behind the wisp, but should be warned against doing the same to sensitive fillies. After he has completed the process and put in whatever quarter marks the trainer approves (in my opinion one large sweep is the most effective), he will probably place a clean rubber over the quarters as he replaces the rug, refastening the girth strap so that it will not mark.

With his dandy brush he brushes out mane, foretop and tail. Only the head man should use the comb scissors to bang the tail to the required length. Then he hurries off to do the same to his second horse. By 5.45 p.m. at the latest he should be finished and both his buckets, now full of clean water, should be standing lined up with those of the other lads opposite their respective boxes on the other side of the walk. The head man will ensure that the yard is swept clean and that each lad, now clean and tidy, is with his first horse. His grooming kit will be laid out neatly on a stable rubber. Both headcollars will have been polished up beforehand. As the trainer approaches the entrance to the yard, the head man blows a blast on his whistle so that each lad is standing to his horse's head ready for the Guv'nor's inspection. The head man reports to the trainer any horses who have left their feeds or have any form of injury or sickness. He carries a bucket of sliced carrots so that the trainer can present each horse with a small handful as he meets him. (Note carrots must be sliced lengthways, not chopped. A hard chopped lump of carrot has been known to stick in a horse's throat.) Then the inspection begins. As the trainer and head man are in the first box, the travelling head man will be standing by the door of the next, so that the lad has time to remove his rug.

This is the one real chance that a trainer has of inspecting his horses and he should take it. Most trainers prefer their lads to stand back from the horse's head while they are making their first all-in appraisal of the animal's appearance and general well-being. The routine of a quick, close inspection soon becomes second nature, starting with the head and looking into each eye, running the fingers across the poll and under the jaw, ostensibly to look for dirt (you'll usually find some on the top of the head and on top of the quarters when a small lad is doing a big horse!), but at the same time feeling for any irregularities such as swollen glands. Always look in the nostrils; although they have been sponged out, there may be some discharge, or they may be flaking. If the horse has been off his feed, it is usually advisable to inspect the teeth and in this case the lad should be instructed to untie the horse before the trainer looks in his mouth, in case the horse runs back on the rack chain.

Then you inspect each foreleg and each fore hoof. Feel each foreleg carefully from and including the knee downwards, looking for any heat or swelling, particularly the knee, main tendon, suspensory, joint, pastern and coronet and, if there is any softness in the frog, smelling it for thrush. Moving upwards to the elbow, you should look particularly for any sign of girth gall, girth pox or ringworm, and, moving upwards, for saddle sores. As you run your hand down the horse's neck and over the flanks, you will hope to find his skin sleek and supple, smoothly loose with fitness over the ribs. By running your hand all over the horse, down the neck and across the back, loins and quarters, you should be able to detect any irregularities such as, for example, an incipient warble fly. You will run your hand over the quarters and hind legs as well before putting him over, looking at him from behind to ensure that the muscle is going on to the right places (to see that he has a 'good pair of breeches'), and then inspect the off side in the same way. It is remarkable how quickly a thorough inspection can be carried out and, once you have established your own sequence of inspection, you are most unlikely to miss anything.

You can always tell a good trainer. Even if he has owners with him, he will have a quick word with each lad as he goes round. This understanding and mutual confidence will produce those vital scraps of information which only the lad knows and without which all the trainer's plans may go astray. As he leaves each box, the lad bundles up his kit and hurries to his second horse to await the Guv'nor's arrival again. When the trainer, after a few words with the head man, leaves the yard, the horses are done up for the night, watered, fed and let down.

Nowadays, however, it is more usual for the trainer to walk round while his horses are being done, rather than have the ceremonial inspection described above. It means that the lads can get away earlier and that they do not feel that they are being subjected to 'bull'. Experience has proved, on the other hand, that smartness and meticulous attention to detail are not 'bull', but make for greater efficiency and, as a result, for all-round success not only in the Services, but in racing stables as well.

I believe that discipline in racing stables, where you are likely to be dealing with horses worth a king's ransom, cannot be relaxed any further without the horses, and consequently those in charge of them, suffering.

Of course, routine will be varied to suit individuals. For example, there will always be some horses who need virtually no work at all and instead of going to the gallops are better being lightly exercised in paddocks, on the road, or even trained on the lunge rein. A good trainer and his staff will quickly discover the needs of each animal. In any case, particularly during the hot summer months when the majority of the string are thoroughly fit, I believe in having as many as possible led out on the easy day of the week, and they should then be allowed to pick grass to freshen them up.

Before closing this chapter a special tip from 'Down Under', which is rarely known in this country but has always been practised by the leading Australian trainers. They used to call it a 'clover leaf'. Immediately after the horse has returned from a race or fast work, the trainer first listens to his breathing and then hurries round behind to look at his quarters. If a horse still has room for improvement, he can see, standing directly behind the horse, that the muscles of his quarters are swollen up like a clover leaf either side of the backbone. If he is absolutely straight in condition, they will not swell up at all. I repeat that this only applies in the first minutes of pulling up. It will not be perceptible later, but it is an invaluable guide, not only to the man who wishes to make money from backing horses.

The French have always held that the well dressed woman is *bien coifée, bien gantée and bien chaussée.* Be that as it may, no horse is any good unless he is well shod and there is little doubt that the trainer should regard this as one of the most important points of horsemastership. Unfortunately, although George Wigg, as Chairman of the Levy Board, started an admirable scheme to encourage the recruitment of farriers, there is a terrifying dearth of good ones in this country today. Those that there are, particularly outside the main training centres, are terribly overworked and are apt to allow their apprentices too much responsibility before they are ready for it, so that a lot of lameness in hunters and ponies is caused by their being pricked or being fitted with shoes that are either too tight or press on the frog.

As we have seen, it is best to fit yearlings with tips in front, provided that most of your exercise is on grass, so that the young foot may be allowed to grow. This will have to be modified, of course, depending on the state of the ground, because you don't want hooves broken up.

Nothing is worse for any type of horse than feet that are too long. They are bound to restrict the animal's action. Fred Pratt used to stand over his farrier whenever he was shoeing his horses, insisting that he cut the toe of the foot back until he could see blood in the same way as you pare the foot of a pony with laminitis. This is probably carrying it too far, but before passing judgment it is as well to remember that Fred was a very experienced and highly successful trainer, otherwise he would not have had the Rothschild horses.

Racehorses are always shod cold, but the major principle of shoeing still applies: that is, you fit the shoe to the foot, not the foot to the shoe.

Normally a pair of light exercise shoes will last for about a month, although if a heavy horse with a shuffling action does a lot of road work, they may not last longer than three weeks. In any case, they need changing once a month, otherwise the feet will grow too long, putting undue strain on the back tendons of the legs. Moreover, shoes left on for any longer are liable to cause corns. The farrier will always hammer the clenches down flush with the hoof, but as time goes by, they may come up and the rough, sharp edge can cut one of the other legs, so the head man should always be ready to hammer down any protruding clenches.

Horses must always race in aluminium plates, which are still the best although experiments have been carried out with various forms of plastic. It is surprising how many trainers, even today, get away with running non-triers in ordinary exercise shoes. My head man, Jack Maisey, one of the best friends I have ever had, used to run professionally as a boy in Wales. Whenever he was 'not off' the trainer would put flat soles of lead inside his spiked running shoes, removing them only for the big day when Jack was fancied and the money was down. Incidentally, the prize money for this form of running in those days was enormous and used to attract professional runners from all over the country, particularly the sprinters of Edinburgh's Powderhall.

Wales has always been a splendid source of racing lads and apprentices who have gone on to make fine jockeys. The prize money for 'flapping' races is large indeed and I have always believed that the Jockey Club should soften their attitude to these unauthorised meetings which are responsible for producing so many of our best young riders. As a little boy in Cornwall, I used to ride in such races, which were sometimes held quite openly and at other times were disguised as Express Letter races at gymkhanas. Everything was just the same, except that, rather like the clip joint that calls itself a club, each competitor was given an old envelope to stuff in his breeches. Looking back now on those appallingly sharp tracks, with stakes and ropes instead of rails and the competition of tiny, tough gipsy boys riding thoroughbred ponies on eight-ounce 'docks', the very thought terrifies me. But between the ages of about eight and thirteen it was great fun and I reckon that I learnt a lot about race riding which has stood me in good stead ever since. One of the chief lessons you learn is that it is vital to lay up and at least keep within striking distance, because a horse who is not in the firing line with his rivals but is trailing in the rear will soon be disappointed and lose interest. Another lesson is that you become accustomed to the body-to-body, horse-to-horse contact when galloping at speed, which is so frightening at first. One of my instructors at this stage of my life was a splendid little spiv who had been a highly successful jockey, first in flapping races and then under Pony Racing rules, until he was warned off the latter. He must have been very naughty, but to this little boy he was inevitably endowed with excitement and glamour. His chief trick that I remember was using your foot under a galloping horse's elbow to turn him over if you are riding a non-trier and all other means of stopping him have failed!

Racing plates will not stand any road work and should be removed except for racing. Although it will be necessary, as has been explained, to rasp down the toes of horses in training, no horn should be taken off the heels, as the plates must often be removed and, owing to the large number of nail holes employed to hold them to the foot, any reduction in the horn, other than at the toe (except when it has obviously grown), is bound to add to the difficulty of shoeing.

Each individual horse's plates must be taken off immediately after the race, marked with his name and kept with the others, either to be fitted before he leaves home for his next public outing, or to be taken by the travelling head man and fitted by the racecourse farrier.

I have always found that farriers know far more about horses' feet than vets and should be consulted in any case of trouble. In fact, any vet who knows his job always calls in the farrier when there is trouble in a foot.

CHAPTER
TEN

Ailments

There have been many changes — not always for the better — in the last twenty years. The emphasis on high academic qualifications has tragically depleted the number of vets who have been born and brought up with horses and cattle. Just as the dapper 'agronomist' has come to govern the land, frequently with disastrous results, so the specialist, theoretical 'expert' has superseded the genuine, practical horse doctor, who had hunted from childhood, often shown and point-to-pointed, with his innate knowledge of animals. The lovely world of James Herriot has been dealt a near-mortal blow, from which we and our animals are suffering.

Veterinary charges are exorbitant and money is in short supply. So, remembering that our forebears necessarily knew more about horses than we can ever learn, and fully aware that many potential trainers are not millionaires, I have written about and stand by some of the old, tried and tested methods. Do it yourself where practicable.

Various forms of vicious virus have crippled great stables, such as that of Major Dick Hern in 1992. These heartbreaking happenings, of course, can only be remedied by rest and by the best available veterinary treatment.

Blood counts are now a way of life in many stables. I am a strong advocate of weighing horses, if you have a weighbridge handy, to determine their state of fitness, a method pioneered by Vincent O'Brien and the late Harry Wragg. And, again if you have the facilities nearby, I know that swimming horses is very beneficial. 'Treadmill'? I'm not all that keen, but it obviously has its uses in convalescence, and an automatic horse-walker can be a great asset.

Finally, I will always be in favour of line-firing by an expert. With local anaesthetic and an electric firing-iron, a horse does not suffer and seldom goes off his feed. It provides a natural bandage and, as the best old vets still maintain, is a visual reminder to the trainer of the need for a long, complete rest as the ultimate cure. It certainly prolongs active life and its banning in 1992 (apparently revoked at the time of writing) was the work of the ignorant urban academic sentimentalists now blighting the veterinary world.

That said, there are still a few — a very few — vets around with a true vocation. Skilled doctors, to whom the treatment of and caring for the animals they love is more important than money. If you are fortunate enough to have one of these, look after him. Give him your best horses to ride and hold on to him. He's worth his weight in diamonds.

I have always said that, if I had my life over again, I would become a vet. I would certainly have liked my son to have become one, because the financial rewards of this hard-worked profession, which has for so long been neglected by the better brains owing to ridiculous social strictures, are now out of all proportion to the skills of most British vets. Old stud grooms simply cannot believe that the managers of famous studs today feel bound to call in the vet for everything, even to tell them when their mares are ready to be covered. The whole thing seems to have got out of hand, with the result that too many trainers know little about the treatment of minor ailments and their owners consequently receive enormous vet's bills.

One well known vet is apt to turn round and say to the trainer. 'What do you think?' My answer was always the same. 'If I had known, I wouldn't have called you in. The only reason you're here is to give me expert assistance, to tell me what you think and to act accordingly.'

The introduction of modern drugs and antibiotics has undoubtedly saved the lives of many animals, but it has had a dangerous effect on the veterinary profession in a number of ways. For example, when faced with ordinary skin diseases like the eczema type in dogs, many vets who should know better, rather than treating the condition from the outside in the old-established way, fly immediately to cortisone, heedless of the side-effects of hormone drugs. This practice is unfortunately all too common with some horse vets, who have come to regard every new antibiotic as a panacea. Nevertheless, the medicine cupboard of a racing stable would necessarily contain some antibiotics and my favourite British vet, Alastair Fraser, if called in an emergency for any big wound, had one invariable rule. 'First inject a massive dose of antibiotic and then think of the best treatment afterwards.' Many tragedies would be avoided if more members of the profession acted on this belief instead of fiddling about while the poison spreads.

The prevention of disease is far more important than its cure. All injuries and diseases have a cause and this can generally be discovered, reducing the risk of similar trouble in the future. When you call in your vet, his opinion of the cause and his advice on the prevention should be sought, as in some cases this may be more valuable in the long run than the successful treatment of that particular patient. However, after this preamble, I cannot emphasise too strongly that if the trainer or his head man has the slightest doubt about any horse's condition, he should always summon the vet at once. In this connection it is worth noting that at long last British vets are specialising and the trainer must immediately find out who are the best horse vets in his area.

Coughs and flu

We seem to have come to such a pass in the last few years that every incidence of the ordinary cough, which has always occurred like the common cold in humans, seems to have acquired the title of 'flu', or 'the virus'. Undoubtedly, there have been some pernicious forms of flu about and the Jockey Club were right in ruling that every horse should be vaccinated. I shall never understand why the veterinary profession was unable to produce a thoroughly satisfactory diagnosis of the virus epidemic which crippled British racing in 1972.

But we still get the old-fashioned type of cough, which takes two forms: a wet one with nasal discharge that normally comes in the spring and a dry one with no nasal discharge, but frequently with the flaking of the skin in and around the nostrils, which occurs as a rule in the latter half of the hot, dry season. Either form may be heralded by the usual symptoms of a horse who is off-colour: he may leave some of his feed, be bad in his coat, and work or race listlessly until found to have a temperature — or, particularly in the backend type of cough, he may just start coughing. Both types are highly infectious and the only cure is rest. Even though this means an inevitable set-back in training, the alternative would probably be a broken-winded horse. If a horse gives a few coughs and blows his nose when he first pulls out in the morning, there is nothing to worry about. But if he coughs more than once while at exercise, without blowing his nose, he is almost certainly sickening and instead of being worked that morning should be sent home. The cough will quickly spread throughout most of the string (as with humans, there will always be a few who will miss it), but if you are in the middle of a busy season you may be able to postpone the evil day by isolating the important runners, like Classic candidates, in a yard away from the main body of the string — if you are lucky enough to possess one. Vincent O'Brien is one big trainer who has frequently and successfully used this method of safe-guarding his Classic hopes.

As long as the horse has a temperature he should be kept warm and comfortable in his box on slightly reduced rations and it is a good idea to give him some Epsom salts in his evening mash. But if and when he has a normal temperature, he can be led out, well rugged up, with an exercise blanket held over his standing rug by a roller and breastgirth. He should, of course, be kept dry; in fact, except for the immediate runners, most Flat trainers prefer to keep their horses inside when it is raining.

The cough will run its course. As with the common cold, it is usually advisable to let it do so, rather than attempt to suppress it with antibiotics; as with the human equivalent, the best you can do is to make the patient as comfortable as possible, take away the irritation and clear the head. In this connection, despite the inevitable mess, I still like old-fashioned electuary, with its treacle base, which the head man can spread on the tongue with a flat stick. It undoubtedly soothes the irritation in the throat and most horses eventually come to look forward to it.

If the cold is reluctant to come away and loosen up, steaming is still as effective as it is with human beings: eucalyptus and boiling water in a bucket three-parts full of hay provide an excellent inhalant which sick horses seldom resent because they must feel it clearing their heads from the first sniff. In any case, during a coughing epidemic, the head man will sponge out the nostrils of the sufferers morning and evening with a solution of Dettol and warm water, then smear them with Vaseline to prevent the discharge from sticking. Atty's immediate reaction to the first sign of coughing was to order the head man to put a teaspoonful of iodine in each horse's water bucket. I have never met any vet who believes that this could do any good, nor have I known any other trainer to do it. It was presumably an old-fashioned Irish idea, probably dating from before the turn of the century.

Provided that the cougher was in hard training before he became a victim, he will not take long to get straight again when he recovers. As soon as he has no temperature he may be given road exercise, walking and trotting; on these occasions the head man must ensure that each lad gives him an accurate report on the animal's progress — for example, 'He coughed six times and did not blow out' or 'He only coughed three times and blew out well each time.'

Occasionally you will run up against a chronic persistent cougher. I have known trainers who, in desperation, take such a horse up to the downs and, because for weeks, despite his cough, he has been jumping and kicking with *joie de vivre*, give him a short sharp gallop. This kill-or-cure method sometimes succeeds in clearing up the animal altogether. But recently a few enterprising vets have diagnosed lungworm in cases of chronic coughing and have been able to clear it up quickly once they have confirmed their diagnosis.

Many trainers, and indeed their vets, have been experiencing great difficulty in recent years in distinguishing between the ordinary cough and the various new types of influenza virus epidemics. Perhaps it is best to say that the vet should be called at the first sign of a sick horse with a high temperature. Let us hope that the inoculations will in the future be effective enough to stop this disease, which is often so difficult to detect. A horse may appear perfectly fit, eating his food and generally showing no signs of debility or even the normal symptoms of lassitude, but in a race he will suddenly and inexplicably run a long way below form. As horses recover, they frequently produce the same type of performance: full of beans at home and seemingly ready to run for their lives, they will go for a short way in a race, only to pack up. The vets must make an absolute priority of getting to the bottom of these diseases, which cost owners so much money in lost opportunities, cripple the industry and provide the inevitable wrong-doers with cast-iron excuses for the non-triers.

As soon as there is the first sign of cough or flu the head man should see that all the horses' temperatures are taken morning and evening. A horse's temperature normally is 100.2 F, his pulse about 40, his breathing about 15 to the minute, and the colour of membranes lining eyes and nostrils, a good pink. The bowels move on an average eight times daily and the droppings are just soft enough to break as they hit the ground. A lad who sees that his horse's droppings are small and hard, full of undigested oats, or covered with slime, should report immediately to the head man.

The urine of a healthy horse, light yellow and somewhat thick in appearance, is passed several times a day in quantities of a quart or more. A lot of clover hay is apt to darken its colour, while grass has the opposite effect. As mentioned previously, in cases of box flooding from excessive urination, misnamed 'diabetes', all forage should be checked at once and the vet called.

Eyes

The vet should also be called for any eye trouble which does not clear up within a few hours after the application of one of the modern eye ointments. It may be that the horse has simply stuck a bit of hay in his eye, but this will soon disappear. Before the First World War, periodical ophthalmia was unknown in this country. It is supposed to have been brought over by the remounts from countries like Australia, but as it is not seemingly infectious, I have never been able to understand this theory and can only assume that the timing of the first case was merely coincidental.

It starts with a slight bluey haze over one eye, which appears to respond to treatment and disappears, only to recur a little worse some time later. This process continues over quite a long period until there is total blindness in that eye. As horses' eyes do not focus together like ours, this is by no means as bad as it would be for a human being, and many horses who are blind in one eye have gone on winning races. The trouble is that periodical ophthalmia is likely to spread to the other eye. Furthermore, in all stages whenever there is a haze over the eye, the animal understandably suffers loss of form.

Perhaps the most famous case was the brilliant Derby winner, Dante, whose defeat by Court Martial in the Two Thousand Guineas was almost certainly due to the initial symptoms of a disease which finally left him totally blind, but still able to cover his mares. It is clearly not hereditary.

Teeth, mouth and throat

The shortage of veterinary dentists is becoming alarming. An experienced head man armed with an efficient ratchet type of gag, two long rasps and a pair of veterinary dental forceps, will be able to keep the teeth of his charges in fairly good order. As the rear molars become too sharp for the horse to masticate properly, he should rasp them and should know enough to remove the shells from young horses' teeth. Nevertheless, I believe that every horse in the yard should have his mouth inspected as matter of routine at least once a year (preferably in the winter for Flat – race horses) by a good veterinary dentist. So many troubles have their origin in teeth that this must be regarded as of the utmost importance. Apart from leaving his feed, a horse will usually show when he has tooth trouble, carrying his head on one side, shaking it and quidding his food or his hay, dropping half-masticated mouthfuls, usually with a discharge of saliva. 'Lampus' is a term for swollen condition of the gums behind the incisor teeth of the upper jaw; young animals get it when they are changing their teeth and old ones when suffering from indigestion. The treatment is a little drastic but most effective and should be well within the scope of any head man. You simply nick the swollen gum in several places and then rub a handful of salt firmly into the bleeding gum. If the condition persists it will probably be necessary to feed the animal on mash for a few days, but I have never known it to continue troubling a horse once it has been spotted and treated.

Other injuries in the mouth are usually caused by the bit and heal quickly once the cause has been removed. For example, the end joints of the bit may become worn so that they and the ring chafe the corners of the mouth. The application of a little antiseptic cream or antibiotic ointment will quickly stop this, as long as you either substitute another bit, preferably a rubber one, or get the saddler to sew leather round the offending joints.

If you feel swellings between the branches of the lower jaw, it is possible that these are the symptoms of strangles, a dreaded disease in pre-war days, but the name, like 'diabetes', is far more alarming than it need be. If the vet is summoned immediately, as he must be, when the abscesses are noted, he will quickly nip the disease in the bud with the aid of injections.

Conditions affecting the limbs

The keen young trainer will pester the vets and the local hunt kennels for as many legs of dead horses as they can supply. This is really the only way in which you can learn as much as you ought to know about legs. It is obviously important, when obtaining the leg of a dead horse, that you should discover from the vet what was wrong with it; then, when you boil it down, you will be able to pinpoint the exact cause.

TENDON, LIGAMENT AND MUSCLE INJURIES.

It is incredible how much work a horse's leg can stand. You may feel a leg every night at evening stables until you know every bump and thickening of the fired and blistered limb, like the back of your own hand. But the horse goes on running and winning, particularly over fences, when the strain of galloping is not as exacting as it is on the Flat, and it is not until the animal is finally put down that you can look at that leg and see the collection of tiny tapes which had been masquerading as a main tendon.

However, the golden rule for ninety-nine per cent of trainers is to call a halt to all work as soon as you feel any heat or thickening. Only a handful of top class jumping trainers have sufficient knowledge and experience to take calculated risks and get away with them.

Sprains of tendons and ligaments are more frequent than those of muscles. They develop gradually as a rule and so detection of the slightest heat or swelling will probably prevent serious breakdown. Do not forget that, at this initial stage, the horse may not be lame and so it is only the sensitive hands of the trainer and his head man which can save the animal.

The golden rule is that, before applying any form of blister, you should always remove the swelling and the heat with fomentation. The object is to get rid of any fluid around the tendon or ligament and to unite any broken fibres. This can be done with either Antiphlogistine or Animalintex. The former is more convenient in that it holds the heat longer, but the latter is infinitely easier to apply. In both cases the dressing should be as hot as it can be borne and should be covered with oiled silk and a cotton wool pad to keep in the heat underneath the bandage.

For cases when the vet applies a heavy blister, you will require a cradle to put round the horse's neck to prevent him from biting his sore legs.

There are, of course, many different ways of treating strains and sprains; for those who have the time and labour, it is often beneficial to allow a horse to stand in cold water for a period, or to keep the hose on his affected legs.

The old trainers cure for swollen knees, joints etc. is still the best — cabbage leaves. Bandage two or three large leaves to the affected place, leave on for twenty-four hours, and repeat until the swelling goes down. This really works, not only on horses, but on people too. Try it.

SORE SHINS

As we have seen, sore shins necessitate a short rest. Over the years the Americans have deliberately galloped sufferers on the hard to buck the shins out. Although unsightly, this method is undoubtedly effective, but it is not popular in this country where, combined with the rest, a little working blister, or Workalin, rubbed in for a short time with a toothbrush on both shins, is probably the best treatment.

INJURIES TO BONE STRUCTURE

SPLINTS are bony growths on the cannon bones which occur chiefly on the inside, although sometimes on the outside, of the forelegs. Provided that they are well forward, they are unlikely to cause much harm as they are coming out, but the further back they are on the leg the more likely they are to produce lameness as they are forming. In the last few years vets have become particularly skilful at removing splints.

BONE SPAVIN is a bony enlargement which forms in the inner and lower side of the hock joint as the result of disease. The two rows of small bones in the hock become inflamed and join into a solid mass, throwing out bony deposits on the inside of the hock. Cow-hocked horses are very liable to contract spavin.

The horse becomes lame and drags his toe, but once the bones have united and the deposit ceases to interfere with the flexion of the joint, they can remain reasonably sound for some time. Many vets still prefer firing as the best treatment of spavin, but in any case, unlike bog spavin, you should always seek expert advice.

RINGBONE. If, when your horse is lame, you discover a bony deposit on the pastern between the fetlock joint and the coronet of the hoof you are in trouble. It is probably ringbone and your horse is unlikely to be any further use for racing; although I believe that a cure is on the way, thanks to the research work of Dr Pouret.

NAVICULAR. The same long-term loss of use unfortunately still applies to navicular, even though with this disease the evil day may be postponed for quite a while.

SLIPPED STIFLE means that the stifle cap is dislocated owing to cramp of the muscles of the quarters, so that the leg is dragged behind and cannot be flexed or brought forward. There is a swelling on the outside of the stifle caused by the displaced bone. This seems alarming but is comparatively common, although the chronic stifle-slippers are happily few and far between. One of Atty Persse's colts, the huge Fairway bay, Fair Speech ('the most beautiful horse I have ever seen in my life'), used to slip his stifle regularly in his box and put it back again as a sort of game to attract attention. But usually when this happens, you can get hold of the leg by the pastern and pull it forward, while at the same time an assistant pushes the displaced bone forwards and downwards until it is replaced.

SOFT TISSUE INJURIES
CAPPED ELBOWS AND CAPPED HOCKS are usually enlargements resulting from bruises. The former are usually caused by lying on an uneven floor from which the horse has pawed the bedding, and the latter by kicking the walls of his box. Both will respond to treatment, but as they are so ugly and can, without attention, become semi-permanent, I always like to call in the vet to get rid of them as quickly as possible.

WINDGALLS are soft swellings on either side of the fetlock joint. They are easily compressed, painless, seldom cause lameness and are usually quickly dispersed with the use of standing bandages.

THOROUGHPIN. This is an enlargement of the hock joint just in front of and above the point of the hock. When pressed with the finger on one side of the leg, it will bulge out on the other and has the feel of a windgall. It is caused by overstrain and once again is not so important in a young Flat-race horse, as it does not usually cause lameness. If it does, it will normally respond to a mild blister once a day for three days, repeated after an interval of a week. During the winter, cork firing (application of a smouldering cork to the bursitis) has been found to be most effective.

CURB. This is an enlargement at the back of the hock, roughly six inches below the point, at what is known as 'the seat of curb'.

It is caused by a sprain of the ligament in this area and frequently causes lameness, which can be cured although the enlargement always remains. Horses with curby-shaped hocks are more liable to curbs and this faulty conformation is often hereditary.

Curbs are not as important in a Flat-race horse as they are in a jumper. After all, the animal is probably running only at a tender age and they are unlikely to do any serious harm to his action. They are, however, a definite unsoundness and, as such, are to be avoided at all costs, particularly if there is any chance of the horse being a jumper. The treatment of curbs is normally a working blister.

BOG SPAVIN. A swelling at the front and under side of the hock, seldom causing lameness. When it does, the swelling will be found hot and painful to the touch. If the horse is rested and the leg is hosed with cold water, followed by the application of a mild blister, all should be well.

Conditions affecting the foot

THRUSH. Racehorses, scrupulously mucked out twice a day, should not contract thrush, a diseased condition of the frog in the hoof which becomes soft and gives off an evil-smelling discharge from the cleft and the sides. The cause is normally negligence − for example, if the horse has been standing in badly drained stables sodden with urine. If you receive a horse with thrush, the hoof will quickly respond to treatment if you wash out the cleft and sides with a flat wooden spatula, soft tow and hot antiseptic water. Then you take away any ragged bits that may be hanging off and dress it daily with Stockholm tar. As a racehorse's hooves are picked out four times a day and washed at least once, this in itself is sufficient prevention.

CORNS are a different matter. Once again this is a misnomer, because, unlike the human growth whose name that they bear, they are bruises on the sensitive sole of the foot, between the wall and the bar at the angle of the heel. The spread of blood in the affected area makes it red and easily recognisable. Horses with weak heels and flat soles are particularly liable to corns. Again, it is usually better to call in the expert, this time the farrier who will remove the cause (the pressure of the shoe) and will probably cut out a small portion of the bruised corn. If pus has formed, he will make sure that it is free to flow out and will instruct on the necessary dressing. A well run yard will normally have one fore and one hind boot to put on over the bandaged hoof in cases where the hoof has been badly bruised, or punctured by nails, broken glass or sharp stones.

'Setfast'

'Setfast' is an alarming but comparatively harmless complaint suffered by horses in training, usually after fast work. The animal appears to be in distress when he arrives back at the stables and is unable to walk properly because he cannot bring the hind legs anywhere near the forelegs − hence the term 'setfast'. This is, in fact, caused by the production of an excessive amount of sugar and is known by the vets as 'azoturia'. Keeping the patient warm and administering a 'setfast drink', which can be bought under that name, has always done the trick in the past. Nowadays, however, with their fanatical zeal for drugs, the vets usually prescribe cortisone, although there is a brand-new American product which has recently arrived on the market in this country. It is worth noting as a typical example of the modern trend, that Atty Persse's head man, Archie Hughes, never called a vet for a horse in this condition, but invariably achieved quick, complete recovery with the aid of a setfast drink. There is a lesson to be learned.

Wounds

Vets usually divide wounds into four types: clean-cut, torn, bruised and punctured.

Clean-cut wounds usually bleed freely. When the bleeding has stopped the cut surfaces, which have been brought together by clips or stitches, heal fairly quickly.

Torn wounds do not bleed as freely. The tearing process will have damaged the flesh, which therefore needs a longer time to rejoin.

Bruised wounds, by far the most common kind, include broken knees, overreaches, treads, girth galls, etc. They bleed only slightly and usually the injured part is swollen.

Punctured wounds are nearly always dangerous because dirt is carried into the wound through a small opening that closes quickly. Horses puncture their feet by treading on sharp stones and nails. Their skins will be punctured if they stake themselves or are pricked by thorns.

If there is the slightest possibility that any foreign matter has entered the hole, the vet should always be called. An immediate antibiotic injection is essential. With all wounds of any size, particularly the puncture variety, you should always demand an immediate anti-tetanus injection as well.

The general first aid for all wounds is to wash out and bathe the injury with a strong solution of warm water and antiseptic. Then, in the case of minor injuries, you can usually apply antibiotic ointment or powder, depending on the position of the injury and whether you wish to keep it open while it heals or dry it up.

In this connection, the introduction of chloromycetin mixed with gentian violet, in aerosol containers, has been a tremendous boon to trainers, who must, however, realise that they are applying a powerful caustic that may create proud flesh.

The other new aid which most vets have recently adopted, and which has been used by hospital surgeons for some time, is the aerosol 'New Skin', which can be sprayed to provide an effective covering on places such as the stifle, where it is impossible to bandage.

All wounds should be dressed at least twice a day, depending on their severity, by the head man, who must decide whether to call for the expert assistance of the vet. With the exception of really minor injuries, however, it is always best to be on the safe side.

Of the common minor injuries, *girth galls* and *saddle sores* can usually be treated by washing out and the application of an antibiotic or antiseptic ointment. Unless they are particularly bad (which should never be allowed to occur in a training stable) they should not interfere with the animal's training programme. Skilful manipulation of blanket pads, or numnahs, should keep the saddle off the affected places and, with the aid of bandage and cotton wool, the girth should be kept off the gall until it is healed.

Although it is not practical to fit the saddle to the horse in a racing stable, it is up to the trainer to see that his exercise saddles are in good condition; that wither pads are used if the front arch shows any sign of pressing on the withers; that a blanket pad is carefully arranged with a channel to keep the centre and rear arch of an offending saddle off the back; that a breastplate (or breastgirth) is employed as soon as a saddle looks like slipping back, and that the lads do not lounge on the back arches as they are inclined to do, particularly with the present trend of riding far too short.

Of course, dressings for leg wounds can usually be bandaged, in which case a cotton wool pad should normally be placed over the dressing first.

Treads are normally minor injuries to the coronet of one foot caused by the other forefoot or the hind foot, or are caused by a tramp from another horse. Wash out and keep clean.

'*Overreach*' is a wound, or bruise, usually on the bulbs of the heel or the sides of the coronet, caused by the shoe on the hind foot and most often occurring when, owing to heavy ground, the foreleg is held and the exit of the forefoot is slightly delayed.

As long as your farrier keeps the hind toes short, you should have little trouble with overreaching. When this does occur, you will often find that the downward stroke of the offending hoof has cut the heel so that a flap of skin is hanging. When bandaging you should see that the cut ends are held in position, which is not so difficult in the rare cases of a cut above the joint, but somewhat tricky in a bad case on the heel. A really serious overreach will entail bandaging under the hoof and all round, and the fitting of a surgical boot to keep the dressing in place. Normally, however, the ordinary overreach can be dressed and the flap of heel will be so small that it can be cut off without doing any damage.

A final word on wounds. It is essential to impress on the head man, or whoever is doing the dressing, that the cleanliness of himself and his clothing should be regarded as of the same importance as in the treatment of human beings. A trainer should always issue his head man, travelling head man and any other lad who may be treating sick horses, with a sufficient supply of kennel coats so that they can always be spotlessly clean.

Conditions affecting the skin

SKIN DISEASES. For a racehorse trainer these can usually be reduced to two: ringworm and what is commonly known as 'girth-pox'. Jockeys' valets, frequently hard-pressed, sometimes may not be quite as meticulous as they usually are and this is why the Jockey Club are rightly so strict about any horse who appears on the course with either of these complaints. At the first sign of girth-pox, the little spots which raise the hair around the girth, the lad must immediately report to the head man, who will ensure that his grooming kit is disinfected and is not used on his other horses. There are many new-fangled cures, but the cheapest and best is undoubtedly a mixture of sulphur and train oil, which has stood the test of time in all the major racing stables.

Ringworm is not serious provided that it is caught in time. Small round or oval areas of raised hair appear which later fall off, leaving bald, grey, scaly patches. The old trainers used to rub soft soap into the skin around the patch and over it for a few minutes. The following day they would wash off the soap with warm water and when it was dry would paint the affected area with strong iodine. This treatment still works, although nowadays it is considered quicker to rub mercurial ointment into the affected area and ring it with strong iodine to prevent it from spreading.

I cannot emphasise too strongly that these skin disease will not be allowed to spread in a good stable, because constant meticulous inspection will obviously discover them.

The spots which sometimes occur, usually in lines over the horse's quarters, should not be confused with either of the other skin diseases. They follow the course of certain veins and are symptomatic of a highly-strung, nervous animal. As such they will not respond to any normal treatment. One of my best horses had these spots for years and they did him no harm.

WARTS. Warts are generally reckoned to be of two types: the 'grass warts' around the horse's nose, lips and eyelids, and the bigger variety on the lower part of the belly, around the sheath and penis of the horse and the udder of a mare.

This distinction is not generally accepted by the veterinary profession, some of whom, including the reviser of Hayes' *Veterinary Notes*, do not favour the castor oil cure. But the old trainers always used it, rubbing it well in to remove grass warts, and I have personally found this treatment extremely effective.

As regards the larger type, it is as well to summon the vet to remove them surgically, although, if your head man is experienced and the wart is in a suitable position, he may remove it by tying with silk thread until it falls off.

WARBLES. This is the least important ailment that affects the horse and, at times, the most irritating and frustrating for the trainer. During the summer months a horse may have picked up warble eggs when cropping grass. At the height of the season, just when the animal is due to run in important races, a swelling may appear and, if you are very unlucky, it will be immediately under the saddle. Continuing to ride the horse could be disastrous. The only solution then is to apply hot fomentations to accelerate the exit of the larva, which pops out like the root of a ripe boil, leaving a hole in the skin which swiftly disappears with normal washing and dressing. The important thing to remember when dealing with these infuriating insects is not to pick and prod, which can damage the tissue of the skin and increase the swelling, but to wait until the larva is absolutely ready to emerge.

Colic and digestive disorders

COLIC is the name loosely given to tummy ache and can be a symptom of various diseases. As most cases of spasmodic colic are caused by diet, faulty stable management, overworking unfit horses, giving large feeds to tired horses, feeding on poor quality forage, sudden changes in the diet, and tooth irregularities which prevent the animal chewing properly, it is comparatively rare in the well run racing stable. Indeed, most cases that I have experienced are self-inflicted by greedy feeders.

I had one two-year-old who possessed a charming temperament, but could not go fast enough to keep himself warm, so that the only time he sweated up was when he had colic. Whatever precaution I took, such as putting large stones or blocks of salt in his manger, nothing could prevent him from bolting his food. He was the greediest horse I have ever known and would impatiently hurl the rocks out of his manger. Almost as soon as he had finished eating, he would lie down on the floor or his box looking at his vastly-distended stomach, which he nibbled occasionally, groaning constantly until he had got rid of the wind from which he was suffering. In this case it was so mild and so frequent that we learnt to ignore it and simply called him a silly old fool. But when horses exhibit these symptoms it is usually as well to get them up, lest they should become cast and twist their guts, and to keep them walking around well rugged up.

There are some excellent colic drinks on the market and a good head man should always have a stock available from which to give the necessary drench in normal cases. Obviously, the more severe and alarming the symptoms — such as violent pawing, throwing himself down and then getting up, only to go down again — the greater the need to call the vet. Even in comparatively mild cases, expert opinion should be sought if the animal does not respond to treatment speedily.

CONSTIPATION should not normally occur in a well run stable, provided that the trainer feeds roughly on the balanced lines laid down in an earlier chapter, and it is unlikely to become extreme if a strict watch is kept on the droppings of each horse. If a horse is impacted you will probably need the vet to back-rake him and give an enema, but in the normal cases slight constipation can be cured by extra mashes, perhaps with the addition of small doses of Epsom salts.

DIARRHOEA. Some nervous horses are inclined to purge when they get into strong work. Obviously, it is advisable to feed the horse in the opposite way from that described for constipation, that is to say with a preponderance of dry food. A solution of flour and water is the old trainers' remedy, and an economical and effective one which I see no need to vary in the light of modern science.

Worm infestation

The chief kinds of worm found inside the horse are the round worm, yellowish white, tough and elastic, varying from 6–14 inches in length; the thread or maw worm, a wiry little creature nearly 2 inches long which frequently, like the round worm, comes away with the dung; and the red worm, which is generally the most common.

The thread worm is not particularly harmful as a rule and is most unlikely to affect the animal's general health. The female deposits her eggs on the horse's dock, where they stick as a light yellow waxy mass. They irritate and cause the animals to rub their tails and quarters. Most head men will treat with an enema of plain water, and then by anointing the inside of the anus with a little mercurial ointment on the end of the finger, to ease the itching.

As regards treatment of the round and red worms, the trainer is best advised to consult his vet. The best method is prevention and I am convinced that the Americans are right when they insist on a nil count pre-natally and throughout the horse's life. It is terrifying how often you still hear repeated the old English argument that an animal should always have a certain amount of worms. 'He does in his natural state and if you take them away he will have no resistance.' That this theory is arrant nonsense is proved, if proof is needed, by the class and hardiness of many American bred horses. After receiving the necessary medicine from his vet and eliminating all worms, the trainer will then be able to prevent their reappearance by regular routine doses.

At least you cannot then be blamed in the normal way if you lose a horse to another member of the profession. Since time began, the new trainer has always told the owners and anyone else who cared to listen: 'You should have seen the state he was in when he arrived. It is a wonder he hadn't died, coat all staring, you could count his ribs, riddled with worms. Vet says it's the biggest count he's ever known. I think I can probably get him right, but it will be little short of a miracle if I do!' In this way, of course, he is safeguarding himself against failure and at the same time paving the way for unstinted praise if the horse does win the race.

Stable and sexual vices

WINDSUCKING AND CRIB-BITING are both legal unsound-nesses which have to be reported when a horse is being offered for sale. They are two forms of the same vice, but are not all that common among racehorses in training. The best cure that I have found is to remove the manger and construct a little concrete border in the corner of the box where the feed can be placed, so that the animal has nothing to grab hold of and feeds naturally off the ground.

WEAVERS should also be fed off the ground. There are few chronic weavers in training, although some horses will weave when they are excited, as, for example, when their food is coming. In the Army, weaving used to be regarded as a major vice because, unless it was stopped, the animal would transmit the habit to his fellows so that, we were told, you might have a whole line of horses weaving from side to side like a line of chorus girls. It sounded very funny, but I have never met anyone who has seen this happen.

There are many cures for weaving, such as painting a white, vertical line on the wall of the box to mesmerise the horse, but I have found that the most effective treatment is to tie bricks from the roof of the box on bits of string, so that every time he weaves he clouts his head. They soon seem to stop.

OTHER STABLE VICES. Horses who tear their clothing can be thwarted by fixing a piece of stout leather to the back of the headcollar, reaching below the level of the lips so that the animal cannot get his teeth into his rugs.

Chewing the box is most common among racehorses. In wooden boxes it can be a devil of a job, because it is wood they like to chew; in the brick variety they will only have a go at the door. In all cases it is essential to have constantly handy a large supply of creosote, which should be brushed as quickly as possible on any area that has been bitten.

Similarly, you should always have a supply of pig dung handy, as a strong solution painted on the outside of bandages will stop a horse gnawing them. I can understand horses hating camels, but I have never really been able to grasp the reason for the thoroughbred's aversion to donkeys, pigs and, as I said earlier, hacks.

Horses who eat their bedding can often be cured by sprinkling the straw with a solution of antiseptic and water. If this fails, it may be necessary to put them on peat or sawdust. Most modern racing stables have no provision for a horse who persists in eating his dung. The correct prevention is to tie him up in a stall by the rack chains, one on either side, which should be sufficiently long to enable him to lie down, but short enough to prevent him from turning to drop the dung in reach of his mouth. It is incredible how acrobatic they can be when executing this manoeuvre. If you are unlucky enough to have such an animal in your stable, the best cure is frequent mucking out and plenty of bedding, sprayed with an antiseptic solution. In any case, you will soon be getting rid of the culprit, because they are seldom any good and usually look in appalling condition. That is the box door that you keep closed when showing owners round stables. 'There is a poor sick horse in there. He's been let down and we don't want to disturb him!'

If you did show him looking like 'the high-mettled racer shortly before his demise', as depicted in the famous old print (a sort of equine equivalent of Shakespeare's 'Seven Ages of Man'), you would not inspire great confidence among your patrons. They will expect to see big, glossy thoroughbreds, shining brilliantly in the glow of 100 watt bulbs.

SEXUAL VICES. The problem of self-abuse does not seem to be as great today as it was once, when tougher horses required tougher measures, such as the remarkable piece of tack resembling a medieval instrument of torture which used to be strapped over a colt's sheath. There are still some in existence. There is a hole in the middle of the leather accoutrement to allow the animal to urinate, but the inside is lined with three-quarter-inch nails to prevent him from drawing. I understand from Atty Persse, however, who had great experience of these fiendish inventions, that although they achieved their object at first, the colt soon learnt to abuse himself without drawing.

I have always believed that too much importance is placed on the dangers of self-abuse. There is no doubt that work dampens most horses' sexual desires. The English public schools, both for girls and for boys, have long realised the truth of this statement. As they say in the Services, the best answer is to send them to bed tired!

Sheaths should be washed out with antiseptic soap and a weak antiseptic solution once a week, to remove the dirt which causes irritation. Although many trainers today do not seem to consider it necessary, I believe that it is still advisable to follow the example of the old masters and to fit an ivory ring over the end of a colt's penis. This prevents its expansion and thereby discourages self-abuse.

Fillies who come in season at the wrong time can be an infernal nuisance. The old trainers had great faith in the nettle treatment. Lads would chase a filly round the box, smacking her quarters with stinging nettles to put her out of season. Today this can be achieved simply by the injection used on studs to produce and burst the egg, but in my experience it is usually better not to interfere with nature, except in extreme cases. I once took a chance and bought a yearling who must have been one of the most precocious fillies ever foaled. Her breeder, the celebrated Irish vet Walt Davison, had had to sew up her vagina early in her yearling summer. Like all the progeny of Lady Dandy, Soliciting was a beautifully-made filly. She was by The Solicitor and I was rather proud of her name! But she was a right little madam, invariably more interested in her sexual organs than in her work. I managed to win with her first time out, but thereafter nymphomania took over and she was no further use on the racecourse despite all the efforts of the vets.

CHAPTER ELEVEN

Schooling over Fences and Hurdles

A natural sprinter is one thing, but a natural jumper, while just as thrilling to watch or to ride, can be an infernal nuisance. He is fine while he is sailing happily over the obstacles with gay abandon. As soon as something goes wrong, however, as it inevitably will before long in his races, he has no resources. His confidence has been upset and he doesn't know what to do. So, however brilliant horses may seem, it is as well to take trouble and to teach them all to jump in the same way.

Before you start schooling him, the horse must be strong in condition, fit and have plenty of impulsion. You are training racehorses, not hunters, and it is important that they should all be well up into their bridles before being taught to jump. Moreover, in consultation with his owner, you should try to envisage the individual's future. You must decide, if possible, whether he is designed to be simply a hurdler or whether he is big enough and strong enough to make a chaser. But, with the disappearance of the Irish Draught mare, the huge, rough, tough type of horse has become rarer. He has to a large extent given way to the wiry, quality sort with the necessary length and scope, who probably starts his career successfully over hurdles.

If, however, you decide to do this with a young horse of ability, beware! After a few runs over hurdles, win or lose, and whatever his hurdling potential, you must stop. Otherwise you will have the devil's own job to get him to jump fences properly. The temptation to carry on over hurdles for a while will be strong, but you must resist it. Of course there are exceptions, but in general a good British hurdler, galloping at two-mile speed and jumping the minor obstacles with dash and economy, gets so much on his forehand that he will never come back on his hocks sufficiently to jump fences well. Most of the great Champion Hurdlers, still young horses though they have lost their edge, have been tried over fences with no success. It is rather pathetic. Ironically, the very technique which has made them champions now prevents them from being anything but clumsy novices.

So to work, with boots all round. Remember that the average horse will take to jumping naturally as long as he does not associate it with pain or fear. It's rather like running-in a motor car. You pay for your mistakes later. As a horse has little brain but much memory, pain or fear, linked with his first lessons in jumping, are likely to make him refuse or rush his fences later.

Since few trainers have loose schools, the majority either profess to disapprove of them or insist that it is even better to teach your horse to jump in the paddocks. When, however, trainers of the calibre of Reg Hobbs and Fred Rimell swore by loose schools, you can be sure that they must be an outstanding form of introduction.

It is no use trying to teach a gassy horse, so first you should give him a decent exercise to get his back down and put him in a sensible, receptive frame of mind. Now, whether the first instruction is to be mounted or loose, I like to give the novice the rudiments of jumping by leading on a lunge rein. For this purpose you need a pole on the ground which can be raised, and perhaps a little ditch, both of which can be easily negotiated by a man on his feet. If you keep a few bits of carrot in your pocket for inducement and reward, he will soon learn to follow you as you step first over the pole, and then over the ditch. As soon as he follows without hesitation, you can raise the pole inch by inch, rewarding him each time with a bit of carrot. In this way he will quickly learn to leave the ground without hesitation or worry and to jump from the walk or trot using his hocks and not relying on sheer speed for momentum to hurl him over. So into the loose school, from which the jumps will have been removed. After lungeing him round a few times to show what you require of him, you will be able to stand in the middle with a long whip and soon have him cantering happily round. You must immediately prevent any attempt to stop or whip round. As soon as he is going easily, you can introduce

Fred Rimell, a great believer in loose schooling his charges over jumps, pictured here with Cheltenham Gold Cup winner Royal Frolic

one or two small fences and let him canter round, negotiating them as he goes. He will soon be enjoying himself so much and performing so well that you will be able to raise the fences. This is the ideal method because the horse teaches himself to come right into his obstacles, shortening or lengthening his stride as necessary to get over comfortably. The Irish Sweeps Hurdle winner Normandy was just one of Fred Rimell's horses who had never been ridden over an obstacle in his life before his first race over hurdles. Normandy proved the value of loose schooling when he won that first race at Kempton, jumping most impressively throughout. Apart from timing, it gives a horse a supreme confidence in his own jumping, which is the one really vital thing.

Meanwhile, the trainer who has no loose school has been riding his horse or having him ridden by a top class lad over similar small obstacles in the paddock, following a sensible lead horse at the trot and at the canter. As soon as they are jumping smoothly, both horses are now trained in the same way. You require three flights of hurdles, adequately spaced and sited to face from west to north so that there is no danger of the jockey and his horse being blinded when galloping into the morning sun. It is better to have two fool-proof horses as schoolmasters ridden by highly competent, sensible lads and, if at all possible, I like the novice to be schooled by the jockey who is going to ride him in his first race. This is really worth waiting for. The top jumping jockeys are always wonderfully co-operative and they always appreciate this opportunity of getting to know their future mounts and teaching them to jump in the way that they ' want. I always like to give them the novices whom they ride schooling and then wait until they are available to give their introductory races. This will affect a horse's entire racing career; his performance and his attitude to jumping and racing through-out the rest of his life. No one can truly appreciate this until he has ridden a novice before and after his introductory race in the hands of a jockey such as Peter Scudamore or Richard Dunwoody.

Always remove any possible source of danger which could permanently damage a horse's confidence. The hurdles must be well sited and the going on the schooling ground must be good. The wings must be really effective. The run to the first hurdle must be long enough to give the novice a good view of the obstacle and there must be a decent pull-up after the last. The

*Richard   Dunwoody;   a   jockey   whose   skills   assist   in   a   horse's
education.*

schooling jockeys must wear crash helmets, but the horses must
never wear night caps, which might fall over their eyes and
blind them just as they are jumping. They should still be equipped
with boots all round. Their bridles should have nosebands and
rings (Irish martingale). They should be fitted with breastplates
because any horse can jump through his girths, causing his
saddle to slip back with disastrous results. When they come on
to the schooling ground, let the novice, in company with the
experienced jumper, have a good look at the hurdle he is going
to be asked to jump. Hold him into his bridle so that he realises
what it consists of. This applies also to the first fence in any
school, although I do not approve of the present system whereby,
before the start of any steeplechase, the jockeys have a fixed
idea that they must show their horses the first fence. With
experienced jumpers this is quite unnecessary and leads to a lot
of kicking.

Take the horses back about a hundred yards from the first hurdle and, with the lead horses in front and the novice tucked in behind, jump the three hurdles at a nice half speed. Do this again, allowing the jockey on the novice to control the speed and, in fact, the whole school. If he is satisfied with this, send them back again and tell them to come over the three hurdles upsides, with the novice between the two experienced jumpers. This requires considerable skill, intelligence and understanding from the lads on the schoolmasters. They must never be thinking of their own horses, but always of the novice. Do it again and the third time that they jump upsides tell them to go faster and keep close to the novice, so that he knows just what it is to jump with other horses almost touching him. The jockey on the novice will soon tell you when he is satisfied. Otherwise you will have to use your own eyes. The golden rule is, as soon as he jumps adequately, stop and leave well alone. If you persist, you will surely find that something goes wrong which will undo all the good that you have done.

Make much of him. He is now fit to race. After his first outing it should not be necessary to school him again unless he has done something wrong. In this case it may be advisable to put him back into the loose school in order to restore his confidence. The one really important thing to remember from the moment that your potential hurdler starts jumping, and the one thing that you have to instil into his jockey, is that you want him to get away from his hurdles like lightning. He must be balanced as he jumps and must never be allowed to sprawl on landing. His jockey must pick him up and ride him away fom the hurdle as hard as he can. Ryan Price, the maestro hurdle trainer, always insisted on this. I had two of Ryan's horses when they retired. They had wonderful manners, like all his charges, and made excellent hunters, but it was a trifle embarrassing in a large field of provincial hunting people. The horses would happily jump their fences, if necessary from a trot, but on landing they would shoot away as though the devil were behind them. This is the way to win hurdle races.

It is necessary to school horses again before the beginning of each season, but, after the first race, you should not need to do it again. The old trainers, however, used to have hurdles well spread out round the gallops, so that a horse would jump in the course of his normal work. There is a lot of sense in this. After all, a human hurdler like David Hemery was always jumping hurdles in order to keep his timing as near perfect as possible. This must apply equally to a horse and, once again, I think that our grandfathers and fathers were right and we are probably wrong in giving our hurdlers only those few schools over three flights. So, if you can build a nice school over five or six flights of hurdles, so much the better.

One year, I had a couple of useful experienced hurdlers. John Bisgood asked if he could borrow them to teach a good novice hurdler on a school which he had constructed in the valley alongside that stiff gallop, Faringdon Road, leading up out of Lambourn towards Wantage. Now John had learned his job partly from Gil Bennett, the highly skilful selling-plate specialist. Apparently Gil, who was a very fine horsemaster, would stand with a 'Long Tom' on a vantage point by the school and crack his whip exactly when he wanted the horse to take off. It was very successful. The Commander, however, had reckoned without the echoes from the valley. Dick Francis and Jack Dowdeswell rode my two horses. They and I had no prior warning of this whip-cracking thing. John stood on a mound some way from the action. Apart from the echoes, he had not reckoned on the time sound takes to travel. Jack and Dick will never forget that horrific school. As they galloped into each hurdle in the winding valley John cracked his whip. The message must have been transmitted at a different time for each obstacle: the result was chaos. The horses were taking off in the most unlikely, almost impossible places, crashing through their hurdles as they went. It was the first time, and the last, that I had seen either of those two jockeys 'falling out of the back door' and holding onto the buckle end of the reins over hurdles.

Nevertheless, as Fulke Walwyn preferred to school over only three flights of hurdles, who am I to judge? After all, he was consistently the greatest jumping trainer of our time. Fulke had three lines, each of three fences, in his schooling ground on Lambourn's Mann Down. Each line consisted of a plain fence, one with a pole in front of it, and an open ditch. Like the three bears, they were graduated small, medium and large. The large fences were originally designed to help trainers schooling for Cheltenham and Liverpool, but Fulke rarely used them. As with distance, it is always better to under-school as far as height is concerned, and he always found the middle fences quite high enough. Walwyn horses seldom fell.

I think those wonderful horsemen and masters, the Australians,

The late Fulke Walwyn, pictured in his riding days on 1936 Grand National winner Reynoldstown, went on to become widely regarded as the greatest jumping trainer of his time.

have an important point in the transition from hurdles to steeplechases. They have the top bar of their hurdles fixed. This teaches a horse to respect any obstacle that he's asked to jump. Anyone who saw that superb steeplechaser Crisp jumping Aintree more fluently than any horse has ever done in the history of the race, as his time proves, will never doubt that the Aussies have the right idea, although there is far too little steeplechasing Down Under.

There have always been mixed feelings about the advantages of hunting as an aid to jumping fences. Ryan Price said that a racehorse must not be allowed to think, otherwise he loses his dash. Although a lifetime hunting man, who rode more than a hundred point-to-point winners in his youth, Ryan maintained that a course of hunting should not be used to teach novices, but rather to revive slightly jaded experienced chasers, such as his Gold Cup winner What a Myth. Most of Ryan's remarkable successes, however, were achieved with hurdlers, whereas a

*The Dikler. Trained by Fulke Walwyn, he graduated from the hunting
field to win the Cheltenham Gold Cup.*

number of Fulke Walwyn's many chase winners, including The
Dikler, were introduced to racing via the hunting field. My own
experience, if compared with either of these two great trainers,
favours Fulke. In the transition period from hurdles to fences a
certain degree of thinking is surely necessary, so that the horse
will learn to respect the larger, stronger obstacles and to place
himself right at them, lengthening his stride or putting in a
short one where necessary. He will not always be able to rely
on his jockey to make up his mind for him, placing him just
right and picking him up beautifully on landing. During his
career he is sure to be ridden at times by some less talented and
forceful pilots.

   If one is available, I like to put the novice chaser back into the
loose school where he originally learnt to jump. Now, however,
the obstacles will be larger and stiffer, so that they will hurt him
if he clouts them hard and he should thus learn to get back on

his hocks to negotiate them safely. On the schooling ground, with the same object in view, most of the leading jockeys like to school at a very steady pace even when they are upsides. Then, with their excellent hands, they can make their horses jump properly off their hocks.

A horse must be able to stretch his neck fully in order to stand back and gain at his fences. Indeed, you can often see a horse losing ground when he is checked by a heavy-handed rider as he jumps. An effortless jumper gets a breather over his fences, but an awkward landing, often through bad jockeyship, can have just the opposite effect. After several such landings in a race, he soon starts to show signs of distress.

When I wrote earlier that a horse should have good exercise before he schools, I did not mean that he should be tired. This would cause him to jump sloppily. However, he must be receptive and sober enough not to charge into his fences with his head in the air. It is essential that the jockey schooling the novice chaser should hold him straight and prevent any tendency to jump crooked. If this is not corrected from the start, the habit will soon develop and, instead of trying to meet his fences right, he will attempt to make the necessary space on the take-off side by jumping sideways. Such horses are a menace to others and to themselves.

The school should be conducted at a level pace throughout, with a tendency to extend the horse's stride, rather than to shorten it, on approaching each fence. Talking one day of the stable lad vice of trying to win the gallop, Phonsie O'Brien told a salutary, though macabre, story of the time when he was training a high class horse for a big race at Punchestown. The school was a galloping course with banks as well as fences, so that the horse would learn to negotiate the notorious Punchestown double. The schoolmasters, two good, experienced horses, did not, however, possess the same degree of brilliance as the young horse they were teaching. They were ridden by Phonsie's two best schooling jockeys. 'Splendid, brave chaps', said Phonsie. 'They had clearly been longing for some time to have a go at me who had been lucky enough to win quite a few races and nearly won the National. They must have seized on this school as a chance to show me how good they really were and possibly take me down a peg.'

The school was being watched from a hill by the lady owner of the good young horse. Phonsie told the lads to stay upsides on either side of him and to take it very steady throughout the school. Now it is very important, when schooling, to be either exactly upsides the lead horse or horses, or behind him. A jumper who finds himself half a length or so behind tends to take off with his companions, with disastrous results. This is the jumping jockey's oldest legitimate strategy. If he can get half a length up on his rival coming into a fence and shout 'Up!' as his horse takes off, the other is liable to do the same, take off just too soon and come to grief.

They jumped off steadily enough, but after a short while the lads started to increase the pace. Phonsie recounted:

> I had no option but to go with them or make a nonsense of the whole school. Fortunately my horse was jumping superbly and still galloping well within himself, although they were almost off the bit. I shouted to them to ease up but they just laughed, went mad and really set their horses alight. I think they thought I was windy. They were dead right. I was terrified when, still trying to pull them back, I found they were coming into the bank completely out of control and I was half a length behind. I had no option. I really kicked on, got upsides and asked my horse for a tremendous leap. He flew over the bank as though he was jumping the Chair and landed way out on the other side. Not so the other two. They had been going far too fast and they never rose at all. They smashed themselves to pieces. One horse was killed outright and the other died soon afterwards. Both of the lads had to be taken off to hospital unconscious.

So school at a steady pace. Let your horse know exactly what he is doing and, once again, ask your jockey whether he is happy to ride the animal in his first novice chase, whether he wants to go again or whether he thinks he would be better off with another day's schooling. He is the man who will be on board in that first race. I think it was poor John Lehane who described the start of a modern novice chase as 'twenty horses you've never heard of ridden by twenty men you've never seen, each with a lethal weapon in his hands!'

Jumpers usually need longer exercise than Flat-race horses and are probably better for being out of their boxes for nearly two hours. Although good hills are not essential, they are certainly of tremendous benefit to the jumping trainer, who inevitably has some bad-legged horses and in, any case, can build up the necessary condition so much better by steady uphill work. When it comes to galloping, the same principles apply as on the

Flat. It is far better to underwork over shorter distances than the horse will be asked to race. Although a number of highly successful jumping trainers practice and preach otherwise (as did the late Ivor Anthony), Fulke Walwyn's jumpers seldom galloped further than one and a quarter or one and a half miles. And, having watched Fulke's methods and results at close quarters for many years, that is good enough for me.

It is always better to castrate horses who are going to jump fences, even though the Grand National winner Battleship and the Gold Cup winner Fortina managed to win their jumping races and then became successful stallions. Most horses understandably fall out of love with the game and turn sour when they scratch their testicles repeatedly on the tops of the fences. Nowadays, unless the animal is a rig, the operation is simple and, as long as you take the vet's advice and give the horse plenty of time to get over it, presents no complications. The important thing is to find the best vet available, who cuts a horse standing.

The same problem does not necessarily apply to hurdlers. In fact, sometimes the entire horse possesses just that bit of extra fire. But he cannot be expected to last as long as a general rule. Moreover, he is surely not worth keeping entire unless he is potentially very good indeed. If he is however, then like Eborneezer, Saucy Kit, Normandy and others, he will still be able to make a successful stallion.

As a general rule, the entire horse keeps his summer coat and does not need clipping. Nearly all other jumpers, however, require clipping out as soon as their winter coats start to appear. If an animal is naturally a cold horse, like Hatton's Grace, he is better off being trace clipped. As far as yearlings are concerned, I used to trace clip those with the heaviest coats and belly clip the others.

When running jumpers in boots, remember to have some pairs of the non-absorbent type for use when the ground is soft or heavy. A sodden boot puts unnecessary weight on a horse's leg.

I don't like the all-elastic girths for jumping but favour those with the elastic insert which gives just that little extra expansion. If you use these, you will definitely need a breastplate, but, as I have said, I believe in fitting them to jumpers in any case.

Cheek martingales (fastened to the rings of the bit) are of great value during the building-up, steady walking and trotting process after a horse has been physicked following a summer on grass but they must, of course, be removed as soon as you are going to start cantering.

Some of the great jumping trainers have always had a rule that every horse returning from a race must be given a cupis ball. They claim it cools him down and settles him after the stress and strains of his outing. I believe this is an excellent system which is equally beneficial on the Flat.

Although it normally takes about two months to get a horse fit when he comes up from grass, think twice before you take on a good show ring performer whose owner wants him converted into a jumper. I learned this lesson when Bill Edwards-Heathcote, subsequently the owner of champion Bula, bought Dorothy Paget's top class show hunter, Prince Stephen, and sent him to me to train. Before I could start on him I found that I had to remove layers of show condition, or hard fat, which only the master showman puts on this type of horse. We tried everything, but eventually the vet advised that plain starvation was the only answer. So we took it off by this method and then had to start all over again building up racing condition. It was worth it in the end. Prince Stephen became an excellent hurdler and effected the introduction between his owner and Fred Winter, who rode him a winner; this association was later to be cemented into such a wonderful partnership when Fred turned trainer.

Many top class Flat trainers do not believe in having their horses' manes plaited for racing. They do not believe that it is necessary and claim that this obvious preparation for a race merely adds to the horse's tension. For jumping races, however, it is absolutely essential that horses' manes should be plaited up. Failure to do so can mean losing a race when the jockey, after slipping his reins over a fence, desperately tries to gather them and pick his horse up, only to find himself clutching handfuls of mane. Similarly you never plait the tails on Flat-race horses, except very roughly when they are in physic and purging, just to keep them clean. But, although it is now almost a lost art, I like to see the tails of jumpers plaited in bad weather to keep them from getting caked with heavy mud. It may come as a surprise to some people to learn that in the United States, when the going report is 'track sloppy', the Flat-race horses all have their tails plaited.

The jumping trainer's life is by no means as comfortable as that of his counterpart on the Flat. He has to race in appalling conditions at times and must exercise in all weathers. Those tough older horses must be kept on the go. Despite the enormous, ever-increasing price of potential jumpers, scarcely any of our chase courses are properly watered and the prize money is generally outrageously low compared with that offered for far inferior races on the Flat. The trainer is constantly worried by bad legs and all too often sees good old friends killed or has to have them put down.

A horse who shies at things in the ledge should never be taken to Aintree. For that course you need a bold, forward-going animal. Indeed, you need to be a bold man to be a jumping trainer today: unless you have a substantial private income, you must bet to live. But, if you can stay the course, surviving months of frost-bound inactivity, overcoming the disappointments and the tragedies, it can be one of the most satisfying jobs open to man today.

CHAPTER TWELVE

Racing Horses in Britain

One of the most important factors in the success of a European trainer is his intimate knowledge of the courses where he will be running his horses. In the United States nearly all the tracks are virtually identical — sharp, although well-banked, and left-handed.

In Europe we have great variety in the length, shape, terrain and soil of our courses, and top class tracks both right- and left-handed. For example, Ascot and Sandown go round to the right; Newbury and Doncaster are left-handed. Longchamp is right and Saint-Cloud is left.

Since it is vital that a horse should run on the type of course that suits him, according to his breeding, conformation, action and stamina, it is extremely difficult for anyone to start training successfully until they have personal experience of these differences, gained either in the saddle or as an assistant trainer.

David Robinson, whose richly-deserved success was the wonder of the racing world, graded racecourses in three colours, as he graded his horses on their ability. Only the red horses ran at the ten red courses in Britain, blue at the twelve blue, and the remainder at green courses. Even jockeys were graded: 'I change the system only if there is a big race at a green meeting. Then a good horse may drop in class.'

Being a businessman, Mr. Robinson left nothing to chance, but it is an undeniable fact that it is frequently easier to win races at some of his red courses than at some of the green ones. The very name of the course seems to frighten off the average trainer, so that one is apt to meet far tougher opposition at

162

Warwick or Windsor than at Newmarket or Kempton — of the big prestige tracks, the last two are undoubtedly the ones at which to win races.

Some of the big maiden events at Newbury, Newmarket and Kempton can be most deceptive, especially at the start of the season. I once beat a big field by eight lengths with a particularly moderate two-year-old who never won another race and I have always been convinced that mine was the only trier!

The following are personal assessments of racecourses in England, Scotland and Wales.

British racecourse locations

ASCOT is a right-handed triangular course of 1 mile 6 furlongs 34 yards, mainly downhill to the start of the old mile, whence it climbs steadily to the finish. There is a straight run-in of two and a half furlongs. A galloping track, but the comparatively short straight means that you must get a position either with, or in close touch with, the leaders before the final turn if you are to win. After many drainage troubles, which Dutch experts were invited to solve, the going is now good, but thunder rain is frequently attracted to Ascot and the ground can become very heavy in parts, especially in Swinley Bottom.

The Royal Hunt Cup course is a straight mile slightly downhill from the start, rising from the 5 furlong gate to the finish. All races of less than a mile are run on this track.

Appropriately, a tough, long-striding horse with guts and stamina is needed to win at Ascot.

Since the course's reconstruction in 1965 the effect of the draw in straight races has depended on the weather. Overall it can be said to have no material effect.

Note that, as long as the Royal Enclosure system remains, trainers should remind their owners to apply for vouchers at the correct time in March and April, as advertised in the prestige papers and *The Sporting Life*.

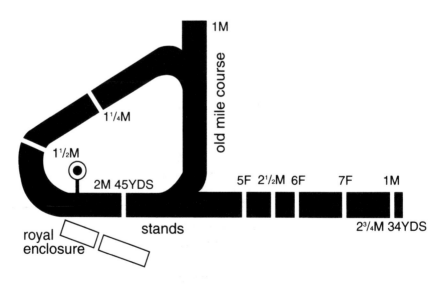

Ascot: right-handed Flat course

The turf transported from Hurst Park in 1965 for the jumping course inside the Flat track has knitted well and the husbandry of Clerk of the Course, Nicky Beaumont, is paying dividends. The going is good, the fences are stiff but fair and the only things that a jumping trainer has to worry about over fences and hurdles are that his horse is good enough and, as on the Flat, that his jockey has got a good forward position before the final turn. This applies even more to jumping because the straight is only two furlongs.

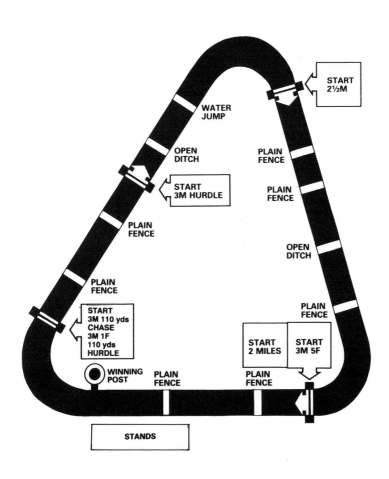

Ascot: right-handed N.H. course

AYR is one of the best courses in Europe under both codes. Benefiting from the Gulf Stream, it seldom suffers from the weather even in the midst of the hardest winter and the sandy soil provides such natural drainage that it is rarely heavy even after heavy rain.

The left-handed, oval Flat course of 1 mile 5 furlongs has a straight run-in of half a mile. Although the turns are well-banked to suit a long-striding galloping horse, it is flat and there is a straight 6 furlongs which is 100 yards wide.

The N.H. course, $1\frac{1}{2}$ miles round, has a run-in of only 210 yards from the last, so that your candidate must be a good jumper as well as a galloper and he must be right there at the second last to be in the shake-up.

The course is so fair under both codes that it is an ideal place for a gamble on a good horse. In Flat races of 7 furlongs and 1 mile, a low number has an advantage, but otherwise the draw makes no difference. There is a good watering system.

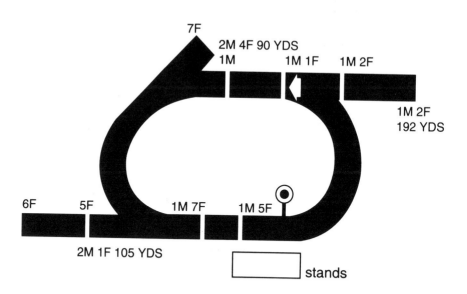

Ayr: left-handed Flat course

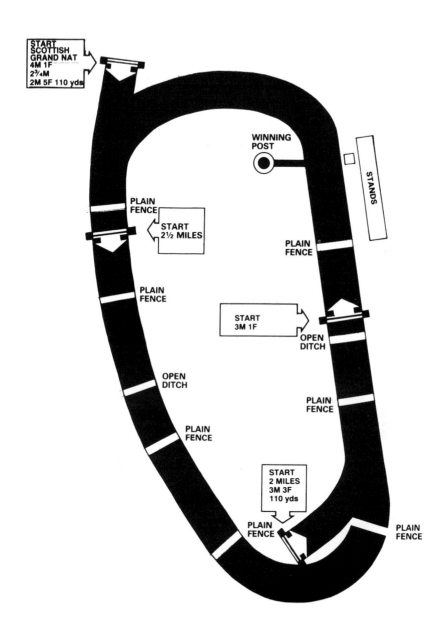

Ayr: left-handed N.H. course

BANGOR-ON-DEE is a little left-handed jumping course, much-maligned chiefly because few general racegoers go there. Situated in a lovely part of the country, it is more like a point-to-point at first sight, but there the resemblance ends. It is an excellent $1\frac{1}{2}$ mile oval course, absolutely flat with a run-in of 325 yards. The ground provides a magnificent natural grandstand, and for those who do not wish to take advantage of the picnic atmosphere there is a lunch room, bars and lavatories and, more important from the trainer's point of view, stabling for eighty horses and a hostel for stable lads (and girls).

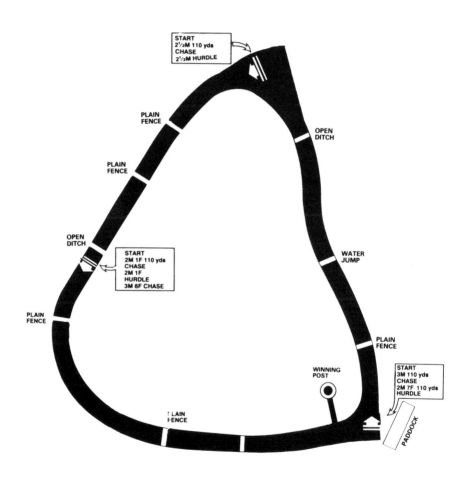

Bangor-on-Dee: left-handed N.H. course

BATH caters for Flat-race horses only and not particularly high-class ones at that. It is a peculiar track, dating back more than two hundred years, situated by Landsdowne high above the old spa city. This height and the downland turf combine to excite horses and you can usually rely on a few loose ones. They feel they are on the gallops at home and this is not at all a bad thing.

The course is almost oval, just over $1\frac{1}{2}$ miles with a dog-leg run-in of nearly half a mile. It is a stiff course on the collar for the last 5 furlongs so that the 5 furlong 167 yards track requires just as much getting as 6 furlongs on most normal courses.

The bend at the bottom of the course has been banked up and in general Bath can be said to suit a galloping horse. It is quite fun in its quaint way, but on the whole, from my experience, you will be helping your owners and yourself more by running elsewhere, particularly since the constant left-hand bias means that low numbers in the draw have an unfair advantage, except in the $1\frac{1}{4}$ mile races.

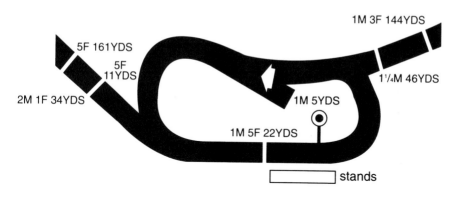

Bath: left-handed Flat course

BEVERLEY, also confined to the Flat, is even older in origin and, though right-handed, has a marked similarity to Bath. It is oval, 1 mile 3 furlongs 44 yards, with a straight run-in of about $3\frac{1}{2}$ furlongs. Here it gains, but the 5 furlong course has to start on a spur and has a distinct bend as it joins the straight. Like Bath, this course is on the collar the whole way to the finish, and I would not recommend Beverley as the ideal course for an early two-year-old; it takes too much out of them. For average horses, however, this is a good stiff galloping track with reasonable bends and a watering system.

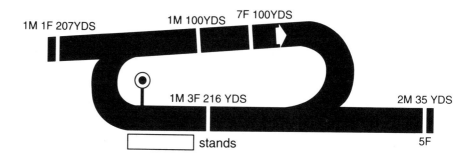

Beverley: right-handed Flat course

BRIGHTON is a left-handed course for Flat racing, but nothing else about it is flat. It is 'Epsom-on-Sea', high up on 'Race Hill' looking over the Channel and, like Epsom, it has long been a cockney sporting paradise. What a shame they have had to spoil the holiday atmosphere by spending nearly half a million pounds on a huge new stand with concrete surrounds which is posh enough to daunt even the most fervent short-sleeved, iced-lolly sucker.

The $1\frac{1}{2}$ mile left-handed track is more like three sides of a square than Epsom's horseshoe. The first 3 furlongs climb, then, after a slight downhill run, the course rises again until 4 furlongs from home, when it runs steeply downhill. 2 furlongs out it rises again, levelling out in the last 100 yards. There is no straight course and, although $3\frac{1}{2}$ furlongs is claimed, as far as horse and rider are concerned the track is always turning left. The sprint course is 5 furlongs 66 yards and even this does not favour the short runner, as the average time of 1 minute 2 seconds testifies. Nor do the hills and bends help a long-striding horse, or one who is big or straight in the shoulder.

The prize money is excellent and, as a result, the class of runners is higher than the nature of the track really deserves. Owners and lads like racing at Brighton and, with a suitable animal, I would pander to their whims in races over 7 furlongs. But in contests below this distance the draw gives low numbers an awfully unfair advantage. There is a watering system.

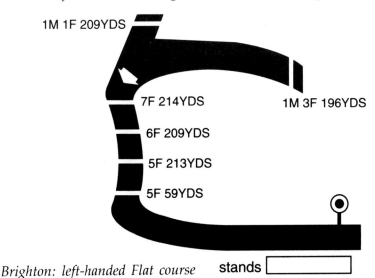

1M 1F 209YDS

7F 214YDS   1M 3F 196YDS

6F 209YDS

5F 213YDS

5F 59YDS

stands

Brighton: left-handed Flat course

CARLISLE is an underrated, right-handed course catering for both codes. It is a stiff galloping, undulating course of about 1 mile 5 furlongs. The hurdle course is on the outside of the Flat and the chase fences are on the inside. The straight is $3\frac{1}{2}$ furlongs, uphill until it almost levels out at the distance. Before entering the straight, both the 6 and 5 furlong courses bear round to the right. As they rise steadily for the last 4 furlongs, both require a pretty strong two-year-old, or sprinter. In the same way, the pull up for home over the last three fences before the 250 yards run-in demands plenty of stamina in all the starters.

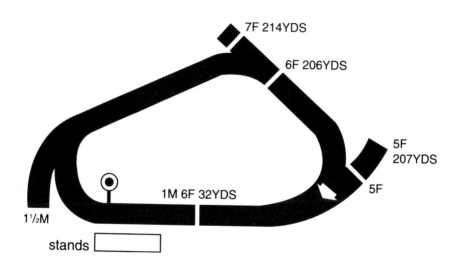

Carlisle: right-handed Flat course

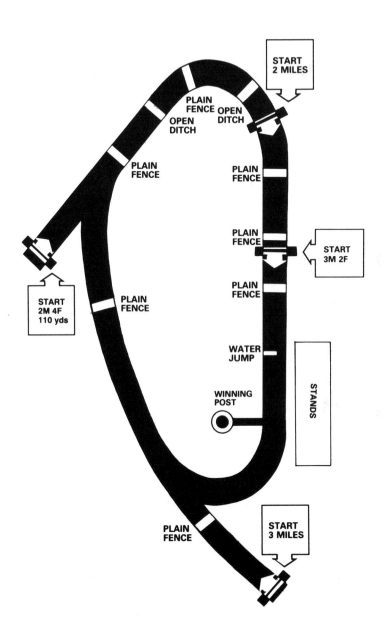

Carlisle: right-handed N.H. course

CARTMEL is a left-handed jumping course with a ridiculously long run-in of nearly half a mile from the last fence. Although the oval circuit is only about 1 mile, the course seems to suit any normal horse. Racing is held on only three days a year, on the spring and summer Bank Holidays.

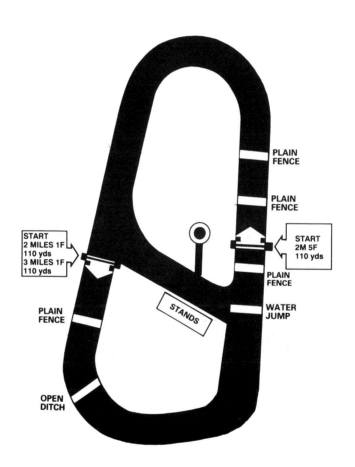

Cartmel: left-handed N.H. course

CATTERICK in Yorkshire is another small track, only just over 1 mile round, but it is very sharp, undulating and left-handed, and caters for both codes. Don't take either an inexperienced apprentice or a big long-striding horse to Catterick, under either code. You want a jockey who is good at the gate on a sharp, nippy sort, or you will be cut off even more effectively than at Chester. The gradients are steep for both types of horse and, although Catterick is now deservedly popular with race-goers, I would not advise any young trainer to send a horse there unless he has a special reason, and then only if he has thoroughly reconnoitred the track beforehand.

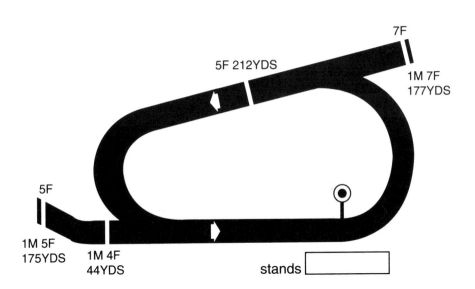

Catterick: left-handed Flat course

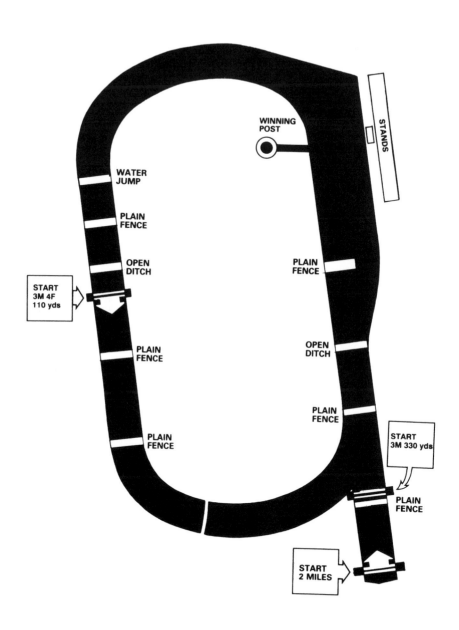

Catterick: left-handed N.H. course

CHELTENHAM is the finest jumping course in the world. Its superiority to those other magnificent left-handed courses, Ayr, Doncaster and Newbury, stems from its hills and its infinite variety.

Since the new 'Park' course came into being, it has become almost impossible to describe the various tracks satisfactorily on paper. The circuit is about $1\frac{1}{2}$ miles with a steady uphill climb in the back stretch, a run down to the last two fences, and then the last four furlongs are steeply uphill again. My only advice to trainers who intend running horses at Cheltenham is that their animals must have guts — no cowardly horse, whatever his class, wins on this course — and that the trainer

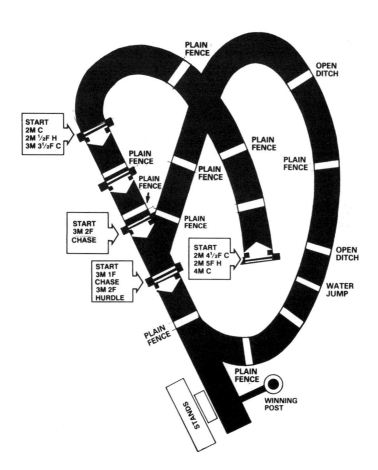

Cheltenham (Old): left-handed N.H. course

and his jockey must find out which course the race is to be run on and must familiarise themselves with every aspect of that course. Although I consider it essential for every trainer and his jockey to walk a course which they do not know, Cheltenham is probably the most important of all in this respect, except perhaps for Aintree, (Liverpool).

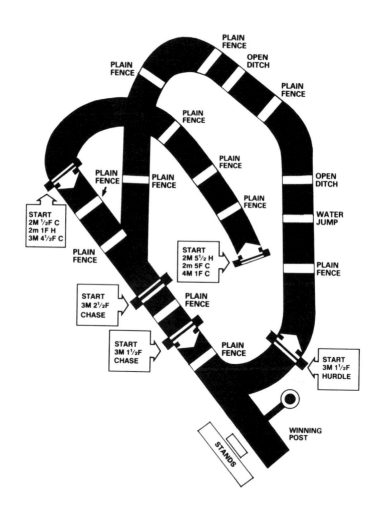

Cheltenham (New): left-handed N.H. course

One last word on the headquarters of National Hunt racing. For the Festival meeting make sure that your owners have all their necessary passes and that your horses and lads are properly accommodated. Then start early. The crowds through Cheltenham, and, indeed, from all approaches, create incredible traffic jams despite all the efforts of the Gloucestershire police (although 1993 showed considerable improvement on previous years).

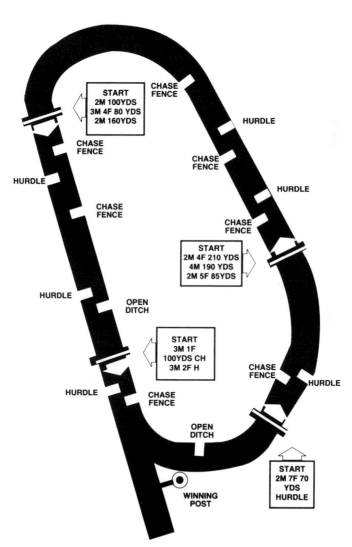

Cheltenham (Park): left-handed N.H. course

CHEPSTOW is fun. Left-handed and catering for jumping and Flat, it is situated in glorious country only a mile from the Severn Bridge where the Wye Valley runs into the Severn Estuary. Owing to the distance, Newmarket horses seldom make the journey and Chepstow has always been a happy hunting-ground for all trainers, including those who are just starting. It is about 2 miles round and undulates sharply, though this does not seem to affect a long-striding animal, as might be expected. In fact, many of this type of horse have won here. I have found that the switch-back straight appeals to most horses. There is a straight mile and all races up to this distance are run over it. Downhill until about half-way, it rises sharply for more than 2 furlongs and then levels out with another slight downhill slant to the winning post. Races on the round course join the straight just after the 5 furlong marker. Although the draw appears to make little difference, statistics seem to show that low numbers are favoured on the round course and high numbers on the straight. The bends are easy and the run-in on the jumping course is about 250 yards. You need a horse with plenty of stamina to win if the going is at all heavy.

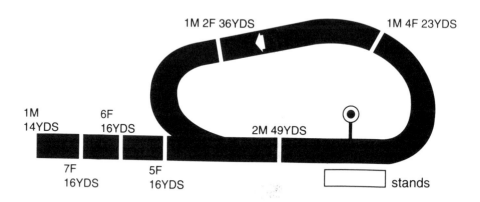

Chepstow: left-handed Flat course

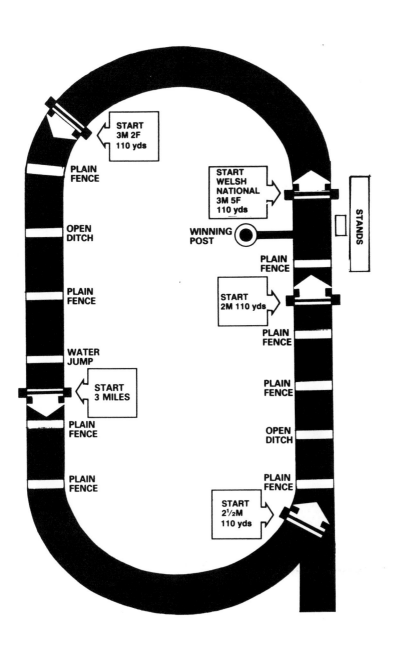

Chepstow: left-handed N.H. course

CHESTER is another 'fun' meeting. It is important for the trainer to realise that a happy day out makes a lot of difference to the owner, particularly if he is disappointed with the running of his horse. The May meeting vies with Ayr's Western meeting and the two main meetings at York and Goodwood as the most enjoyable fixture of the Flat-race season. Owners can stay at Chester's well run hotels, which are usually in gala mood, and walk down the 'Rows' to the delightful little amphitheatre on the outskirts of the town. The course is flat and only 1 mile 73 yards round. And it *is* round, just like a saucer. Left-handed, it is no place for a big, long-striding horse, but the value and prestige of the races, plus the fact that Cheshire cheeses are given to the contestants who win at the May meeting, attract many top class performers and Classic hopes. A low draw and a fast break are essential for all races up to 7 furlongs 22 yards. You need a nippy horse and a jockey with guts and dash. Chester is no place for chicken-hearted riders; those tight bends soon find them out. The watering system is excellent.

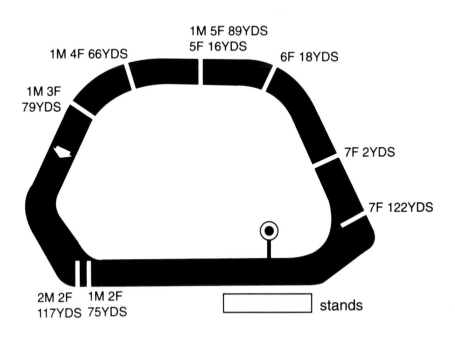

Chester: left-handed Flat course

DEVON AND EXETER, running right-handed on Haldon Hill, is a most attractive jumping course. Undulating and about 2 miles round, it was particularly popular with the late Lord Mildmay, who hoped to stage trials for Cheltenham here. Unfortunately, he died before these ideas could be put into practice. It is an ideal galloping track for a long-striding horse and the long pull up to the finish enables a jockey to ride a race. Although not as springy as it used to be, the going is nearly always good.

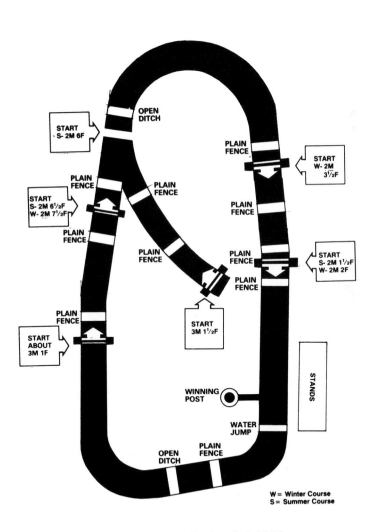

Devon and Exeter: right-handed N.H. course

DONCASTER is one of the world's great racecourses for both codes. Flat and wide, and about 1 mile 7½ furlongs round, this pear-shaped track is one of the fairest in the country, except for events on the straight mile, when the draw makes far too much difference. Owing to the terrain, high numbers on the straight course were ridiculously favoured, but recent efforts have helped to solve the problem. When the round course joins the straight there is a run-in of about 4½ furlongs. An ideal track for the high class, big, long-striding horse. The only rising ground is on the far side of the course.

The jumping track is laid inside the Flat and the same remarks apply. In fact if Aintree were to close down, Doncaster would be the ideal course on which to run a substitute for the Grand National. In many respects it would be a better race — certainly from the spectators' point of view. As there are four fences in the long straight, a horse can be ridden from behind. The run-in from the last is 247 yards.

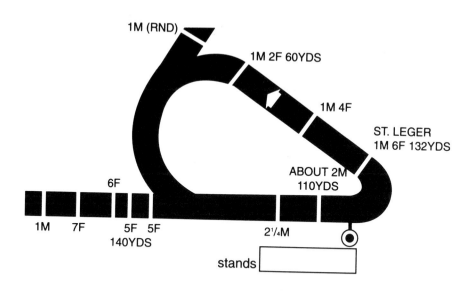

Doncaster: left-handed Flat course

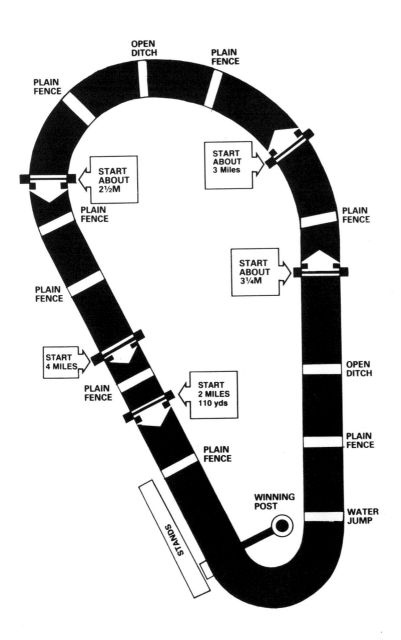

Doncaster: left-handed N.H. course

EDINBURGH was nearly closed, but Lord Rosebery's intervention and the subsequent management of Bill McHarg gave the little right-handed course near Musselburgh a new lease of life. I know it well because I was at school next door for five years, and whenever we had ten minutes free we were made to run round the racecourse. The atmosphere is good and the sharp course of under $1\frac{1}{4}$ miles is adequate for the moderate nippy horses who race there. The long-striding animals should keep well away. Apart from a slight rise to the winning post over the last $1\frac{1}{2}$ furlongs, the course is flat.

An excellent watering system has transformed it, so that now it is always good. The 4 furlong straight is a continuation of the 5 furlong course, which has a slight elbow as it joins the round track. High numbers in the draw are favoured in 7 furlong and 1 mile races and have an immense advantage over 5 furlongs, owing to this elbow. That 5 furlongs alongside of the Great North Road is very fast. The National Hunt course now provides excellent sport.

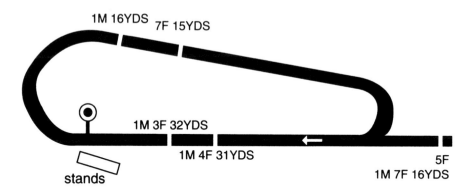

Edinburgh: right-handed Flat course

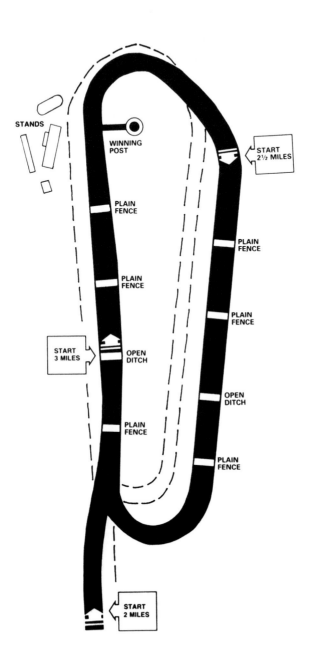

STANDS

WINNING POST

START 2½ MILES

PLAIN FENCE

PLAIN FENCE

PLAIN FENCE

PLAIN FENCE

START 3 MILES

OPEN DITCH

OPEN DITCH

PLAIN FENCE

PLAIN FENCE

START 2 MILES

Edinburgh: right-handed N.H. course

EPSOM may be the most famous racecourse in the world, but it is a long way from being the best. It is an anachronism which survives through the legend of the Derby, the world's greatest Classic race. The undulating, turning, left-handed $1\frac{1}{2}$ mile Derby course was once claimed to demand all the qualities essential in the Thoroughbred racehorse, but horses like Sir Ivor, who according to Lester Piggott 'never got an inch above one mile and a quarter', have proved this a fallacy. Indeed, milers such as Mahmoud have been successful in the Derby. This may not be a bad thing at a time when the emphasis in the international market is on speedy middle distance horses and when the ability to stay a mile and three-quarters is the kiss of death.

Epsom is no longer as ruinous to horses' forelegs as it used to be. The only straight course is the fastest 5 furlongs in the world. The average time is 56 seconds. The $1\frac{1}{2}$ mile horseshoe circuit rises steeply for the first half mile, levels out over the top of Tattenham Hill and then, as it turns sharply left, plunges downhill to Tattenham Corner where another sharp left turn carries it into the straight with about $3\frac{1}{2}$ furlongs to the finish. The 6 and 7 furlong courses enter the main track from spurs, as seen on the plan. Low numbers are best in races up to $1\frac{1}{4}$ miles, but in fair-sized fields on the Derby course it is better to be drawn in the middle. Never run a green horse at Epsom, or one who is outclassed. As we have seen many times in the Derby, such horses can be a real danger to their rivals. They begin to tire and drop back down Tattenham Hill, just as the good horses are getting into top gear and making their run.

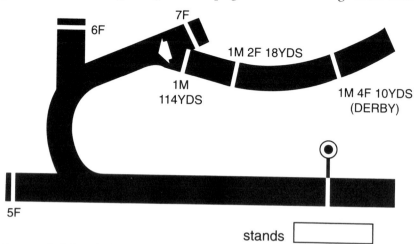

Epsom: left-handed Flat course

Sir Ivor wins the Derby in the hands of Lester Piggott.

There is no set way to ride Epsom. In the sprint races, speed at the gate and balance are essential. Over the longer courses, Lester Piggott, the Epsom master, seems to prefer to make his run in the middle of the track. Right on the rails in the straight there is a slight camber and it is possible to be caught in a pocket there as a tired horse rolls towards the fence in the last furlongs. The going now is generally good. After really heavy rain, however, when the ground is sodden, remember that water drains down the hill towards the inside of the course, and as your jockey comes round Tattenham Corner he may be well advised to come over to the firmer ground on the stand rails; several big races have been won by this tactic. Horses generally need a longer rest than usual after running at Epsom, and keep an eye on those legs. Despite a good watering system, there can still be some jar in the ground when a tired horse is changing legs towards his stable, as he pulls up in the paddock area.

FAKENHAM is a sharp left-handed Norfolk jumping circuit of about 1 mile, undulating and finishing uphill with a run-in of just over a furlong. The competition is not high and the course suits front runners. Watering has been installed.

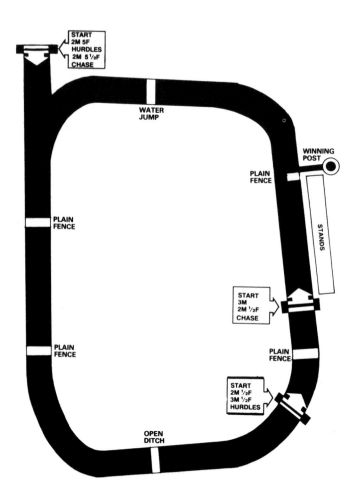

Fakenham: left-handed N.H. course

FOLKESTONE, like Edinburgh, was reprieved from the Levy Board's axe. It also attracts moderate horses and caters for both codes. Right-handed, about 1 mile 3 furlongs round, its undulating circuit lies by the London-Folkestone road, six miles out of Folkestone, and it has the advantage of its own station at Westenhanger, which is handy for owners travelling from London; in fact, one of Folkestone's chief drawbacks is the arduous journey from most parts of the country. The sprint courses, starting downhill, suit short runners when the going is on top. It is frequently hard, although a watering system has been installed. The straight is about 3 furlongs and the run-in from the last on the jumping course is just over a furlong.

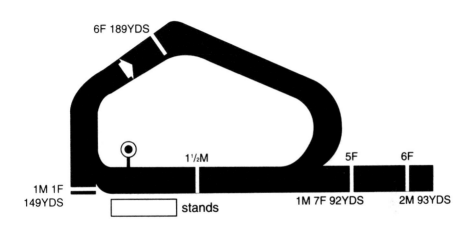

Folkestone: right-handed Flat course

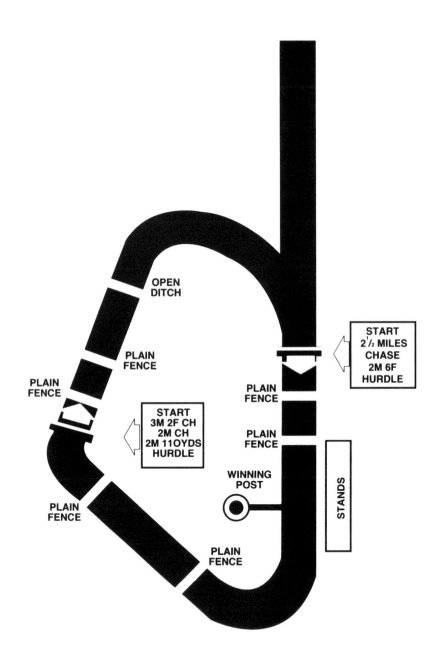

Folkestone: right-handed N.H. course

FONTWELL, confined to jumping, is a much more attractive course than Folkestone and is situated on the main road between Chichester and Arundel. The hurdle course is only a mile round, left-handed. The chase course describes a figure of eight. Although the standard of racing is fairly moderate, Fontwell's atmosphere and accessibility make it popular with owners. The course is best suited to an average handy horse. The run-in is 230 yards. Despite a watering system, the going can be very firm in places. But this is definitely a 'fun' track. If I wanted to show off a little British country meeting to a foreigner, I would bring him here.

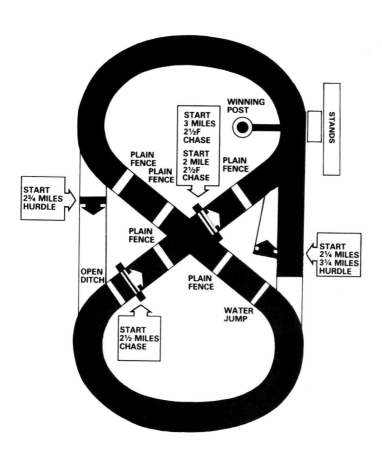

Fontwell: figure of eight N.H. course

GOODWOOD, not far from Fontwell, is another 'fun' track, even though it caters only for Flat racing. Although the main meeting at the end of July and beginning of August is, as it has long been, a prestige festival fixture for top class horses, the other meetings are ideal for the average trainer, and his owners will love coming to the track high on the Sussex downs which so richly deserves its title 'glorious Goodwood'.

It is easy to assume from their downhill gradients that the 6 and 5 furlong courses are ideal for short runners. The average time of 1 minute one-fifth seconds for the 5 furlongs belies this. You still need a horse who gets the trip. On the whole, high numbers have an advantage in a big field over these sprint tracks. As at Cheltenham, trainers and jockeys should be well acquainted with the course before they compete here. Races below $1\frac{3}{4}$ miles are right-handed all the way, but events over 2 miles and 2 miles 5 furlongs (the famous Goodwood Cup course) run backwards up the track until they branch off left, wind through the heather on the hill and describe a sharp loop before returning on the upper course into the straight. Provided that they are run at a decent gallop, these races are true tests of stamina.

The watering is now much better than it has been. Rightly a favourite with owners, Goodwood even has its own airport with a charter service, two miles south of the course. Start in good time every day of the main meeting, for the traffic can be desperate. This is one course where you won't mind arriving too early.

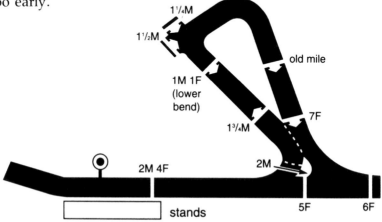

Goodwood: right- and left-handed Flat course

HAMILTON PARK is a delightful little Scottish course catering only for Flat racing. Perhaps in shape it somewhat resembles the now defunct 'Ally Pally', and in races of 1 mile 3 furlongs and upward, right- and left-handed bends are encountered. The maximum distance is 1 mile 5 furlongs, starting in front of the stands. The straight run-in is more than half a mile; this is part of the dead straight 6 furlongs over which the sprint races are run. From a decided dip $3\frac{1}{2}$ furlongs out, the course rises steeply to the finish, making Hamilton a very stiff track. When the going is heavy, you need a really tough horse with loads of stamina to win here. Middle to high numbers have the advantage of the draw in the shorter races.

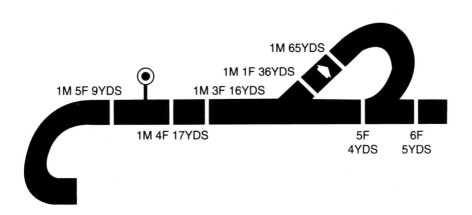

Hamilton Park: right- and left-handed Flat course

HAYDOCK PARK, a left-handed oval circuit of 1 mile 5 furlongs, is one of the best courses in the country for both codes. It is situated within a stone's throw of the M6 and equidistant from Liverpool and Manchester just off the East Lancs road. The big crowds who attend every meeting are proof of its good racing and its accessibility.

The course is generally flat and the turns are good. It is ideal for any type of horse, particularly the long-striding, galloping sort. Moreover, since from the turn into the $4\frac{1}{2}$ furlong straight to the winning post, you are always just on the collar, it takes some getting. The 5 furlong course is straight, but the 6 furlong starts from a spur. This can give low numbers a decided advantage, particularly if horse and jockey are quick beginners. Haydock's jumping track is dramatic. In common with many other trainers, I believe that we are playing a confidence trick on horses if we run them at Aintree without appearing first at Haydock. The first time that the average racehorse knows what a drop fence means is when he finds himself hurtling over Becher's and looks down to find there is nothing below him. Haydock remedies this with two nice drop fences in the back stretch, so the National Trial is a good test for Aintree. The whole course is a racing success story. It is deservedly popular with owners, trainers, jockeys, horses and stable lads alike.

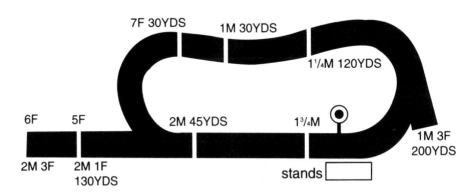

Haydock Park: left-handed Flat course

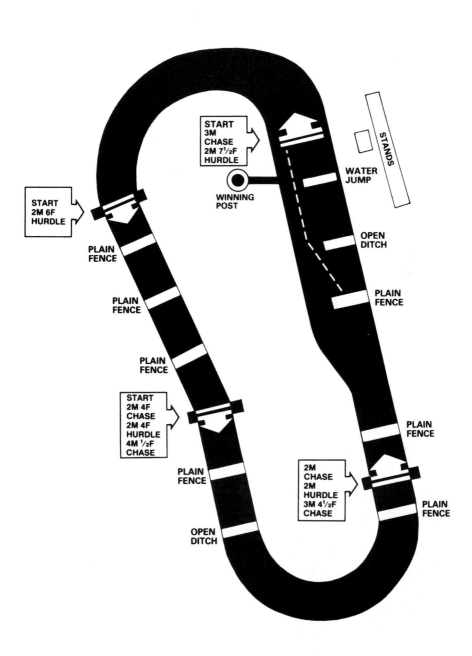

Haydock Park: left-handed N.H. course

HEREFORD. Although the circuit of this fair right-handed jumping course is 1½ miles, it is essentially a minor course. The track is popular with local trainers, although the going can be very hard. The run-in is 300 yards. Watch that fence after the winning post; you have to take it on the turn.

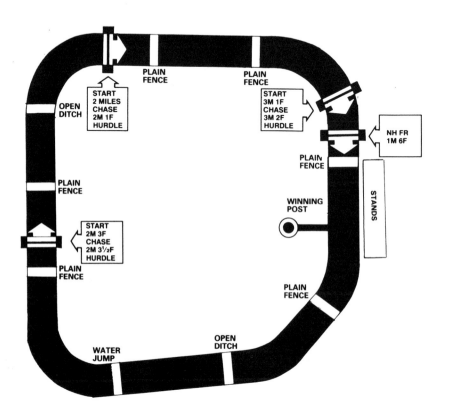

Hereford: right-handed N.H. course

HEXHAM is another of our small jumping courses with a circuit of $1\frac{1}{2}$ miles. Left-handed and undulating with a climb to the last fence and a run-in of 250 yards.

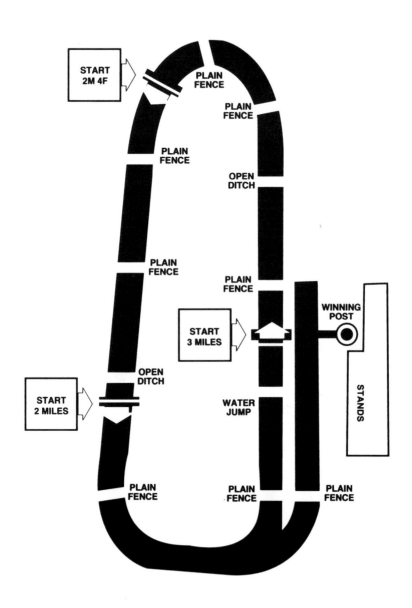

Hexham: left-handed N.H. course

HUNTINGDON is the third little jumping meeting beginning with 'H' and is somewhat classier than the other two. Although the atmosphere is that of a point-to-point, the course's proximity to Newmarket ensures a fair smattering of professionals and in the past one or two highly successful gambles have been brought off here. The oval, right-handed track is flat, $1\frac{1}{2}$ miles and very fast. A horse must stay the trip. Although the fences are not particularly stiff, a chaser must be a fair jumper too, because the run-in is only 200 yards.

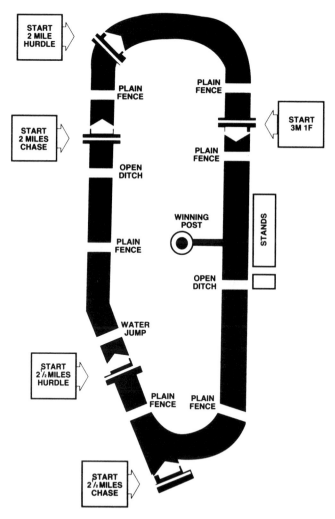

Huntingdon: right-handed N.H. course

KELSO is a charming little left-handed jumping course with two separate tracks. For hurdles, an oval circuit of 1 mile $1\frac{1}{2}$ furlongs; for chasing, a rectangular track of $1\frac{1}{4}$ miles and 160 yards. This has a run-in of a quarter of a mile, which I consider too long because this puts too large a premium on speed and less on jumping. However it also calls for a fair degree of stamina. Northern trainers regard Kelso highly and frequently run some of their best chasers here in preparation for big events.

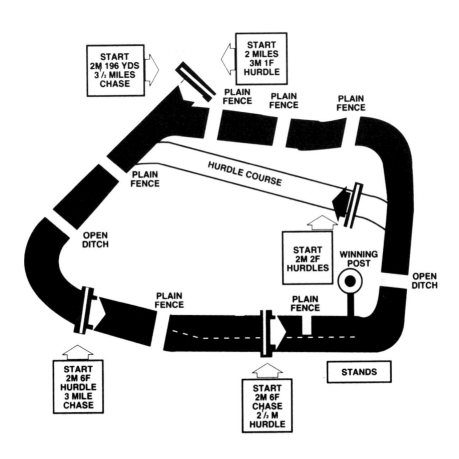

Kelso: left-handed N.H. course

KEMPTON PARK is like a 'talking horse'. It has all the advantages, but seldom seems able to live up to them. As a result,
trainers should not be daunted by the name and the assumed
prestige of this big right-handed track catering for both codes
so near to London at Sunbury-on-Thames. If there is a suitable
race for any of your horses at Kempton, run him; you'll probably
win. My main criticism of this flat triangular 1 mile 5 furlong
circuit is that for a galloping course, which it undoubtedly
should be, the bends are far too sharp. The chief advantage of
the course has always been the gravel subsoil, which drains
magnificently, so that, even after the heaviest rain, horses can
always get through it and it is fair to say that Kempton going
never gets heavy. Now, vast quantities of gravel are being
quarried out and moved on the far side of the course for commercial purposes. I cannot see how this can fail to affect the
racecourse itself in the long run.

The sprint track runs diagonally across the centre of the
round course, finishing in such a way that the angle is almost
impossible to judge from the stand. This is accentuated because
the draw makes no difference and you can have a close finish
between horses on either side of the wide track without the
slightest idea of who has won. Perhaps this was one of the reasons
for Kempton's unpopularity. Under both codes it lacks drama
because it is so impersonal and far away. The $1\frac{3}{4}$ mile jumping

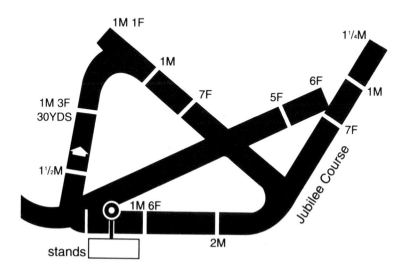

Kempton Park: right-handed Flat course

course has fair fences and a shortish run-in. What was formerly the most dangerous obstacle has been removed. This was an open ditch in the back stretch just by the way into the racecourse stables. As you approached it your horse's mind was not on what he was doing; he was thinking only about his stables and his ears flicked backwards and forwards as he came into the fence, usually with disastrous results. The siting of that fence showed an incredible ignorance of horses and lack of imagination. Perhaps this has been the trouble over the years. It is to be hoped that United Racecourses will be able to provide the necessary imagination, particularly in the framing of races, and bring the crowds and the horses back to Kempton. Happily, under Tim Neligan, this is happening.

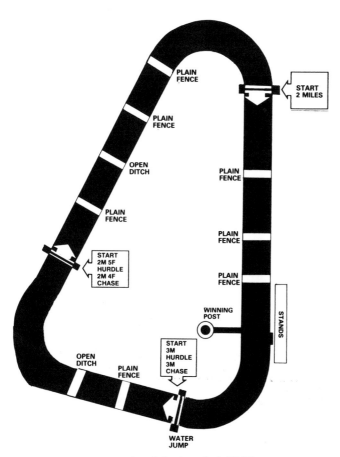

Kempton Park: right-handed N.H. course

LEICESTER. Known by the pedantic old-time journalists as the 'Oadby track', it is situated 2 miles south of Leicester. The Flat course is nearly 2 miles round with a straight of 5 furlongs. The jumping course inside it is 1 mile 6 furlongs. To the spectator, the turns of this undulating, stiff circuit look suitable for the big, long-striding horse which the track demands. In practice I have never found this type of animal particularly happy negotiating them.

Races up to 1 mile are run on the straight course which runs steeply downhill for 4 furlongs and then climbs gradually until it levels out at the distance. No part of Leicester suits a short runner, but the 5 furlongs is ideal for a two-year-old who just gets the distance. The draw appears to make no difference at all.

The fences have always been stiff. There are four close together at the end of the back stretch and the run-in from the last is 250 yards. Leicester has always been a good track to run at before going to Cheltenham or Liverpool. The watering system is the most modern available and the going, particularly on the Flat and hurdle circuits, is always perfect in the hottest summer. For some reason the course has always had a rather forbidding atmosphere. I advise trainers to use Leicester a lot, but don't expect your owners to have a carefree, happy day even if they win.

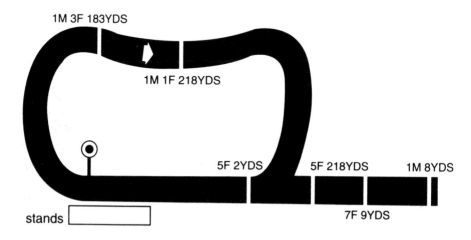

Leicester: right-handed Flat course

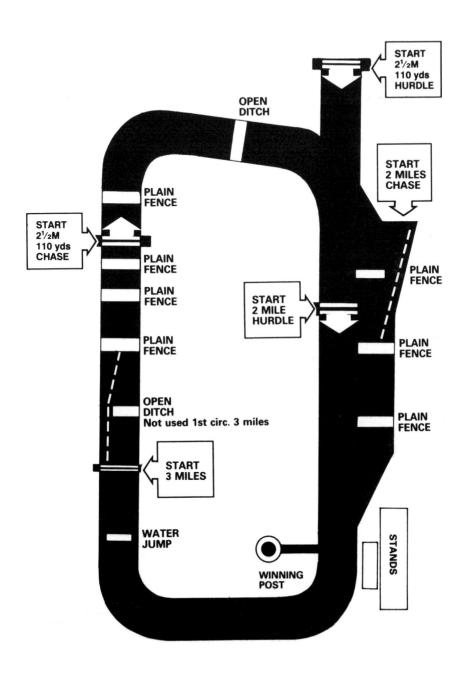

Leicester: right-handed N.H. course

LINGFIELD PARK deserves its title 'lovely Lingfield'. Left-handed and undulating, it caters for both codes. Its chief disadvantage is the clay soil which holds water, becomes very heavy in wet weather and indeed frequently caused racing to be abandoned because, if there are floods anywhere, they always seem to be at Lingfield. Otherwise, particularly on the Flat, it is a 'fun' course, easily accessible from London, with its own railway station a quarter of a mile away and a covered walk to the entrance. Those who travel by car from far afield, however, are not so fortunate.

The straight, 7 furlongs 149 yards, undulates but is easy, and to all races up to this distance, the quick, balanced horse is well suited, even if he is a short runner. The round course of about $1\frac{1}{2}$ miles, over which the Derby and Oaks Trials are staged, slightly resembles Epsom in that the back stretch climbs to the top of a hill and then runs down to a corner turning into the straight about 2 furlongs from home. But Lingfield is a much better racecourse than Epsom. The Derby Trial course starts half way up the straight, cuts left before the stands across the bottom and joins the round course. On normal going, high numbers have an advantage in straight races, and low numbers when the ground is heavy.

The chase course follows the round circuit but takes in the sharp bottom bend past the stands. It is $1\frac{1}{4}$ miles round and has a run-in of just 200 yards, so you would hope to have your race won before coming to the last.

The all-weather course is becoming increasingly popular.

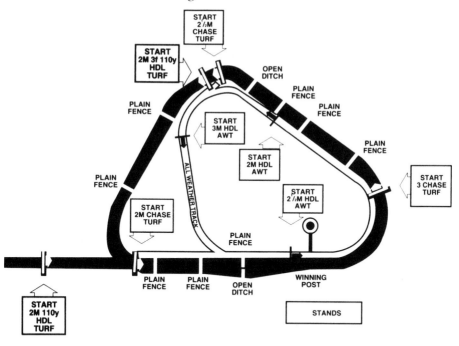

Lingfield Park: left-handed N.H. course

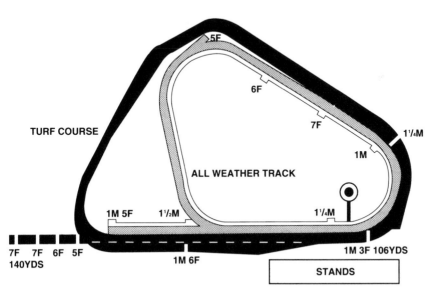

Lingfield Park: left-handed Flat course

LIVERPOOL (AINTREE), once again has two meetings a year. It is a bad hurdle course and a unique steeplechase circuit which, however, is far from ideal for the spectator. The turf drains on to the now disused motor-racing circuit and even in the worst weather conditions the going is nearly always perfect for any horse, except the high-actioned mudlark. The hurdle course, 1 mile 3 furlongs 74 yards, is oval with a straight of just under $4\frac{1}{2}$ furlongs. The bends are tight.

Two complete circuits of the steeplechase course complete the 4 mile 856 yards Grand National trip. As you walk the course you will find that some big fences appear to be sited at awkward slants. In practice you meet them all just right. Now that they have been sloped and bushed out, they are nowhere near as formidable as they used to be and, provided that you have a strong, bold horse (not the kind who shies at things in the hedge), who has won the necessary qualifying race, or has been placed in a chase at Aintree, there is no reason why you should not run him in the Grand National. The only advice that I can give is that of the master, Fred Winter, who preferred to jump the whole way round at about the middle of the left half of each fence. As most of the jockeys tended to keep away from the part of the fence nearest the inside rail, because the drop in the landing side is greater there, he was free from interference from other horses. Moreover, Fred and that other wonderful chase jockey Pat Taaffe, following the advice of Dan Moore, always practised what they preached: 'At Liverpool you want to hunt and hunt and hunt until you come onto the racecourse and then you can start thinking about being a jockey.'

I have long believed that the run-in from the last of 494 yards is unfair. Far too many great steeplechasers, after negotiating thirty formidable fences, have been robbed of their greatest triumph as the weight has told on the flat. The Grand National is the most wonderful race in the world for riders and television viewers, but a hopeless spectacle for today's sophisticated racegoers when it is wet or misty. Nowhere else in the world, except at the start of a long distance event at Newmarket, would you see the world's Press standing with their backs to the great race they have been paid to watch. As the field approaches Becher's in these conditions the only way they can see is on the television set.

Running adjacent to the hurdle course, the Mildmay course, conceived by Anthony Mildmay as an introduction to Liverpool, does not quite achieve its object. It certainly causes plenty of grief because the fences, made like those on the main course, are smaller (and therefore do not command so much respect from horses) but stiff.

Anyway, most trainers find themselves at Aintree at some time during their careers. Many owners like to have a runner at Liverpool on Grand National day, even if it is not in the big race. In this case make sure of your owner's car labels and badges as well as your own car label, stabling and lads' accommodation. Although the fences have got smaller, and Becher's has been filled in, it's still Aintree.

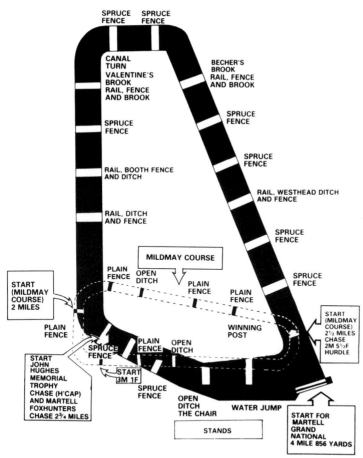

Liverpool (Aintree): left-handed N.H. course

LUDLOW, an oval right-handed jumping track of $1\frac{1}{2}$ miles, is deservedly popular with trainers. Although the chase course is flat, the hurdle circuit is slightly undulating. The run-in is too long at 450 yards, but this is definitely a 'fun' course set in lovely countryside. Your chaser needs to jump and stay. Unhappily, the going can become very hard.

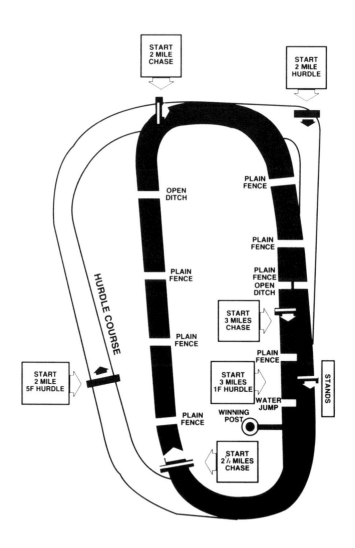

Ludlow: right-handed N.H. course

MARKET RASEN is a popular right-handed jumping track. The slightly undulating, oval circuit of about 1½ miles suits any type of horse. Only the fence past the stands is jumped on the turn. To avoid running wide on the final bend, good jockeys make a special effort to keep close to the inside rail. The run-in is 220 yards. A watering system has been installed and is used when necessary.

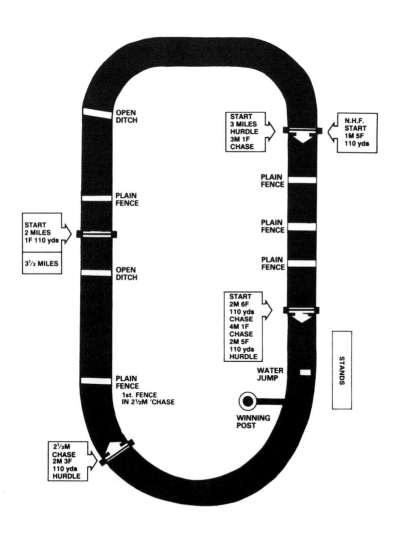

Market Rasen: right-handed N.H. course

NEWBURY is one of the world's great racecourses. A left-handed oval of about 1 mile 7 furlongs, it is a wide, fair track for Flat and jumping horses of the highest quality. From the spectators' point of view, the amenities are superbly arranged and trainers can bring owners of any nationality to the Berkshire course, confident that they will have a good day out. As at Doncaster, however, there is just one snag. Despite the erection of a running rail on the stand side to offset the effect, the draw of races on the straight course with large fields still favours the high numbers although not as much as in the past.

There is a straight mile over part of which the sprint races are also run. Longer races are run on the round course, which joins the straight track about 5 furlongs from the finish. With such a long straight and a stiff course, jockeys must be well coached. As we saw when Newbury reopened after the war, even the top class riders will start to ride a finish too early until they are fully acquainted with the course. The undulations on the straight mile are gradual enough for the biggest, longest-striding animal and the same applies to Newbury's turns.

Racing from Newbury. Prego (Pat Eddery) wins the Trusthouse Forte Stakes from Never So Bold (Steve Cauthen).

You can see every inch of the Flat and jumping circuits from any part of the stands, or on the lawns below. Moreover, Newbury is an ideal course for watching steeplechases by a fence in the field. The fences are stiff but fair. The island 'cross' fence, half-way round the home turn, seems to give most trouble to horses. Accommodation for horses and lads is excellent. Trains from London and the West Country run direct to the racecourse station. If you have a decent, fit horse, take him to Newbury. The watering system is excellent and the new stand is superb.

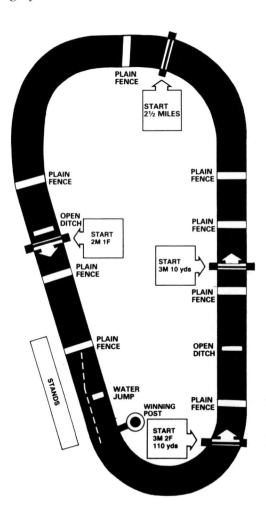

Newbury: left-handed N.H. course

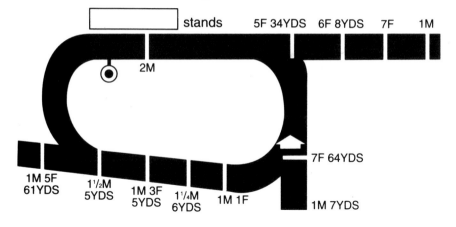

Newbury: left-handed Flat course

NEWCASTLE is another first class, left-handed course catering for both codes: $1\frac{3}{4}$ miles, oval and flat apart from a slight rise in the 4 furlong straight.

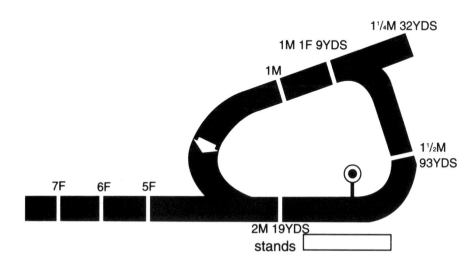

Newcastle: left-handed Flat course

As at Newbury, the straight mile joins the round course at this juncture. A stiff galloping track suitable for top class horses; although the turn into the straight on the chase course may be a little sharp, it is not enough to worry any normal horse and the same applies to the Flat. The amenities are excellent all round. The comprehensive watering system is typical of the rest of the course arrangements − in short, first class.

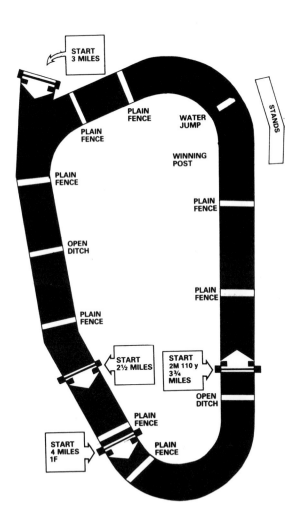

Newcastle: left-handed N.H. course

NEWMARKET is a splendid, ridiculous British anachronism which, despite its recent face-lift, still requires some modification. Freed at last from the shackles of puerile pomposity, both courses have an atmosphere of great tradition which should be maintained. Both courses branch off the same stem. Arriving from London or Cambridge, the first course on the left by the National Stud is the July Course, where the amenities have not been altered. Apart from plagues of small black flies on really hot days, this is a 'fun' course for owners and trainers in fine weather. Just over 2 miles in extent, the first mile is on the Cesarewitch course and bends right at half way, where it joins the Bunbury Mile. The first half of this straight mile undulates slightly, but the course then runs downhill until the final furlong, where it rises again to the finish. The going is generally good.

Continuing along the main road towards Newmarket town you pass, on your right, the Links stables where your horses will be accommodated if you come from afar, and then, on your left, just before the entrance to the town, is the road leading down to the main course, the celebrated Rowley Mile.

Valiant and successful attempts have been made to modernise and, at least in part, to democratise the amenities. Once again the Cesarewitch course bends right after a mile, this time more gradually, and the last $1\frac{1}{4}$ miles run straight across the Flat. This becomes the Rowley Mile from the mile post. Undulating slightly until just after the Bushes, the course runs downhill into the Dip for a furlong and then up a fairly steep hill for the same distance to the winning post.

If you find a suitable race for an average horse, take him to Newmarket. Some races there are not too hard to win and your owner will probably enjoy his day out. Fred Darling told Sir Gordon Richards never to hold a horse up on the Rowley Mile. This advice still holds good. It is fatal to pull him back and disappoint him. A jockey should sit into his horse, allowing him to run on the bridle down into the Dip and make his best way up the hill. The expert starts his run soon after the Bushes to achieve the necessary balanced momentum to carry him home. The going, thanks to a watering system and supporting natural drainage, is nearly always very good indeed. The division of the Rowley Mile has done much to offset the effect of the draw. Weather conditions can alter this, however, and the trainer is advised to enquire locally on the day. Do not run your horse too often at Newmarket: he is entitled to get bored with being asked to race on these straight, wide-open courses. This is natural, not a sign of lack of courage.

Strange to think that, until a few years ago, a trainer was not allowed to watch a race at Newmarket with his wife — the sexes were segregated. Nevertheless, for all its peculiarities, it has a strange magnetism. Like Paris, Newmarket draws you back. Throughout a long life, I've always loved the place and — for all its faults — I always will.

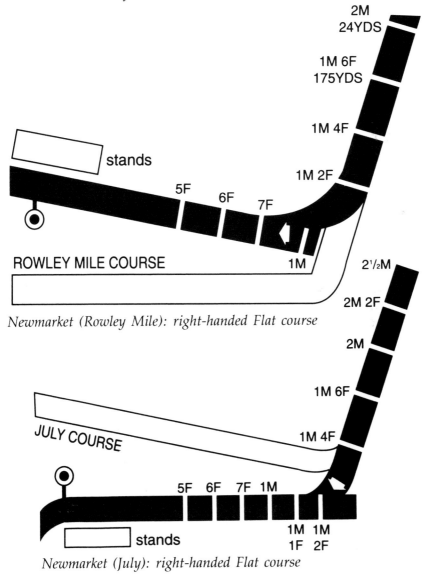

Newmarket (Rowley Mile): right-handed Flat course

Newmarket (July): right-handed Flat course

NEWTON ABBOT is left-handed and sharp, just over 1 mile round. It caters only for jumping and is suited to sharp, nippy horses. If you have that sort of horse, this is a 'fun' course in the summer; Torquay and the other South Devon resorts are close at hand. But do not think you can take any old 'gaff' horse to Newton Abbot and win. There are now some very good local trainers. Remember, it is a tight circuit. Going can be firm and the worst hazard, I used to find, was when the spring tide was up and the take-off side of the plain fence on the home turn suddenly became wet and slippery. You still landed and fell on the hard! The run-in is about 300 yards.

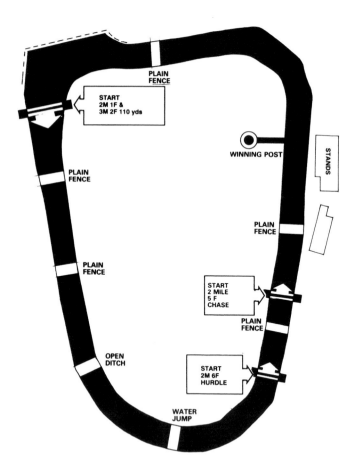

Newton Abbot: left-handed N.H. course

NOTTINGHAM, left-handed, jumping and Flat, is $1\frac{1}{2}$ miles, oval, with $4\frac{1}{2}$ furlongs straight and a straight mile. Like Leicester (owing, I believe, to the same previous moderate management), it has a depressing atmosphere which somehow refuses to disappear. Otherwise it is a fairly good course under both codes. Since they removed the hump in the middle of the 5 furlong course, it has become more suited to a long-striding horse than before, when such an animal was inevitably thrown off balance. The run-in on the chase course is 240 yards. High numbers have a slight advantage on the straight course. Considering that the River Trent is adjacent, the watering system is still not as good as it should be. The amenities are moderate. Not at all a bad course for the trainer and his horse, but not much fun for the owner.

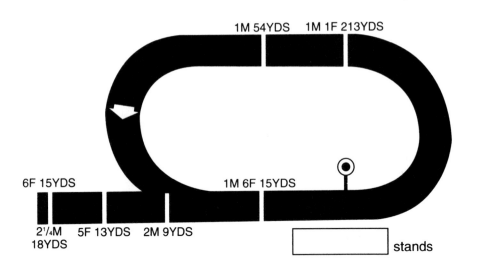

Nottingham: left-handed Flat course

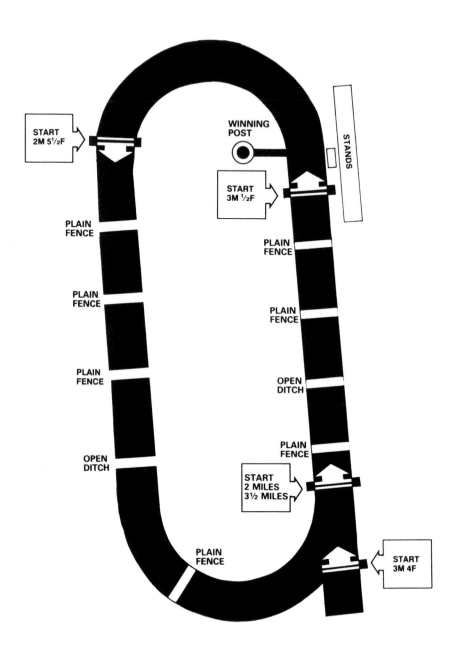

START
2M 5½F

WINNING
POST

STANDS

START
3M ½F

PLAIN
FENCE

PLAIN
FENCE

PLAIN
FENCE

PLAIN
FENCE

PLAIN
FENCE

OPEN
DITCH

OPEN
DITCH

PLAIN
FENCE

START
2 MILES
3½ MILES

PLAIN
FENCE

START
3M 4F

Nottingham: left-handed N.H. course

PERTH HUNT, a right-handed jumping course, oval, $1\frac{1}{2}$ miles, is most attractive and lies by Scone Palace. A bit far north for southern horses, but a good day out and a fair track for Scottish and northern owners and trainers.

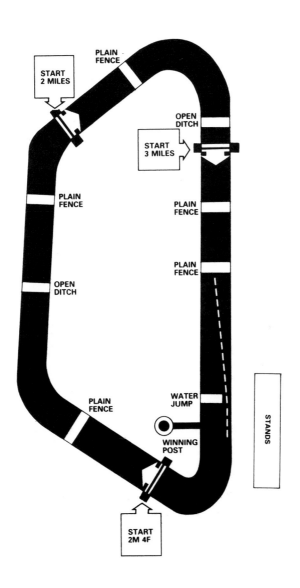

Perth Hunt: right-handed N.H. course

PLUMPTON is like Newton Abbot tipped up on end. Left-handed, 1 mile 1 furlong round, it is a sharp, undulating track which has always been unpopular with most riders — even the greatest of them. It is, however, surprisingly popular with southern race-goers. Any trainer who finds a horse and jockey suited to the track should persevere; it is a rare combination which will continue to win at Plumpton. The track can be said to run steeply downhill on the back stretch and round two sharp bends into the uphill straight. The run-in from the last fence is 200 yards on the collar, so you want to get a good position before the last. The fences are on the stiff side; I would never take a good horse to Plumpton.

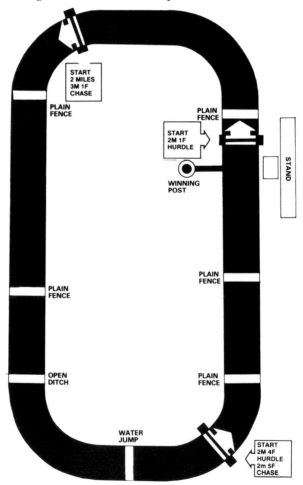

Plumpton: left-handed N.H. course

PONTEFRACT was traditionally popular with the older, northern journalists. Their southern counterparts enjoyed a similar, incomprehensible nostalgia for Alexandra Park. An undulating, pear-shaped course of about $1\frac{1}{2}$ miles, it has a sharp bend into the 2 furlong straight. The 5 and 6 furlong courses are part of the main track, of which the last 3 furlongs are on the collar. Low numbers therefore enjoy a considerable advantage in sprint races and you need a horse who really gets the trip, especially when the going is soft, but it is no track for a long-striding animal.

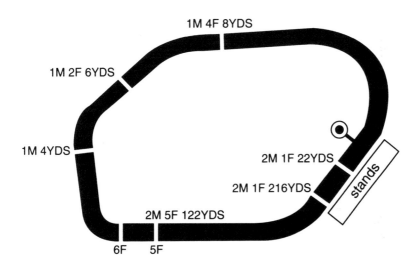

Pontefract: left-handed Flat course

REDCAR, thanks to Lord Zetland, is a splendid 'fun' course by the sea in Yorkshire, which always deservedly attracts good crowds. The sandy turf provides good going and is well watered on the rare occasions when it becomes firm. Left-handed, flat, oval, 2 miles round, it has a 5 furlong straight and all races up to a mile are run on a straight mile which joins the main course at this juncture. The draw has no material advantage. This is a fair track which suits any type of animal. If you have a good horse you can take him to Redcar. Your owner will enjoy himself.

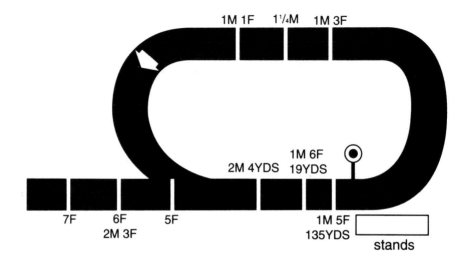

Redcar: left-handed Flat course

RIPON, like Redcar, caters only for Flat racing. It is oval, right-handed, 1 mile and 5 furlongs, and has a straight of 5 furlongs, at which point the straight 6 furlong course joins the main circuit. The straight is slightly on the collar except for a shallow dip at the distance. The draw makes no difference on the straight track, but high numbers are favoured in 1 mile races on the round course. Ripon boasts a watering system and is well run. Despite its size the bends are a bit sharp and it is not the ideal course for a big, long-striding horse.

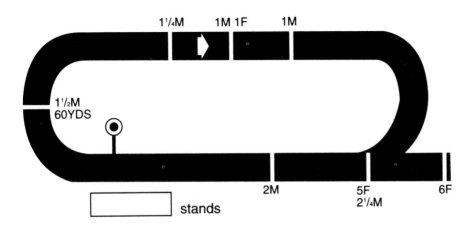

Ripon: right-handed Flat course

SALISBURY is one of those courses which make a horse feel at home, particularly if he is trained on the local downland gallops. It is decidedly a 'fun' course with a fine picnic atmosphere on a lovely summer day, but not too enjoyable in wind and rain. A strangely shaped course high above Wilton, it has a right-handed loop on the main mile course, which is almost straight except for a slight right-handed elbow at half way in $1\frac{3}{4}$ mile races. Horses start opposite the stands, run back up the course, bearing left on to the loop and re-entering the straight at the 7 furlong gate. The course is on the collar from 5 furlongs out, until it levels just before the finish, so that a sprinter who has established an advantage seems to gain momentum to win more easily than on most other tracks. Nevertheless, this is a stiff course and a horse must get the full trip. An ideal course for south-western horses, particularly two-year-olds first time out.

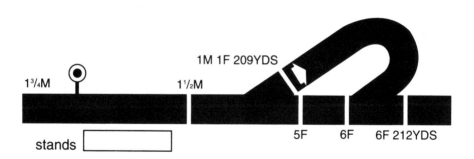

Salisbury: right-handed Flat course

SANDOWN PARK is the most dramatic racecourse in the world. It is also the nicest, the most fun and most probably the best test of a horse jumping or on the Flat. I agree entirely with Etienne Pollet who described it as *'la piste la plus sympathique du monde'*. The new stands do not detract from this charm, but rather enhance it. As for the drama, this is gained because you

Sir Gordon Richards; many times champion, and the first jockey to be knighted. A master of Sandown's stiff 5 furlongs.

are looking down on your sport at Sandown. A right-handed course of more than 1 mile 5 furlongs, it has a straight run-in of $4\frac{1}{2}$ furlongs. This is on the collar nearly the whole way to the winning post. The straight 5 furlongs, which runs across the centre of the track, is probably the stiffest in the world. Stand at the start looking up towards the finish and you will see what I mean. Only here could The Tetrarch have been caught in the tapes, left twenty lengths and still won the most valuable two-year-old race of the season. The draw makes no difference on this track, although the high numbers are naturally favoured on the turning 7 and 8 furlong courses. Since the 5 furlong course finishes well past the stands, jockeys frequently start getting at their mounts too soon. Sir Gordon Richards used to say that you must never start riding until you have passed the Tote building in the centre of the course. So you must sit and suffer until a furlong or less from home. The turns are well banked and it is a great galloping course. The chase circuit of about $1\frac{1}{2}$ miles has more character than any others except Aintree and Cheltenham. There are eleven fences to a circuit and the most awkward are probably the one down the hill away from the stands, when the sun is shining full on it, and the notorious

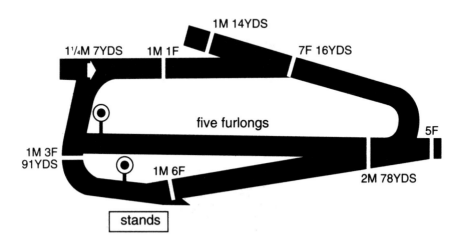

Sandown Park: right-handed Flat course

'Sandown Treble' of three fences very close together alongside the railway before the turn for home. These three fences are so close together that if you meet the first wrong you have almost certainly had it over the last two. A wonderful racecourse. Bring your best horses and your best owners and enjoy yourselves. An ideal train service from Waterloo to Esher lands the racegoer on the track in half an hour.

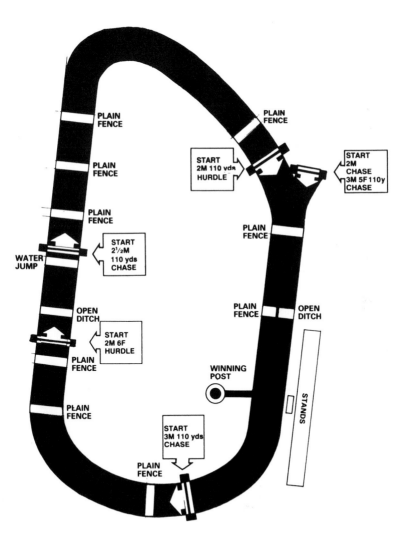

Sandown Park: right-handed N.H. course

SEDGEFIELD is just the opposite of Sandown. Although I have
found some northern racing men who enjoy it, I find it a dull
little meeting. It is a sharp, left-handed rectangular course of
about $1\frac{1}{4}$ miles. The track rises in the back straight and runs
down between the last two fences. The old 500 yards run-in
from the last fence was too long, and an extra portable fence
now forms a new 'last'. In hurdles you must have won your race
before the last, because the run-in is only 200 yards. Unless you
are desperate for a race and there is an ideal event for you, it is
not worth making the journey from the Midlands or the South.
There are a number of high class local trainers.

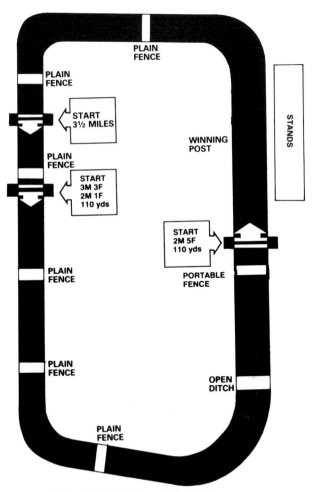

Sedgefield: left-handed N.H. course

SOUTHWELL was a slightly better Midlands equivalent of Sedgefield, left-handed, $1\frac{1}{4}$ miles triangular with seven fences to a circuit. It is, however, suitable for any kind of horse, because the course is easy and the bends are not too sharp. The run-in from the last is 250 yards. Like Sedgefield, it is hell in the rain and for many years the amenities were not worthy of the name. It was no place to bring an owner unless you were certain that he would have a winner. However, the introduction of all-weather racing under both codes has involved a complete facelift and, whatever I feel about it, the course now has a valuable place.

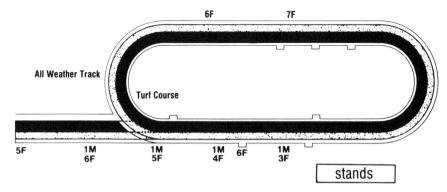

Southwell: left-handed Flat course

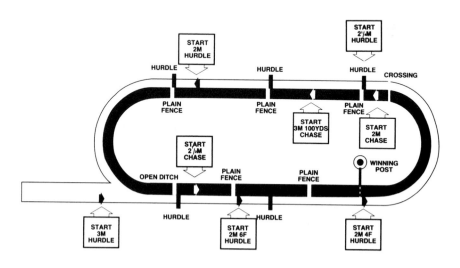

Southwell: left-handed N.H. course

STRATFORD-UPON-AVON, a left-handed jumping track, 1 mile 3 furlongs, almost flat, with a run-in of 200 yards, is a 'fun' course where any owner will have a happy afternoon. Perhaps I am biased because I trained successfully for the late Chairman and his Directors. But, apart from all the imaginative amentities, the intimacy of the sport and the thrill of watching from a fence and still seeing most of the way round, it is an excellent fast circuit which suits any horse. Surprisingly, Stratford winners go on to win at Cheltenham. This is because the back stretch is so fast and the straight so short that you have to ride two races. You must get a position before the turn and then ride your finish in the straight; so, in the better class races, speed and stamina are at premium. But during the season there are races which suit every class of horse, including all-too-rare hurdle contests confined to fillies, which are so valuable for jumping breeders. The catering both here and at Warwick is outstanding value. Watering has been installed. A surprising feature of Stratford is that, even when water is lying in the back stretch, horses are able to gallop through it. No wonder they received no fewer than 805 entires for one projected race.

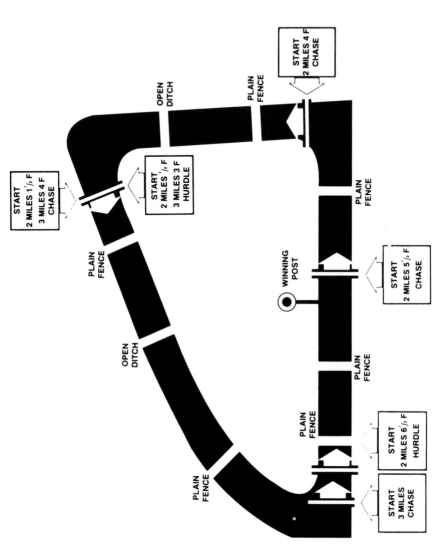

START
2 MILES 4 F
CHASE

OPEN
DITCH

PLAIN
FENCE

START
2 MILES 1½ F
3 MILES 4 F
CHASE

START
2 MILES ½ F
3 MILES 3 F
HURDLE

PLAIN
FENCE

PLAIN
FENCE

WINNING
POST

START
2 MILES 5½ F
CHASE

OPEN
DITCH

PLAIN
FENCE

PLAIN
FENCE

PLAIN
FENCE

START
2 MILES 6½ F
HURDLE

START
3 MILES
CHASE

Stratford upon Avon: left-handed N.H. course

TAUNTON, a right-handed jumping track, is a charming little meeting. A $1\frac{1}{4}$ mile, oval circuit with an uphill run-in of 200 yards, it is a trifle sharp, but nevertheless a reliable course for a trainer who wishes to have a bet, unless the going is very heavy. Then, owing to the clay, you are well advised to take your horse out unless he is a genuine high-actioned mudlark.

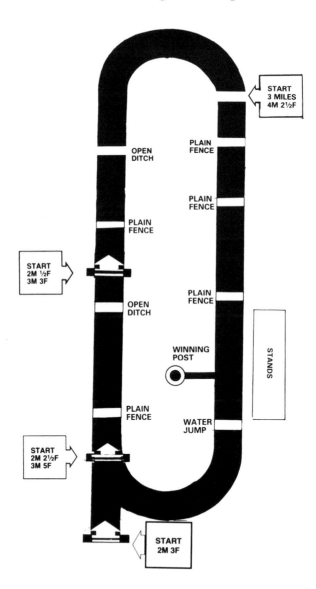

Taunton: right-handed N.H. course

THIRSK is a 'fun', northern Flat course, where any owner will be happy. Quite flat, oval, 1 mile 2 furlongs, with a straight of 4 furlongs. The 5 and 6 furlong courses are straight, undulating until they join the round course 4 furlongs from home. On the left-handed round course in races of 7 furlongs and 1 mile, low numbers are naturally favoured, but in the straight sprint events high numbers appear to have an advantage. The round course is a bit sharp for a long-striding horse, but the sprint tracks are really fast. You bounce out of the gate and come the whole way, and a brilliant short runner may last home. Even the most hardened professional without a runner enjoys an afternoon out at Thirsk, helped by the excellent catering common to so many northern tracks.

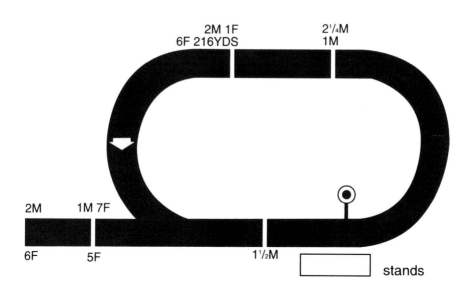

Thirsk: left-handed Flat course

TOWCESTER is a 'fun' course and a fine right-handed testing jumping track. An easily accessible course where trials could be run for Cheltenham, before splendid crowds. Witness the attendance for motor-racing at nearby Silverstone.

A square galloping circuit of about $1\frac{3}{4}$ miles, it has similar gradients to Devon and Exeter or an exaggerated Sandown. When the course turns right after passing the stands, it bends sharply until, from the dip in the back stretch, three furlongs from home, it starts to rise. From here onwards it is on the collar almost to the winning post. The run-in is 300 yards. A splendid test for a brave stayer. Avoid it in very wet weather because the clay becomes extra heavy. If only the spark can be rekindled it is a course of great potential and one which is well worth patronising.

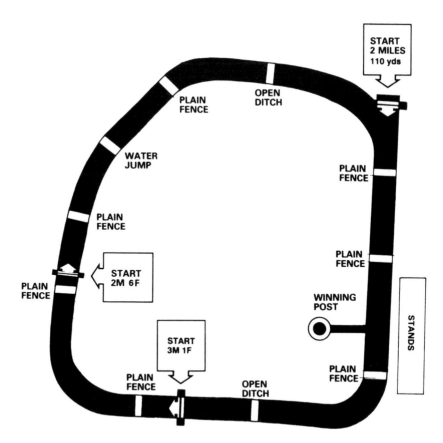

Towcester: right-handed N.H. course

UTTOXETER is readily accessible from the North and Midlands and is well run. It is left-handed, oval, approximately $1\frac{1}{2}$ miles with a run-in of 300 yards and stiff fences. It is a fair test for a good horse. For this reason some of the top trainers like to run their Grand National candidates here. But, unless your horse is a high-actioned mudlark, avoid it when the going is heavy. If you have children, they can spend a wonderful day at nearby Alton Towers.

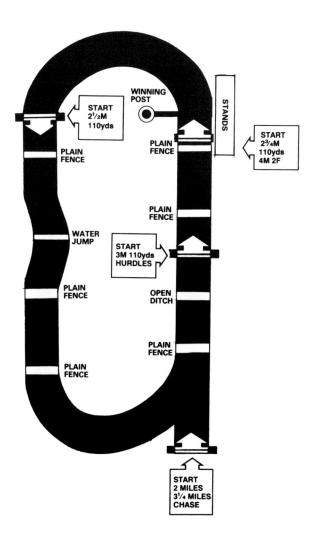

Uttoxeter: left-handed N.H. course

WARWICK was one of my happy hunting grounds with sharp, nippy two-year-olds. It is left-handed, almost circular, $1\frac{3}{4}$ miles, Flat and jumping. The course climbs after passing the stands, levelling out as it turns into the straight back stretch, which turns sharp left into the final $2\frac{1}{2}$ furlong straight. This fast straight forms the second half of the dog-leg 5 furlongs (there is no straight course at Warwick), which starts from a spur. A low draw, out of the stalls like lightning, and you can have your race won by this point. The jumping course has a run-in of 450 yards. Both Flat and jumping, apart from the 5 furlong track, Warwick is a fair course for the average well balanced horse. Only the big, gangly, long-striding animal may find himself at sea. A happy atmosphere.

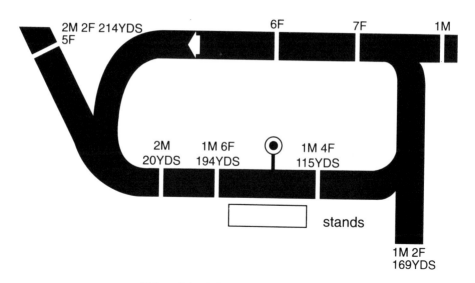

Warwick: left-handed Flat course

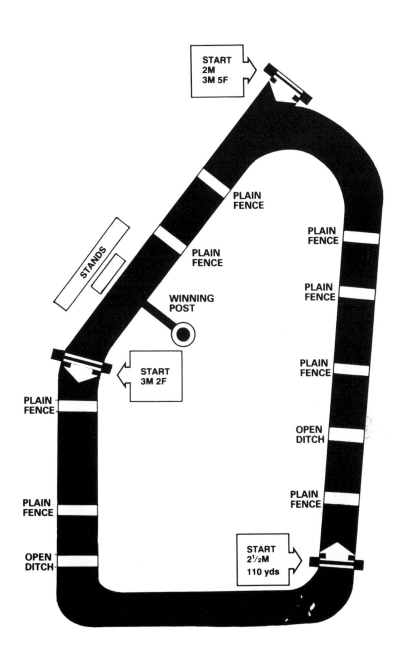

Warwick: left-handed N.H. course

WETHERBY, situated beside the Al, is a good, stiff, left-handed, oval jumping course of $1\frac{1}{2}$ miles. It has a very short run-in from the last of only 190 yards uphill. The fences are not as stiff as they were, but the course takes some knowing and southern trainers are well advised to book northern jockeys if they run here.

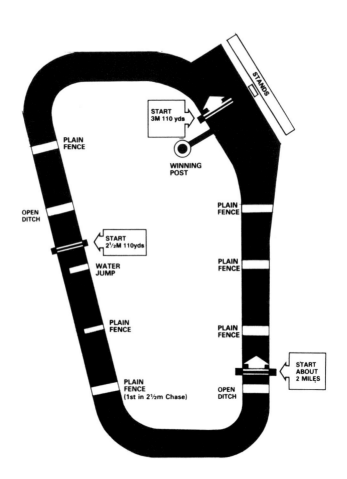

Wetherby: left-handed N.H. course

WINCANTON is a tough, right-handed, rectangular galloping course, 1 mile 3 furlongs, with a run-in of about 200 yards. The straight is undulating and the run-in is slightly uphill. Despite recent improvements, it is not much fun in bad weather, but otherwise it is deservedly popular with owners, trainers and the sporting West Country public in general. It is a fair course for any horse. Recently the drainage of the track has been considerably improved, but still the one time to avoid it is when the going is really heavy. Then the soil is so holding that you will do your horse no good by running him.

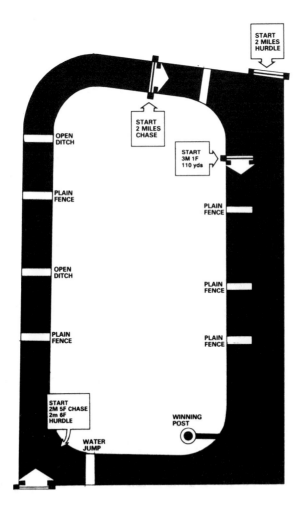

Wincanton: right-handed N.H. course

WINDSOR, Flat and jumping, is a figure of eight, level, $1\frac{1}{2}$ mile circuit with sharp bends, a nearly straight 6 furlongs and a run-in from the last fence of just 1 furlong.

Situated just off the M4 in a picturesque riverside setting, it is only half an hour from London and is therefore popular with owners. Summer evening meetings are a success here. You need a handy horse to win at Windsor. For some reason it is not the most popular course with the animals themselves, even those who love Fontwell's figure of eight. High numbers are favoured in the sprint races. A good place for trainers to run their moderate horses with a fair hope of success.

The watering system is good and the going, helped by the new, efficient Thames control, is generally among the best in the country.

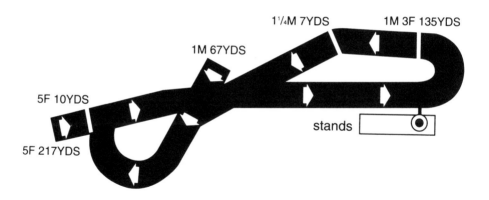

Windsor: right- and left-handed Flat course

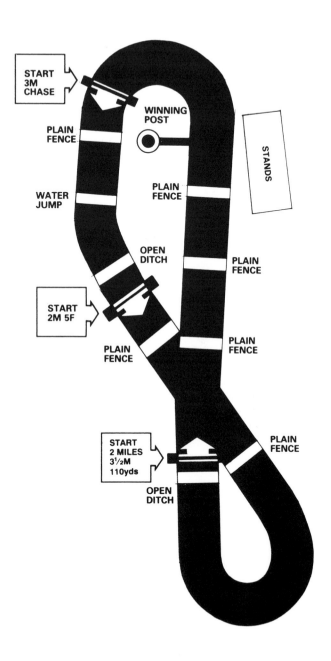

Windsor: right- and left-handed N.H. course

WOLVERHAMPTON, left-handed, $1\frac{1}{2}$ miles, almost flat, triangular, has a straight of 5 furlongs and a run-in on the chase course of about a furlong. It is a course for all seasons.

Under both codes this is a fast, fair track and, as there is no advantage in the draw, it is a good place for a trainer who wants to have a bet. Although the entrance and surroundings are not too prepossessing, Wolverhampton is quite popular with owners, particularly as the catering is good and reasonable. An all-weather complex with floodlighting is under construction at the time of writing.

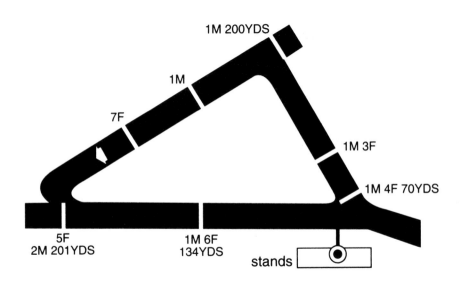

Wolverhampton: left-handed Flat course

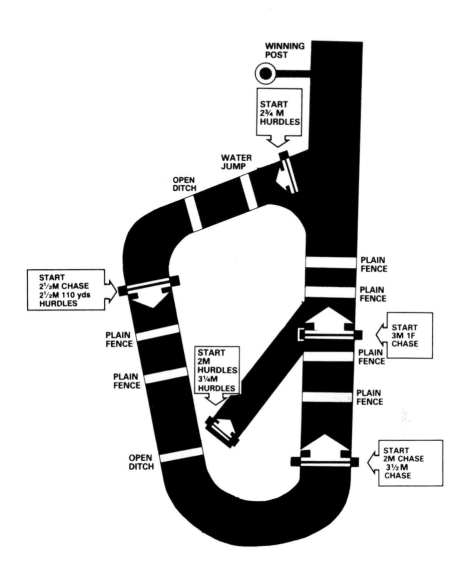

Wolverhampton: left-handed N.H. course

WORCESTER, now only jumping, is a flat, oval, left-handed track of 1 mile 5 furlongs with a run-in of 220 yards. It is improving and is now one of the best courses in the country for a novice, as the fences are well sited, fair and comparatively easy. Situated alongside the River Severn, which used to flood the course with monotonous regularity, and into which sprinters periodically used to gallop, Worcester has a watering system. As at Windsor, the river is now efficiently controlled so that flooding has become a rarity. A good 'fun' course for all and suitable for any kind of horse.

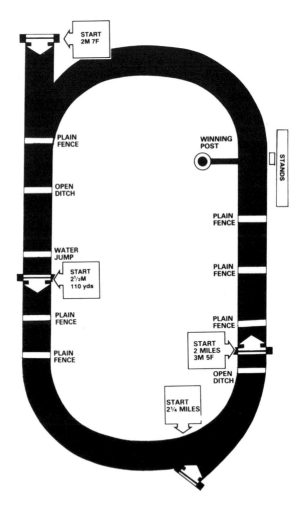

Worcester: left-handed N.H. course

YARMOUTH is a good, fair, level, 1½ mile, oblong, left-handed, Flat course with a straight mile and a straight run-in of 5 furlongs. Races up to 1 mile are run on the straight course. The sprint course is 5 furlongs and 25 yards. Yarmouth is almost monopolised by Newmarket trainers, who regard it as their local track. In fact, it is about the same distance from Headquarters as Leicester. An excellent watering system and the sandy soil always produce good ground, the draw has no effect and the course is admirably suited to any kind of horse.

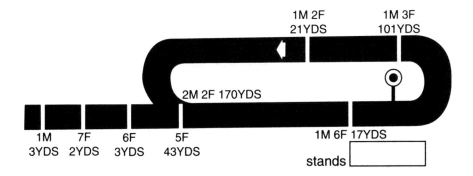

Yarmouth: left-handed Flat course

YORK, a left-handed, flat, wide 2 mile course, shaped like an elongated horseshoe, with a straight run-in of 5 furlongs, is one of the world's greatest racecourses. The 5 and 6 furlong courses are dead straight. There is a short left-handed bend in the 7 furlong course as it joins them. The draw has no effect, except in soft or heavy conditions when high numbers are favoured. A glamorous, lavishly decorated 'fun' course with an excellent watering system admirably suited to the highest quality horses. Only in really heavy conditions would I advise a trainer to ignore York. What more need I say? Bring your horses and their owners, stay on in this wonderful old city, visit the glorious countryside and make the most of a memorable trip.

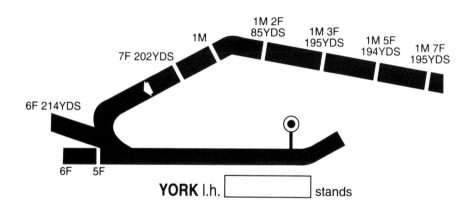

York: left-handed Flat course

CHAPTER
THIRTEEN
Racing Horses Abroad

'Abroad is bloody!' The sentiments of Uncle Matthew in Nancy Mitford's *The Pursuit of Love* have been echoed over the years by a number of British trainers, including that master of his craft, the late George Todd. 'When I came home from France after the first war,' said George, 'I swore I wouldn't leave England again. And, unless I have to, I'm damned if I will!'

To most members of his profession, however, 'abroad' is France, which in turn means Paris or, in August, Deauville. It means glamorous, fun weekends and, above all, the chance to win substantial prize money for contented owners.

Although some trainers may find suitable races in different countries, notably Italy, Germany and the United States, and others may send runners to Ireland for the Classics or the big jumping events, it is really France that matters week in and week out, from early March right through to December.

For some strange reason our grandfathers and great-grand-fathers raced their horses across the Channel far more than our fathers, who remained at home before the last war and suffered the crippling French invasion after the conflict. Now that the Tote monopoly and the Tiercé have boosted French prize money far above ours, the traffic, except in the Classic races, is nearly all one way.

Racing in France today is splendid for owners, trainers, jockeys (who are never maligned for not trying) and journalists, but very bad for our racegoers who seldom have the chance to see their own real stars in action. For example, in 1970, when David Robinson's magnificent My Swallow was breaking all two-year-old records and amassing a total of £88,000, the British racegoer only knew what he read in the papers. He was denied the opportunity of applauding Lester Piggott on the big day because only the French crowds had this privilege. Moreover, although we know that jockeys draw crowds, their favourite stars are so often absent on overseas duty.

The huge prize money, however, had an unexpected effect which soured off the French owners and trainers. Condition races and the weights carried in them were normally governed by the amount of prize money won by each of the candidates. In this respect, a high class horse who had raced in England was a pauper compared with a horse of the same standard in France. My Swallow, for instance, would probably have earned only a quarter of his total if he had been confined to this country.

Thus for some years high class English horses were able to compete not just on level terms, but receiving lumps of weight from inferior rivals trained across the Channel. So we won a lot of races and, since place money, including that for finishing fourth, was incredibly generous, our owners netted huge sums in francs.

The French authorities have taken certain steps to counteract this, but the English trainer is still favoured. You must study the conditions of each French race carefully before making an entry. In fact, until you have acquired experience by running a number of horses abroad I would advise consulting the International Racing Bureau which was the brainchild of the late David Hedges. They will advise on race conditions, entries, forfeits, penalties, travel allowance, air freight, stabling, accommodation for lads, insurance, the necessary travel documents and all other matters connected with the trip.

A few words of warning. First, however well your horse may be treated by the conditions, you must know that he is a good horse with guts and stamina, capable of getting every inch of the distance over which he is expected to run. Secondly, you should choose a jockey who knows the track and French racing intimately. At least half-a-dozen of our own English-based top jockeys are riding in France regularly.

Time spent in reconnaissance is seldom wasted. In this case it is essential that the trainer himself should know French racecourses really well and I recommend a long weekend exploring the different tracks before you even contemplate sending a horse to race over there. Hire a car and carry out a detailed examination of Longchamp, Saint-Cloud, Maisons-Laffitte and Evry. Then motor down to Deauville and inspect the main track and the little jumping course at Clairefontaine. Walk the circuits, inspect the turns and gradients and have a look at the stabling and the lads' accommodation. It will pay handsome dividends. I always had the utmost co-operation from the French authorities, particularly from Jean Romanet, Director General of the main society, the Societe d'Encouragement, and Jean's son Louis Romanet has stepped admirably into his father's shoes.

A few points to remember. The French watering systems are more efficient than ours. They saturate every inch of the track so that you can easily find the ground much softer than you expected, especially when there has been recent rain. It is advisable, therefore, to obtain an accurate, up-to-the-minute report on the going before you send your horse. Like most civilised countries, the French have long had overnight declaration of jockeys. Their names are printed on the racecards and woe betide you if you make a mistake. The late Ernie Fellows earned a heavy suspension because his apprentice had been declared in error for his runner in the Tiercé race on the Sunday at Deauville, only for Bill Williamson to ride the horse and win a dramatic finish at very, very long odds. 'You'd think I'd robbed the Bank of France', said Ernie. 'I don't think they'll ever believe that I did it by mistake. They treat me like a criminal.' The system has now, at last, been introduced in this country.

The patrol cameras are still more efficient than ours. They cover every race from a number of different angles and do not miss an inch of the running. If you have an English jockey with little experience of racing abroad, you must impress on him that he must keep his place. He may not cross over to the rails or take another jockey's ground. If he does, he will not only lose the race but will be suspended, and such a suspension is valid in every other country by reciprocal agreement. We are still far too lax in this country.

Then, before you allow your owner to have a bet, if you think it really necessary with all that prize money, you must ascertain the effect of the draw in races over short distances. The sprint tracks at Longchamp and Deauville are notorious.

As far as racing over obstacles is concerned, experience seems to show that, unless you have a high class French-bred jumper, you will do better to remain at home. Horses like Mandarin and Beaver returned to triumph in their native land, although

God knows how Fred Winter and little Mandarin achieved that miracle. But other British champions seem to run out of stamina as soon as they turn the tap on well before the last. English horses trained in France, however, have been doing particularly well. The lesson seems to be that the animal must be fully accustomed to the French type of obstacle and to the way in which the races are run. In addition, to win over hurdles round the Paris circuits like Auteuil and Enghien, he must be a pretty high class performer over a distance of ground on the Flat in England. You need at least a mile and a quarter horse and are better with a good winner over one and a half miles.

Racing in Ireland is, of course, much the same as in England. Do not imagine for one moment that you can get away with a short runner at the Curragh. You can't. You need a horse who stays every inch of the trip. Lester Piggott said that Sir Ivor never got further than one and a quarter miles. He could win at Epsom convincingly, but he was well beaten up that stiff Curragh straight.

The few Irish courses over which an English trainer is likely to have runners are all very fair. The Curragh, Leopardstown and Fairyhouse are excellent tracks. But, once again, carry out that reconnaissance beforehand and employ a jockey who knows his way round.

This applies equally to all courses abroad where you may contemplate running. Never be afraid to ask for advice from an old trainer who has experience of running horses on those particular tracks. For example, if you are invited to run in the United States, you will find that trainers who have already been there will have had a number of problems to overcome: the long journey, possible delays, food, and so on. My experience has been that such people are only too willing to help. Do not be frightened of the American bends. They are so well banked that they counteract the sharpness of the circuit, but you need a balanced horse with a fair degree of brilliance to win over there.

Nick Clarke, enthusiastic, ultra-effcient boss of that admirable organisation, the International Racing Bureau, says:

> There are so many more opportunities for British horses to race abroad and quite often the cost of travel is very reasonable or even free. For example, a free charter plane is laid on for racing in Turkey and, generally, transport is paid. It is essential for the trainer to know all the formalities and mechanics such as penalties, etc. in the country where he intends to compete. We advise and

take care of every detail and, wherever you go, there will be one of our people to meet you and your horse at the other end and advise you on the going, etc.

Take my advice. Use the I.R.B. and trust them to arrange every-thing for you. You can consult the International Racing Bureau at Rookery House, Newmarket, Suffolk, CB8 8EQ. Telephone 0638 665032.

One of the chief differences a trainer will notice racing abroad is a far higher standard of starting. Every horse enters his stall as nonchalantly as if he were walking down Newmarket High Street — straight in with no fuss and straight out. Indeed, the quiet efficiency of starts in France, the United States and Australia has to be seen to be believed. The English trainer must therefore ensure that his animals are just as well schooled in this depart-ment as their foreign rivals. The reason for our comparative inefficiency is chiefly financial; we have not had starting stalls for as long as the other countries. This was largely the Jockey Club's fault.

Seeking advice 'from the horse's mouth', I consulted Paddy Prendergast, whose runners were always brilliant at the gate. He had his own set of four stalls in his large indoor ride. This is what he said:

It is essential that a horse take no notice of the stalls and that he should regard them as a normal part of his life. So I start my stalls training even before they are ridden away. From the first day on long reins my yearlings are driven in and out of the open stalls until they are no more worried about them than about going in through their own stable door. If any one is at all nervous, I have the ropes taken off and lead him through, making a fuss of him, until he has lost all signs of apprehension.

I carry on the same process after they have been backed and ridden away. Within as little as a week I have them closed in the stalls and leave them there while their lads crawl over to each other's horses. Then, when they are thoroughly used to this, I take them into the stalls, close the back door behind them and allow them to walk out. Then they will trot out and a little later they will canter out. Then we'll walk out again, nothing special about it, just daily routine. And we carry on as part of normal exercise whenever they are confined to the indoor school through bad weather. By the spring, far from having any fear of the stalls, they are taking no notice of them whatsoever.

In Ireland every horse has to have a certificate from the Official

Paddy Prendergast; a top trainer whose charges were well educated in the starting stalls.

Starter before he is allowed to run in a race. So in March a week before the Starter comes down to test them, I spring them from the gate outside. Huby Tyrrell doesn't mind how fast they are as long as they make no fuss and obviously know their jobs. Mine are usually good as gold.

He can say that again. Like Atty Persse, Paddy had his first-time two-year-olds flying from the stalls straight into their strides. They had the necessary impulsion and were well up to their bits.

Remember how Atty's yearlings used to gallop two and three furlongs flat out, so that as soon as you picked them up they went straight into their bits? The Guv'nor showed his two-year-olds the old-fashioned starting gate only once, just a week before they ran. He never used a sprung gate. 'Damned sophisticated things, which can go wrong and damage a horse's confidence irreparably!' He had a gate on which the tapes were pulled up by hand.

Two two-year-olds, on either side of an older horse, would first walk backwards and forwards under the raised tapes. These were then lowered and the three horses stood with their noses on the tapes, which were waggled about while you made a fuss of the youngsters and gave them an occasional handful of grass. While they were all standing there, you raised the gate and lowered it quietly a few times. As soon as they were accustomed to this, you raised the tapes and brought them down sharply in their faces with as much of a bang as possible. They would normally jump, but you made a fuss of them again and they realised there was nothing to fear. We would take them back, bring them in again and, as they got to the tapes, raise them and let them walk out. The process would be repeated, allowing them to trot or canter out. After one or two more times one could raise the tapes sharply and jump them off, letting them gallop for a furlong. It was important not to pull them up too quickly. We would go back and do it again and that was all; they were fit to run.

The principle was the same as Paddy's with the stalls. The trainer gives the horses impulsion and he shows them the worst that the mechanical contrivance can do, so that they will never fear it for the rest of their lives.

It always gave me a thrill putting the young produce of a long line of sprinters under the gate or springing him from the stalls for the first time. He seemed to have done it all in a previous life. He knew all about it and was just waiting to go by instinct. Sadly, owing primarily to cost with the subsequent need to travel from course to course, British stalls on the racecourse are still too flimsy. Those used at home are usually even lighter and are therefore inclined to move and sway when pushed, which can terrify a young horse. If he is going to be enclosed, let it be by something firm, solid and immobile.

Conclusion

Morning mists on the downs and that the vague hint of autumn in the air tell us we're back where we came in — on our way to Doncaster for the St Leger meeting and the first yearling sales.

The last weeks have been a time of decision — which to keep and which to cull. You must harden your heart and remember that bad horses eat as much as good ones and do you no good at all. It is fair to say that, on the whole, even the most backward ones should by now have shown you something, if only a faint glimmer of promise.

Even if you have been unable to persuade an owner to replace, do not keep his bad horses. You may not believe it at the time, but you will be better off with empty boxes. Unfortunately for the breed, any filly with reasonable breeding now fetches a lot of money, even if she has been a poor performer. But charity begins at home and you must try to dissuade your breeding owners from taking such animals back to their studs. You will suffer later on when you have to train the progeny. As the late Mat Dawson used to say, 'She's a damned bad specimen of a damned good breed. Get out of her.'

Try not to train four-year-old fillies. But, if an owner has a decent horse who always gives him a run for his money and wins sometimes, even if not really high class, think twice before exchanging for a yearling who, for all your careful buying, may turn out to be useless.

A trainer's licence now entitles you to train anywhere over obstacles or on the level. Make use of it. It is bad for the horse, the trainer, his staff and the owner if there has to be a change of stable. There's nothing like a few jumping winners to keep a Flat yard happy through the winter.

Training racehorses in Britain today is a hard, exacting job for both the trainer and his wife. On the Flat, however, the rewards are beginning to make sense, particularly if you are prepared to take your horses to France.

Any young men or women wishing to enter the profession should learn the job thoroughly from first class established trainers before setting up on their own. Then they must be prepared to work really hard for the rest of their lives, studying the interests of their horses, their owners, their lads and themselves, in that order.

One of the major tragedies of the British racing scene today is that, owing to the property shortage, some of the best potential trainers are being denied the facilities which they deserve because a number of the better training establishments have fallen into the hands of men with little ability but plenty of money. Stable lads are still paid far too little for dedicated men who have served a five-year apprenticeship.

There is only one solution. It is absolutely essential that the Jockey Club should forget that they themselves are owners of racehorses and should establish a minimum training fee which is reviewed every year. This must be based on the actual cost of keeping a horse in training, plus a salary for the trainer. Such a step, which would only be justice, would put out of the game a large number of undesirable owners who have no right to be in it; it would also get rid of a lot of bad horses, ensure that the lads are adequately paid, and bring the good trainer into his own again. No one will bother to pay those fees to playboys and spivs.

The Jockey Club must also realise that it is the trainer and his staff, not the owner or the jockey, who are the backbone of British racing. They must therefore change their whole outlook and study the trainers' interests before those of anyone else in the sport. This is the quickest way to make British racing healthy and wealthy again. I say this advisedly. It is vital to remember that in the days when British racing led the world — up to 1939 — apart from the somewhat nebulous owners, the trainer was the boss. It was he who produced the jockeys, as he still does today. But at that time, unlike today, he also remained the boss.

Now we are faced with a ridiculous situation. The trainer takes on and tutors the apprentice, training him as a jockey at considerable cost. It is the trainer who buys, breaks and produces the horses. It is he who has to keep the owners satisfied. It is he who gives the orders and carries all the responsibilities. But in the end it is the Flat-race jockey who, owing to his financial position, can laugh at all but the very top trainers.

Perhaps, when all Flat-race jockeys follow Lester Piggott's example and become freelances, trainers will concentrate more on their work riders, as they do in the United States, and the jockeys will therefore have to rely more on the trainers' selection. This would undoubtedly help to rectify the situation.

In the meantime I would like to express my gratitude to all the trainers in these islands who have stuck it out through the most difficult times with skill, hard work and extraordinary integrity.

A shabby little interloper, who has muddied the waters, is the 'jockey's agent', a totally unnecessary percentage spiv, who comes between the trainer and his rider, qualifying for the title of 'the lowest form of animal life in racing'.

Atty Persse gave this description to the racing manager, who comes between the trainer and his owner. How he hated them! The great old man would never have recognised or dealt with any 'jockey's agent' and God help any member of the breed who tried to interfere with him, Sir Noel Murless or any of the masters.

Index

Page numbers in *italics* refer to diagrams and photographs